PERNILLE STENSGAARD

WHEN LOUISIANA STOLE THE PICTURE

TRANSLATION: JOHN KENDAL

GYLDENDAL

WHEN LOUISIANA STOLE THE PICTURE

c) 2008 Pernille Stensgaard and Gyldendalske
Boghandel, Nordisk Forlag A/S, Copenhagen

Original title: *Da Louisiana stjal billedet*.
Translated from the Danish by John Kendal
Graphic design: Bettina Kjærulff-Schmidt
Picture editors: Annette Ekstrand and the author
Editor: Lisbeth Frimodt
Front and back cover photos: Louisiana's photo
archive

Set in FF Din and printed by Narayana Press,
Gylling
Printed in Denmark 2008

1st edition, 1st impression

Isbn 978-87-02-06705-7

THANKS to
The Augustinus Foundation
The New Carlsberg Foundation

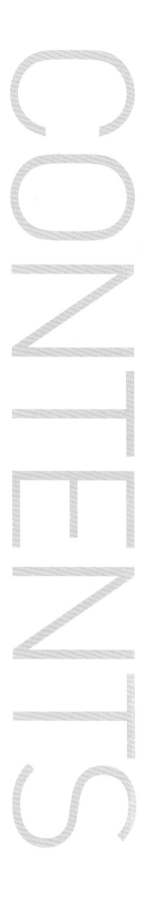

Foreword

Already on that summer day in 1958 when Knud W. Jensen opened Louisiana, he had a scintillatingly clear sense of what it was he held in his hands. From the rostrum in the long tent on the lawn he said almost prophetically: "Louisiana must be *used*, be an artistic environment and a framework around a piece of life where things happen." He adhered to this vision until his death, and it became Louisiana's fundamental principle.

Without having any idea about how to run a museum, he nevertheless knew intuitively how he should steal the picture and revolutionise the Danish museum world. He had only just sold his huge, well run cheese firm to the Americans and left his desk at the factory down by Copenhagen Harbour, but from the very first day he had an unsurpassed ability to know how he could conquer the very different world of art and the public.

With Louisiana he launched an attack on the classical museum with its stiff silence, its Olympian marble stairs and attendants dressed as admirals. Out went reverence and awe. In came cheerful uninhibitedness. He dreamt of a secure, homely, pleasant place, where the attendants walked around in their own clothes, and where smoking was permitted. Even the Communist newspaper *Land og Folk* had to surrender to this "museum for joie de vivre" which turned everything upside down – even though the revolution was financed by a private capitalist fortune and was taking place at a country estate in North Zealand.

In 1958 no serious museum or university course dealt with contemporary art. The Now evoked either scepticism or shyness. One preferred to wait a bit rather than seize upon some fashionable trend buzzing confusedly around on the surface. But it was the Now that Knud W. Jensen wanted, and it was part of his enthusiasm for his fellow human beings and of his criterion for success to think: What is important right at this moment?

Coffee, pastries and art in one mouthful was regarded as an unheard-of provocation 50 years ago, but this was only the start of a sequence of events that in time gave Louisiana normative status, introduced a ground-breaking new concept of the museum – and changed the way in which Danes looked at art.

I am not involved in the story that I am now going to tell in any other way than anybody else might be. Born in 1960 on the threshold to the good times, I grew up with Louisiana which arrived in the very middle of Social-Democratic, prospering, highly taxed and motorised welfare Denmark. On a Sunday my mother would stick her head into my room and ask: "The zoo or Louisiana?" And it would be Louisiana – there was always something to see there. Her father lived on Funen and was a waiter on the ferry to Zealand. Every time he visited us, we drove slavishly up to Humlebæk, and every time he said that if he lived nearby he would always drink his Sunday coffee and read his newspaper at the museum. He felt a natural sense of belonging at Louisiana. He felt at home there. We all did. Only later did I discover that one can also adopt a critical approach and maintain a certain distance to this supremely successful museum.

The present book was written at Louisiana's invitation, but quite independently of the museum. I made it a condition that I should have access to the archives and full control over the content of the book, and these conditions were accepted. The manuscript has been delivered to my usual editor at Gyldendal which though it is owned by Louisiana is editorially autonomous. At the museum I have met nothing but open doors, good will and patience. I have interviewed many people at Louisiana and outside, and have been much encouraged by the interest they have shown. Their help has been indispensable since only a small part of Louisiana's motley history is official and in writing.

To make the text more reader-friendly references do not appear in the actual text, and my oral and written sources are to found at the back of the book.

And so it only remains to say together with Knud W. Jensen: Onwards! Onwards! Onwards!

Louisiana

Samling af nutidskunst og kunsthåndværk

ENTRÉ KR. 2.00 · BØRN UNDER 16 ÅR GRATIS

GL. STRANDVEJ 13, HUMLEBÆK · VED ØRESUNDSKYSTEN, 9 KM SYD FOR HELSINGØR · CAFETERIA · PARK

ÅBNINGSTIDER
16. MAJ - 15. AUGUST
KL. 10-21
16. AUGUST - 14. MAJ
KL. 10-18
ALLE UGENS
DAGE

Busky-Neergaard is a heavily built man with a silver-mounted cane, a light jacket, a waistcoat and knickerbockers with sharp creases. His fleshy knees stick out above the stockings. It is summer after all. Summer 1942. He stands on the steps leading up to Louisiana with his two white Scotties looking just like the well-to-do North Zealand landowner he is. The journalist from the ladies' magazine *Tidens Kvinder* admires his beautiful white house – named by the first owner after his wives, all three of whom bore the name of Louise. It is as if all the peace and beauty of summer are contained in the extensive park. From the Sound can be heard the chugging of a motorboat, otherwise all is still. Then they go inside. Passing through the white hall they enter a "splendid" French drawing-room where a large painting in clear colours – Philipsen's calves on grass – has a cooling effect in the heat. In the window stand costly pieces of porcelain and on a "delightful" French chest of drawers a slender, gracious clock from 1790. Then one turns round and catches sight of the "amusing" figures on the mantelpiece – and so it continues.

Here is everything that a generation later makes the writer Carsten Jensen utter his so typical of his time "North Zealand makes me want to throw up!" But as yet the region has not been transformed from a landscape designed for pure and unadulterated pleasure with its royal palaces and sophisticated bourgeoisie into an object of envy and contempt. This did not happen until the 1960s.

Tidens Kvinder enjoys the visit to Louisiana where everything bears the stamp of "fine old culture and quiet distinction." The garden room is all in white with squares of gold, the dining-room is dignified as in old manor houses, and on the first floor hang the big names of the Golden Age of Danish art with their easily understood mountainous coasts and island girls, farms, basket weavers and 'Glimpse into a Sunlit Room'.

The best thing about it all, writes the coquette signature Lancette, is that nothing in the white house seems overdone. She emphasises her point: "This is not a museum."

Landowner and dentist Busky-Neergaard on the steps in front of Louisiana in 1942. He would be the villa's last resident.

"North Zealand makes me want to throw up!"

Before Louisiana
became modern: the
big drawing-room with
French furniture.

The beginning

On a summer afternoon heavy with rain sixteen years later, Louisiana opens as a museum – the very concept that *Tidens Kvinder* associated with something overdone, unwanted and moribund. On the big day, 14 August 1958, the correspondent from *Skånska Dagbladet* refrains from calling Louisiana a museum. He does not have the heart to do so, cannot get the word past his lips, for "there is an interplay of art and nature that completely expels the museum fatigue most of us know," he reports in surprise and together with 400 other guests wanders slowly down the glass corridors in Scandinavia's only museum of modern art directly built for that purpose. Not as when the Swedes inaugurated their Moderna Museet in Stockholm a couple of months earlier. It is situated in what was formerly the Navy's gymnasium on Skeppsholmen. Here in Humlebæk, the new art has for the first time not been stuffed into old premises that smell from afar of times gone by and the salon art of the haute bourgeoisie. Here the new is enveloped in the new. No one has seen anything like it.

"From the moment the stream of invited guests began to glide down through the long, airy rooms, a festive atmosphere spread among all those with whom Knud W. Jensen had wished to share his pleasure, and it intensified in the course of the afternoon as the impressions gradually settled. One felt almost like one big elated family," writes *Politiken's* man on the spot.

There is a bang – a crowd collects. A guest – now with broken spectacles and a bleeding bump on his forehead – has tried to go out into the park at a place where there was no door, but a big glass pane. Denmark has not yet become accustomed to double-glazed windows from floor to ceiling. They have just arrived in the country, and there is *a lot* of glass in Louisiana. One architectural reviewer mentions "the glass wall" in the cafeteria, another the "sky-high glass wall in the room facing the woodland lake", and in *Bo Bedre* Louisiana's architects defend the new glass walls against a sceptical housewife who had criticised them under the heading "Do we want to live in aquariums?" The men smoke uninhibitedly, dropping their ash on the red-violet tiled floors. The women are in suits and with hats, and some types from the third category, the artists, wear beards and sandals, as they should. Some of them even look at the pictures on the white brick walls. Except for a couple of Swedish and Norwegian artists, these are all by Danish painters, for Louisiana has been conceived as a fortress of new Danish art. To fill the rooms and supplement his own collection Knud W. Jensen has been round to borrow from private collectors and the Carlsberg Foundation. The art is uninsistent, far from the sensational. Nothing disturbing here, but delightful paintings of women, of landscapes, of still-lifes. An "uncomplicated enjoyment" is promised by the first catalogue which describes their creators as artists who

Knud W. Jensen speaking about his museum which surprised everybody by immediately stealing the picture. In the first row sits Minister
of Education Jørgen Jørgensen, also called the peasant from Lejre
(furthest left), next Vivi Jensen in a white suit and her mother with hat.

have matured in independence, "indeed at a distance from the period's avant-garde". They do not belong to the avantgarde, but to something more peaceful. The "heavily reliable" is what many years later Hans Edvard Nørregård-Nielsen calls the first art at Louisiana.

In the high-ceilinged room looking out over the woodland lake hang Niels Larsen Stevns' five large preliminary studies for his decoration of Ranum Church in the 1920s. And then, of course, there is the sadly missed abstract art that has nowhere else to be. Ten years earlier the director of *Statens Museum for Kunst* had been forced to accept the purchase of an abstract painting. He hated it, but the acquisitions committee forced through the purchase because irritatingly enough this was a trend in Danish and international art that could not possibly be ignored any longer.

Louisiana's collection begins with Larsen Stevns and Poul S. Christiansen, goes on via Isakson, Weie, Lundstrøm and Astrid Noack and ends with "the most recent moderns" Preben Hornung, Robert Jacobsen and Richard Mortensen, whose long composition "Normandie" would later survive the purge of Danish art at Louisiana together with a very few of the others from the great day.

"In this museum – it is so vital that one can hardly bear to call it a museum – one is continuously in a strangely delusive way both inside and outside at the same time," writes the journalist from *Kristeligt Dagblad*. He is on a walking tour, but the tour has a calming and enriching effect, he notes. He has time to breathe between the many impressions. The moment he leaves the closed block of the classical house, he is off on a journey in a varied zigzag of galleries, rooms, courtyards, atriums and terraces which offer diverse competitions between the art works on the whitewashed brick walls and the landscape outside. And then the walk ends "in a kind of convalescent room" with a view and a grand piano, books and the profane cafeteria which constantly has to be apologised for and explained by the director:

"It may seem peculiar, but is it so strange? The Museum is situated about 30 km from the metropolis, and whether we're thinking of Copenhageners or foreign tourists, why shouldn't they be able to enjoy their tea or coffee in beautiful civilised surroundings? I think one can permit oneself materialism in this form."

Louisiana is the place where sixth formers taste Earl Grey for the first time. They come into a pleasant middle-class setting that is new to many of them, and for some of them the museum has a formative function. "A visit to Louisiana was nice – it did *not* make you feel socially inferior," says Dan Tschernia, one of these very young men or big boys who took the train to Humlebæk voluntarily. Also because it was an excellent place to meet girls.

Louisiana is the place where sixt

People poured in and the wear and tear was so great that the designer furniture could not stand up to the treatment and had to be removed.

ormers taste Earl Grey for the first time

Classical music, speeches,
light refreshments and 400
guests for the inauguration
of Louisiana, the museum
for Danish contemporary art
and handicrafts, as it was
then called. Both designations disappeared later.

The Wind Quintet of 1932 is playing Haydn and Carl Nielsen, and it appears to have been a surprise for the chairman of the parish council that the host has had the unheard-of idea to invite everyone who has been involved with the creation of the museum, even the artists. So when he catches sight of the painter Jeppe Von-tillius, he asks quite spontaneously: "What on earth are you doing here?"

The company is a bit mixed for a society event, but to *Information*'s relief there is nevertheless a décolletée lady present clad in a living poodle puppy. The fashionable newspaper artists nose around among high and low. Even the Communist paper *Land og Folk* surrenders to this "painting museum for joie de vivre" which is entirely successful in avoiding the usual boring effect of old fogies hanging in golden frames on the walls – sore feet and mortal weariness. "It deserves to become a real people's museum."

On one hand, the whole experience is luxurious – a country house with a park, expensive Danish Design strewn around with a generous hand, soft carpets and a genuine private capitalist, even if he is shy and becomingly restrained. On the other hand, the materials are unadorned: raw beams, brick, tiles on the floor. There is nothing ostentatious or superfluous. But then you may get a little shock when you go outside and see that the ends of the roof beams have been gilded.

In the long tent on the lawn the glad amateur Knud W. Jensen says from the podium that "Louisiana must be *used*, must be an artistic environment and the framework around a piece of life where things happen." He barely uses the word *museum* – it's so tainted, so repugnant to him in its classical form as an overfilled treasury with Olympian marble staircases, palm gardens and pillars, frozen in reverent silence and guarded by attendants in admirals' uniforms. The public go around with funereal faces!

With Louisiana he has launched a direct attack on that whole way of regarding art. A museum should not have an exhausting, humiliating or claustrophobic effect on its visitors, but seem secure, homely and pleasant. And do smoke by all means! He dreams of a museum without attendants as a declaration of trust in other people. And the reviewers feel that they understand him completely. They note that the new museum is simple and unpompous. That here the experience of painting, sculpture, design and architecture enters into an organic connection with concerts, enjoyment of the beautiful landscape, Sunday coffee and bathing on the beach. In this way, a blow has been delivered at the exclusiveness of the art specialists, writes one. Louisiana illustrates that art and culture are part of a happy and active life on earth.

In the old main building Busky-Neergaard's delightful chests of drawers and amusing pieces of porcelain have been replaced by modern sofa arrangements, small lamps, ashtrays and potted plants. Physically, only Knud W. Jensen himself with pipe and his Airedale Terrier Trofast [Faithful] at his feet are missing, and it is an excellent thing if one can really imagine him there since the furnishing is meant to bring out the atmosphere of a hospitable home that he is aiming at. Over the next 40 years, he uses the same picture to describe the aim of Louisiana: "It should be like visiting a slightly eccentric uncle in the country." You are invited to come in and look at the collection, feel at home, make yourself comfortable, and you don't leave again without having had a rest, a beer and some sandwiches, for now you've travelled all the way to Humlebæk, and the visit must certainly not be tiring. "You must see the garden too!"

The hospitable, eccentric uncle is central to the new museum. He is a vivid host figure with personal care for his guests, an eye for detail and is as such an unusual phenomenon. You won't find him in other museums. Knud W. Jensen is a skilled mythologist and succeeds in planting the uncle in most later Danish and foreign descriptions of his lifework. The message is received from Day 1:

"You do not have the impression that you are in a museum. There is no control at the entrance to make sure that you have paid for admission. There is not a single sign telling you not to touch the exhibited objects. On the contrary, round about in the museum on small tables one finds books and magazines that you can immerse yourself in during a short rest, comfortably lounging in one of the many armchairs. You do not meet an attendant in each room who stares down the visitors if they depart in the slightest from the strict house rules," writes a journalist, who like the others is especially struck by the difference between the new museum and the old ones.

Next day the palpable absence of museum weariness is a major news item in the Danish press along with its most extravagant innovation – the cafeteria. Coffee, cake and art in one mouthful is an unheard of provocation for the art experts in 1958, but this is only the beginning for a sequence of events that will in time make Louisiana a norm-setter, introduce a ground-breaking new museal concept – and change the way in which Danes look at art.

The simple outdoor ter-
race with serving tables.
The Danish museum world
found it profane to serve a
cup of coffee so close to art.

Resistance I

Louisiana's sudden appearance coincided with almost uncanny precision with another revolution – the 1960s. They began already in 1958. That year Denmark's slow, weak economic progress changed character, and became dynamic, rapid and so overwhelming that a Danish historian compares this tiger's leap with the transition from hunting to farming 6000 years ago.

Denmark sprang from agriculture to industry, from the country to the towns, from shortage to abundance, from savings to borrowings. It was like moving from East to West Berlin, and the effect could immediately be seen in the stream of people towards Humlebæk where Knud W. Jensen had spent 1.6 million kroner of his own money on an idea his friends thought was hopeless.

They were afraid that he was squandering his entire fortune, earned from cheese, and advised him against going any further. At the start nobody supported him. The museum was situated far too far away. It was a whole journey to get there and just think of Nivaagaard which was closer to Copenhagen, but still had to be warned by telephone if one wanted to see the collection on a Sunday. And Humlebæk was a hole in the ground inhabited by peculiar fishermen, neglected children and a handful of wealthy families in the summer villas on the beach side of the old coast road. The only culture in the place emanated from Krogerup Højskole, the church and Karen Blixen further in towards town. Moreover, most of his friends and acquaintances were critics and writers, not painters, and therefore they naturally focused on their own interests in the shape of Denmark's largest publishing house, Gyldendal, which Knud W. Jensen had bought in 1952, and on the extreme generosity with which their patron had hitherto met them. He carried out his risky enterprise despite warnings and resistance and tried to calm them by saying "people will get cars", but no one believed that this would happen. He expected crowds of visitors and exclaimed triumphantly to his friends: "You can say what you like, but one day Louisiana will be visited just as much as Kronborg."

"Knud was right. People bought cars, and they drove to Louisiana to an extent that none of us, not even Knud, had expected," says Vivi Jensen, who married him in 1957. At the beginning of the decade, the whole country contained only 100,000 private cars – twenty years later there were 1.3 million. Louisiana was well adapted to the coming years' Social Democratic, thriving, highly taxed and motorised Scandinavia with more free time and shorter working hours.

That this castle-in-Spain of a museum would get so far occurred to none of his friends when they celebrated Knud W. Jensen's 40th birthday in the empty rooms of the main building in 1956. On tables knocked up for the occasion from planks and covered in paper they ate food brought in from outside off paper plates.

The friends Thorkild Bjørnvig, Knud W. Jensen and Ole Wivel in front of Louisiana in the opening year 1958. The price of the new museum buildings totalling 11,000 square feet was 1.6 million kroner.

Der synes nu at skulle falde Ro over Gyldendals Forlag, efter at Aktie-majoriteten er købt af den stærkt litterært interesserede Ostegrosserer Knud W. Jensen.

The young poet and critic Niels Barfoed was sitting in the crowd and found the atmosphere strange:

"I remember it as if into his new house Knud had dragged a circle of "Heretics" plus others who were not actually an integral part of his plans. They were writers and their wives and they had worn down each other's and *Heretica*'s ideas. There was something absurd about the company. They were not excited by Knud's vision. They just sat there knocking over bottles and throwing bottle tops around as they usually did. It must have been a bit of a disappointing inauguration for Knud."

He wanted to do considerably more than anyone, himself included, realised. 1.6 million kroner was a lot of money at that time, also for the wealthy, and "there were quite a few people who shook their heads at such boldness, not to say irresponsibility," remarks one of the museum's architects Vilhelm Wohlert.

In 1950 Bo Bjørnvig moved with his parents to nearby Sletten into a house that Knud W. Jensen had bought for his father, the poet Thorkild Bjørnvig. The boy noticed that some people condescendingly called Knud Cheese-Jensen. Perhaps they didn't directly laugh at him, but they smiled a little. "They underestimated him. Only when Louisiana became a success did they take their hats off to him. They all believed that they could cultivate him and milk him, but later they found out that he was in fact strong. You could be hard on him, also at a personal level, but no one was allowed to touch Louisiana. "

An inevitable cheese cartoon after Knud W. Jensen's purchase of Gyldendal in 1952.

Say CHEESE-

Aktiemajoriteten i Gyldendal er nu erhvervet af en ostegrosserer.

In the newspapers, journalists, critics and opinion-makers also found it difficult to write about Knud W. Jensen without mentioning the tempting figure of Cheese-Jensen:

"It may seem immaterial, but I know that in the long run it irritated him," remarks Klaus Rifbjerg. "Not because Knud W. Jensen can't tolerate being called names; there's enough stuffing in him to tolerate the crudest attacks – what bothered him – and with good reason – is the attitude that the repeated associations reveal. If you haven't been to university, but have money on the other hand and also ideas about how it can be used in a sensible way, you are not merely slightly comic, but also suspect."

Fifty years later, Cheese-Jensen still existed in spite of Louisiana's enormous success and the shower of honours accorded to its founder. All his life it bothered him, not that he had been a cheese wholesaler, but that some people continued to believe that he still was: "It doesn't matter how much I read, learn and distance myself from my past, I am and will remain a cheese merchant in some people's heads," he said as an 82-year-old to Karen Fougner, who got to know him when she made two TV specials about him. Cheese-Jensen was not a friendly nickname – it stank of disrespect. His money was a disadvantage. Here came the spoilt scion of a millionaire, and bought a new sandbox and some new and amusing friends to play with. Only one person was enthusiastic – himself. And that was enough.

Yet another cheese cartoon. The director of Gyldendal, Ingeborg Andersen, had to make way for the young leadership trio.

Cheese wholesaler Knud W. Jensen photographed for the ladies' magazine *Tidens Kvinder*
with dog and pipe in the drawing-room at Louisiana in 1958. He saw himself as the attentive host to the museum's visitors and throughout his life said that a visit to Louisiana should
be like dropping in on an eccentric uncle. Pleasant and relaxed as in a private home.

Only one person was enthusiastic

At the opening of Louisiana in 1958 litterateur Torben Brostrøm was 30 years old and deeply involved in the journal *Hvedekorn*, which saw itself as coarse, proletarian and revolutionary, potatoes and gravy, while Gyldendal and Louisiana were labelled as well off, established and devoted to elite culture: "The opposition is comic, for Knud W. Jensen was an avantgardist," says Brostrøm today. "He came from the top of society and was revolutionary in his own way. He opened a window to the world and let it in, and he risked his money with gusto."

At that time, Danish cultural life consisted of circles that were not in contact with, but peered suspiciously at, one another. The split between deep provincialism, conservative tradition, massive moralising, hesitant modernism and consummated international avantgardism was extreme. For this reason, Brostrøm gasped in astonishment when in the middle of the 1950s he suddenly caught sight of a man in a light, well fitting suit who was walking around staring intensely at the pictures of "the enemy", namely *Hvedekorn*, which exhibited graphic art from the journal in auction rooms in Bredgade. "Christ, that was Knud W. Jensen!" his co-arranger said. It seemed like a visit from another world.

The 1950s were a modest time, in which Danes were still waiting for rump steak and artichokes, holidays in Spain, jet planes and parking houses. Knud W. Jensen called the decade a prelude and a strange transitional period, monotonous and colourless in comparison with the 1960s. The mood was low key and all good things, except for love, were rationed. Industry kept a low profile. But the new era began. Panduro wrote "Kick Me in the Traditions", and that is precisely what Jensen did. At one and the same time, he was in tune with the economic boom that had come to Denmark and in marked opposition to the otherwise unbudgeable way of exhibiting art in the country. He profiled the museum by breaking with the old. At the core of Louisiana's success is its breach with that which had gone before.

Resistance II

Already in its first year, the new museum north of Copenhagen attracted more visitors than the monopoly in the capital, *Statens Museum for Kunst* (The Danish National Gallery). The success proved to be a reflection neither of beginner's luck nor of the public's short-lived curiosity – that's how it continued each and every year ever since. In some years, Louisiana had twice as many visitors; in other years, three or four times as many – humiliatingly for such a dignified museum with a colossal and rich collection, state backing it, real art historians and a central address. Louisiana's staff numbered seven employees. Open every day.

Knud W. Jensen grew up with *Statens Museum for Kunst* which for him, despite his dislike of thinking in terms of confrontation, represented how *not*

imself

to run a museum. This applied all the way from the stiff and boring stylised garden filled with bad sculptures. At the steps and the entrance portal one was received by the pompous attendant in scarlet cloak and three-cornered hat. His distrustful eyes would follow the young fellow up the marble stairs until in the colonnade around the vestibule he was met by other zealous guardians in black silver-buttoned uniforms. They were everywhere and affected the atmosphere. Knud W. Jensen came to see Matisse, Weie, Giersing, Lundstrøm, Høst, Hoppe and a few others in the modern department. Abstract art and surrealism were not to be found.

On the way back he looked with repulsion at the ground floor's dusty plaster casts crowded together in some of the museum's best rooms. In the vestibule there lay a couple of old catalogues for inspection on a counter with some post-cards to liven things up.

Although he was too cultivated and diplomatic to openly express his plea-sure that Louisiana's example was used against the old museums, which all of a sudden made a very boring effect, there is no doubt that his intention was to challenge Denmark's major art museum and the highest art-historical expertise in the country. Louisiana was a direct reaction to the classical museum. A cor-rective, quite simply. No one thought for a moment that Louisiana would become anything more than a little private supplement to *Statens Museum for Kunst*, but it became its main competitor. When at the end of the 1950s, art historian Hanne Finsen went to work at *Statens Museum for Kunst*, the art historians were discussing the new museum at lunch:

"They agreed that Louisiana was not really first-rate. Director Jørn Rubow was a witty and intelligent man, but he did not care for these modern activities. He and most of the other museum directors and art historians turned up their noses at Louisiana's exhibitions and cafeteria, and they did so for many years. The mu-seum world was a cultivated world, closed towards the general public. Working hours were from 10 to 3, lunch included. If one had acquired a picture or had one cleaned, one could sit looking at it a whole afternoon, discussing it and drinking tea. Nothing happened. Rubow was also opposed to exhibitions which is difficult to understand, and there was a general lack of interest in spreading knowledge about art. Today, I can't understand that sort of thing took place in my lifetime. It's also absurd to think that there was so much opposition to Knud W. Jensen at the start when we imitate him today and have done so for many years."

A museum was regarded as a temple, elevated and sacral, where those who were specially interested immersed themselves in art. Art was presented as some-thing impressive and unapproachable – one came to it in reverence and as quietly as in a church. It was necessary to have eaten at least a snack beforehand because

Already in the first year the little museum in the provinces attracted more visitors than the monopoly in the capital, *Statens Museum for Kunst*. And went on doing so.

of course you couldn't get any refreshments for miles around. All references to a
world outside had been removed since the works demanded a hypnotic concentration that apparently risked being disturbed by the fragrance of coffee or the
sight of a park with trees. It was different at Louisiana where the door to the park
stood open so you could go in and out as you wished, and friendly attendants wandered around in their own clothes. The critics feared that the actual framework
was stealing all attention, that people came to admire the coffee and the trees,
but they forgot that classical museums are also frameworks. They are built like
high-ceilinged church interiors where the original homage to Our Lord rubs off
on the art and elevates it. At Louisiana the framework elevates first and foremost
the wellbeing of the visitors.

   "A valuable art work can be trodden flat in tumultuous surroundings," was
the view of Erik Fischer from *Statens Museum for Kunst*. "Despite all the success
of the modern exhibition business, one shouldn't entirely forget the importance
of being able calmly to immerse oneself year after year in the works that *Statens
Museum*, *Glyptoteket*, Hirschsprung's Collection and Ordrupgaard possess."

Jazz at Louisiana:
"There were people
who found this use of
a museum offensive,
and in their honour that
we bring the picture
below!" Knud W. Jensen
wrote in the *Louisiana
Årbog* [Louisiana
Yearbook] 1959. The
painting is William
Scharff's 'Legend'.

Young men at a jazz
evening in the 1950s,
when smoking was
quite OK. Louisiana was
to be the place where
things happened.

One Sunday at the beginning of the 1960s Jørgen Nørgaard was going round in the rooms in Sølvgade with his little boy Mads by his side. The boy began to sing, and a second later an attendant announced that this was not permitted. "But art and singing go together well," the father suggested optimistically, but no, it was out of the question. That was not the kind of thing you did in a place where they were watching over the Holy Grail.

"Louisiana was a breach with all that we knew. There were many of us who had expectations of a new way of looking at art – a freer way. *Statens Museum for Kunst* was very disciplined, but the spirit of the times was moving towards greater freedom. At Louisiana, there was a mood of cheerfulness all the way through," says Jørgen Nørgaard, who in 1958 opened his equally oppositional clothes store Nørgaard in his father's discreet and sombre shop for mourning clothes in the centre of town.

In 1958, no serious museum or university course of study was concerned with contemporary art. The now evoked scepticism or embarrassment, and a kind of deliberate retarding mechanism set in. The idea was to take one's time, not just fall for some *fashionable trend* that was whizzing confusedly around on the surface. But it was this very now that Knud W. Jensen wanted – it was part of his relish for people and criterion for success to think: What is important right now?

Statens Museum for Kunst did not take its responsibility for also buying and showing contemporary art seriously. Leo Svane, the director up to 1952, couldn't stand Picasso and abstract art, but did like Matisse and other contemporary French artists, and his successor Jørn Rubow couldn't stand the public who disturbed the museum's most important task: the collection and preservation of art. It was said of him that he wanted to have the museum for himself.

When at last in 1970 the public stormed the museum to see a Matisse exhibition and formed queues in front of the ticket office, in front of the toilets and in front of the pictures, the irritated wife of one of the museum's inspectors asked Hanne Finsen, who had cobbled the success together: "Is it you who are to blame for this?" She became a kind of fifth column working within the rigid *Statens Museum for Kunst* and trying to do the same thing as Louisiana: to open the doors and invite people inside, an endeavour that was thoroughly sabotaged by her own chiefs.

At the big state museum paid for by the taxpayers, visitors were preferably expected to know something about art. At Louisiana, the private director Knud W. Jensen changed the order of the factors and placed the communication of knowledge about art above everything else. He took up arms against "arrogant laziness", as art historian Hans Edvard Nørregård-Nielsen, with an expression

The pompous *Statens Museum for Kunst* that Louisiana is a direct reaction to. "It was a true chamber of horrors," said Knud W. Jensen.

Louisiana quickly understood that people would not keep on coming just to see the new buildings and the museum's own pictures. Something had to happen. The museum began to look outwards and to present exhibitions, lectures and concerts.

borrowed from Hans Scherfig, calls the attitude of the period to the general public. Louisiana's attitude was the opposite; a friendly invitation:

"At Louisiana importance was attached from the start to catalogues that in a reader-friendly fashion cast light on the art works in time and space. Indeed, what else, an undaunted soul might exclaim today, but a generation ago this was far from the norm at the other art museums. There was an aura of condescending expertise that was hostile to life and thereby to art about the collections, which ordinary people ought to view only after having removed their clogs."

Louisiana's problem seemed fairly simple to the critics: It was too beautiful. There were complaints about the distracting effect and unfair competition offered by the natural surroundings. What discreet little landscape painting measuring 46 cm x 38 cm could compete with the park, the woodland lake and the Sound? It was too much. When *Moderna Museet* from Stockholm visited Louisiana in 1960, the Swedes proposed toning down the view by darkening the window in the high-ceilinged room looking out onto the woodland lake because "otherwise one might easily forget the art adorning the other walls".

An important person like Thorlacius-Ussing, chairman of the Carlsberg Foundation looked with scepticism at the new boy in the class. It was one thing that Louisiana was one more mouth to feed, but the surroundings up there seemed to the modestly brought up clergyman's son to be a little too stylish and distracting. His official excuse for not supporting the museum was that one art patron does not support another, but like so many other people in the frugal 1950s he could not help adopting a puritanical view on the place.

"The effect of good art is diminished in unattractive and dingy surroundings. The framework is not unimportant. That is something that "Louisiana" has understood – excessively so, since for the ordinary visitor the framework simply takes the sheen off the works," was the view expressed by Thorlacius-Ussing. Not until 1961 did the Foundation's board of directors visit Louisiana. Five years had passed since Knud W. Jensen wrote an enthusiastic letter to the Foundation about his plans.

The fluxus artist Arthur Køpcke joked that Louisiana was not so bad at all, but "Jensen must find some tricks to make people look at the pictures as well. Paint the windows black, put an emetic in the coffee." To this very day, the museum inspectors realise that Louisiana is a *very nice* place, and that it can be too much of a good thing with all that chamber music and elegant white modernism. They are afraid to wrap the delicious up deliciously and therefore hesitated for a moment before the idea of an Arne Jacobsen exhibition in 2002. But only for a moment.

The criticism of excess continues to be heard. At regular intervals this slightly self-flagellating school rejects the idea that one can show raw, revolutionary and

Concert by the sea. Critics were initially worried that the surroundings would get all the attention so people admired the view and trees instead of art. Conversely, Knud W. Jensen thought that the landscape and the distractions meant that people could endure seeing all that art.

dirty art in beautiful, friendly surroundings without pulling out teeth and rendering the art innocuous. Placing yourself in North Zealand does not immediately give street credibility, and Louisiana has an atmosphere of the coastal road and white garden walls about it. There the art is "given a calm setting as the pleasant furnishings of a magnificent house, but is also deprived of its force. One feels comfortable in Humlebæk – too comfortable, as if that was good enough," writes the German critic Peter Iden in *Frankfurter Rundschau* 15 years later under the headline "Schönes Haus der falschen Versöhnung"[Beautiful house of false reconciliation].

Another irritating thing about the hardworking new creation was its focus on the public and how many people bought tickets. Suddenly the concept of "visitor figures" appeared and created unrest both in the sweetly slumbering museum world and in the press, which realised that people's interest in art was much greater than anyone had thought. They were pouring in up north and by sheer weight of numbers exerting such wear and tear on Børge Mogensen, Wegner and the others that the museum had to give up having Danish designer furniture freely available. The things could not bear the "visitor figures". The founder had calculated with 40,000 visitors a year, and there were 240,000. A permanent cause for complaint for some critics was and is the popularity of the place, and this was immediately equated with populism. It is suspect to have a large number of visitors, because then the museum has not "moved far enough away". Then it is all too easy. If an exhibition appeals to many people, it must be hopeless, for most people are idiots.

A year after the opening the papers were writing about "the Louisiana lesson", which the other museums had to take note of. They also stopped putting the name of the museum in inverted commas – Louisiana now had a place in Danish consciousness. Very early the press and politicians used Louisiana's success as a stick with which to beat *Statens Museum for Kunst*. While Louisiana was being overwhelmed by visitors, wounded museum specialists called it Circusiana, "a museum business", "a supermarket" and a place that "drains the seriousness from art and transforms it into a commodity".

As the 1950s turned into the 1960s, the newspaper *Politiken* compared Louisiana with a supermarket because both institutions arose in the same decade and both tempted and irritated:

"Both places have lots of glass, openness, a multiplicity of wares, self-service, the consumer's belief in his own free will and the owner's pedagogical sureness of touch. The customer is led in such a way that he thinks he is independent.

At Louisiana what is on offer is artistic. Things are individual, originality is the trademark, and nevertheless all these unique objects become one big modernistic unity, the harmony of conformity.

Louisiana is both elitist and popular. The majesty of art resident in a one-family house only a little larger than normal houses, democracy invited into the homes of those that count.

It is said that society was atomised in the 50s. There are indications that the particles are reuniting to form new patterns. The success of the museum in Humlebæk and of the superstores on every street corner is more than just a fashionable phenomenon. They do something for the soul."

When on the first anniversary of the museum its founder, happy and in fine fettle, invited the press and his friends to an informal buffet lunch with cold and hot food, Mosel and beer, he was virtually bubbling over with new ideas – Louisiana gramophone records, Louisiana theatre, Louisiana design – this was just another provocation from beyond the fringe. In comparison with the sleepy level at the other museums the activity had also been fairly extreme: 64 arrangements in the first twelve months and the following year continued in top gear with twelve-tone jazz, readings of modern poetry and a young public who danced in the big paintings room. "There were people who were shocked at this use of a museum, and it is for their pleasure that we bring the picture below!" the museum reflected in its yearbook from 1959 and showed the unthinkable event.

Knud W. Jensen assumed a jaunty position on the delicate question of pure art and dirty money. On the whole grubby market in Humlebæk, where someone had had the idea of selling things to earn money for buying art, central heating or more bricks. He couldn't understand the others' fear of contamination. "I think that art is better served by being a business than by having to run around begging for public subsidies for everything," he defended himself.

At the Royal Academy of Fine Art, Egill Jacobsen was appointed Professor of Painting in 1959 as the first abstract artist to hold the post and commented on the criticism of Louisiana by saying that the real scandal was at *Statens Museum for Kunst*, where new Danish art lay stored in the basement while the exhibition rooms were filled with older and very dead masters:

"The debate on "Louisiana" came to concern trivialities," he said. "People criticised the lighting and the acquisitions, but forgot to mention that the whole thing was created by one man and in one year. The discussion then went on to be about whether coffee should be served at all among art works and whether people looked pleased when they came out of "Louisiana", while they looked sour when they came out of other museums. Wasn't it time to promote a rather different form of criticism about other things? For the idea of "Louisiana" is of course wonderful in itself. Here a private person creates a museum, in which one can go around freely among the works as opposed to a state museum where you of course have to have attendants to keep an eye on the valuables. The public museums are dependent on that kind of thing, whereas Knud W. Jensen can more or less disregard it."

It was as if a little private TV channel of art had challenged the state-run monopoly and brought competition with it by being radically different, profiled and popular. It stood the existing state of things on its head even though the revolution took place on a country estate in North Zealand. As a patron of the arts and a person Knud W. Jensen was "a piece of filthy luck" for Denmark, as Hans Edvard Nørregård-Nielsen, who became chairman of the Carlsberg Foundation in 1988, puts it. Here at last was a man who instead of just thinking about his own private interests placed himself and his money at the disposition of the general public. A small, amiable man with the best of intentions and a secret that very few people heard anything abut before he was dead.

Knud W. Jensen's life – first half

At Louisiana's opening Knud W. Jensen was 41 years old and about halfway through his life. Slim and light on his feet, always dressed in a suit, he had no trouble smoking 40 plus cigarettes a day in addition to his pipe and wore his hair combed straight back like everyone else. He could have spent his time relaxing at Vedbæk Tennis Club, clad in white flannels with red clay on them, looking at the girls from the upper layers of society, but it was something else that got him out of bed in the morning and drew him on. Around him quivered a restlessness so strong that it made some people want to take him by the shoulders and forcibly sit him down. An adrenalin-powered motor that worked at high pressure and made him leap from fire to fire, from one infatuated idea to the next. He let himself be seduced, *wanted* to be seduced, and also seduced others. Everything had to go quickly, always there were unused ideas ready to be taken up. To be near him could be intolerable and fantastic. At night he slept very little, read all the more and knocked on the doors of overnighting guests with articles they ought to look at.

Inculcated in him from childhood was the value of hard toil and common sense, of working from morning to night. His father was a reserved gentleman, but his mother had a soft temperament; there was much laughter between them and his way through life was easy and untroubled. If he met a new person, he invited that person home with him. When he was enthusiastic, he couldn't imagine that that wasn't the case for everyone else. For this reason he could be tough on his staff, while others further up in the hierarchy or outside the house never heard him raise his voice or say an unfriendly word. He might found the association "Art at the Workplace", but democracy at the workplace – no way. This was oligarchy in practice. In that respect he was the product of his childhood home and of his

Knud W. Jensen came from on one of Denmark's wealthiest families. His grandfather had worked his way up from dairy worker to dairy owner and retired as a rentier in Copenhagen at the age of only 45.

position as only son and adored latecomer to the family. He had his socks ironed and was accustomed to getting whatever he asked for. Without delay. That it worked at Louisiana was only because he was open and flexible. He preserved his ability to be persuaded, to apologise and to listen to others, but for the most part he opted for his own idea. Karen Blixen saw through his special way of asking others for advice. "Why are you asking? You know the answer yourself," she said, meaning that since he could formulate the question, he had the answer in himself.

In many ways he seemed clearly overworked, a little absent-minded and en route somewhere else. He had an awe-inspiring capacity for work, and he might appear weary to the bone, but not worried. In money matters he was almost carefree. He just wanted to get things going and then speed them up.

Karen Blixen and Benedicte Jensen on the trip to Greece. In Knud W. Jensen's book "Mit Louisiana-liv" [My Louisiana Life] his ex-wife has been cut out of the picture.

It always surprised people, especially writers and artists, that a rich man should be so restrained and modest. That a man who in the frugal 1950s already had floor heating and a chauffeur for his Mercedes could be passionately concerned with lyric poetry and archaic Greek art. That a man with a yacht, horses and fluent French, German and English in his head bought houses for poor poets and drove them round to superb meals at North Zealand inns. He received letters from astonished people who had never dreamed that a capitalist could behave so generously. They enjoyed it and allowed themselves to be carried away by the *Grand-Seigneur* atmosphere that arose around him. Many felt that they actually became better and kinder persons from being under his roof. From going around in a strangely free atmosphere from reception room to kitchen, establishing depots of brandy and entering into special agreements with Elly, the housekeeper, who ran the house until their host married for the second time in 1957. He was the glad giver, the master of ceremonies.

Knud W. Jensen took this quality with him to Humlebæk in its purest form: all that is mine is yours. He collected people and by cosseting them brought out the best in them, enjoyed seeing other people find one another, talk together and enjoy themselves. When Louisiana's young architect Vilhelm Wohlert turned 80, Knud W. Jensen sent him a compliment in the form of a pile of photographs of relaxed people in the park and the museum. They look as if they were at home. Louisiana reflected his own extravagant and hospitable temperament, his sense of quality down to the smallest door handle.

"Lottery winners always say that they will give their grandchildren new bikes and put the rest of their winnings in the bank. The brilliant thing about Knud was that he knew what he wanted to spend the millions on. He had mastered the art of being rich," says Werner Svendsen, who got to know Knud W. Jensen in 1958.

Karen Blixen presented the same picture of him. She saw him as a divinely favoured person who sheds his gifts on others. Officially at any rate. In her private letters to other people she was harder on him and his restless activity, which made her anxious as opposed to "the slow and organic power that makes the acorn turn into an oak tree." In Blixen's eyes he was well behaved, nice, good and energetic, but nothing more. In a private letter from 1953 she complained of the stingy conditions in the Danish Broadcasting Corporation and drew an unflattering parallel: "The radio is such a miserable institution; it is always the same with it – just like, I think, with Knud Jensen – the way of thinking: 1.97 kroner, and that's no good in life; you have to put a two-kroner piece on the table!"

But Knud W. Jensen sent her oysters, champagne and flower bulbs. He provided the trappings for her Shrovetide children's party at Rungstedlund, on an excursion spontaneously bought a pedal-driven vehicle for her housekeeper's son, picked up the pampered but impecunious writer in his nice big car and had enough money to meet her wish for *first class* travel. In 1951 he invited her for three weeks to Greece and Italy together with his first wife Benedicte. It was a strenuous trip – the young host and hostess had prepared an ambitious programme. Exhausted, Karen Blixen wrote home to her secretary that she didn't know what to do with "such a spiritual pachyderm" as Knud W. Jensen. In his own view he performed as helper, midwife and mediator. Deep inside him his central project was to contribute to her art and get it to move on. To make something happen. For the same reason he installed poets in houses around him: to generate renewal, to create events.

In the same way he sent 20.year-old Niels Barfoed on a month-long trip to Greece with everything paid because they were both interested in Antiquity, and Barfoed had of course not been in Greece and had no prospect of going there. "You'd better be off," said Knud W. Jensen. This was characteristic of him, but crucial for Barfoed, whose direction in life was changed. It was as if Knud W. Jensen had picked him up and said: "What have we got here, and how can we get more out of it?"

"We freely spent Knud's money, which was also what he wanted," explained the writer Ole Wivel. The parties flowed with live music (Mozart), Steinwein and vintage red wine. Everything was in flagrant contrast with the guests' own miserable economic circumstances. On one occasion he hung bottles of beer up in the trees of the garden like fruit: one tree with ordinary strength lager, one with strong beer and one with apple juice for the children.

"Suddenly you were in safety, an entirely new place, happier and wiser in particular than in your daily life" another writer Tage Skou-Hansen recalls. "There was an excess in the world, a surplus of felicity and wellbeing that Knud with his generosity gave you access to, if not permanent residence in."

At home, he had been well brought up and was the type who once drew his friend Jørgen Gustava Brandt aside and asked him not to use the word *tits* in the presence of women. His guests naturally wore dinner jackets on New Year's Eve, and in 1951 for the sake of the entertainment he took part in the performance of "As You Like It". The writer Frank Jæger refused downright:

"Thank you for the letter with the invitation. It would never occur to me to play the fool in Shakespeare's exceptionally stupid and infantile slapstick farce. Nor would it ever occur to me to put on a dinner jacket because of the New Year. I have never worn black, neither for my christening, confirmation nor wedding, so why the hell should I do so at New Year? Idiotic. So thanks for the invitation, but no thank you then on my part."

The patron of the arts

Knud W. Jensen behaved as a patron of the arts even though he did not like the idealism contained in the term. As if he did it to be good. "All this is just due to the fact that it amused me so indescribably," he said before Louisiana opened. Only after his death did the idea occur to some people that the museum might have been a form of expiation for his conduct prior to and during the Occupation.

1939 was a decisive year. Knud W. Jensen returned home to Denmark after two years' apprenticeship in Switzerland, England and Germany and entered his father's cheese firm, but he oscillated between duty and the wish to study art history: "These were difficult years, for all the time I was longing to study," he wrote to Uffe Harder many years later.

That summer he had met Ole Wivel on the tennis courts in Vedbæk, where both their families lived in splendid villas on the shore of the Sound in the warm summer months. The two privileged and intelligent upper-class boys started a friendship that had consequences that went far beyond their own relationship. Wivel happened to have Johannes V. Jensen's *Digte [Poems]* (1906) on him, and they began talking. In Knud's car they drove to Sjælsø and sat by the lake talking

45

Awarding Louisiana's writer's prize in 1961. From the left:
Knud W. Jensen, Maria Giacobbe, Ivan Malinovski, Ruth
Malinovski, Erik Knudsen, Uffe Harder and Lise Sørensen.
Nearly all of them wrote for Louisiana's publications.

"Visions with an unclear outline ros

about poetry and painting. As darkness fell, Knud W. Jensen sketched his plans for the future of his new friend, who later described them as follows:

"We should find out, he thought, who we were irrespective of upbringing and environment – an obvious idea that was not alien to me although I had never formulated it for myself. But it dawned on me as he smoked one cigarette after the other keeping the mosquitoes away with a banner of smoke that identity problems had got their hook into him and itched continuously. Not that he felt unqualified for trade, but imagination ruled too strongly in him, the fear of a bourgeois style of life and too early resignation made him desperate. Visions with an unclear outline rose like the mists about us and surged over his defined path in life. He was a young man obsessed by expectations and dreams."

Young Knud W. Jensen wanted a different life from the one he already had. He wanted to get away from the cheese exports and the farmers, the trade and the dairies in the Danish provinces. And into a different world, a different existence. He met Ole Wivel, who became his entry to all that he wished for. And Knud W. Jensen could pay for Wivel's Publishing House, he could buy Gyldendal. Mutual friends sensed that Knud W. Jensen placed his spiritual life in pawn with him. They were as closely merged as brothers and they took turns to stand on each other's shoulders for the next 40 years until the friendship collapsed in 1982 after having been under pressure for years.

The patronage of the arts began in earnest after the war. Knud W. Jensen's father died in 1944, and his son inherited the biggest cheese firm in the country, the two sisters receiving a number of properties. The young director began by paying off the deficits for seven successive years at Wivel's Publishing House, founded in 1945 together with Ole Wivel, who also came from a tremendously rich family but felt no obligation to spend his own money. "Why shouldn't it be called Jensen's Publishing House?" asked one of Knud W. Jensen's sisters without getting an answer. The firm published beautiful and necessary, but deeply unprofitable art books, new Danish literature, poetry translations of major writers. Serious matters in the wake of the great catastrophe.

Three years later the patronage of the arts continued with the trend-setting journal *Heretica*, which grafted upon the profound pessimism of the period. The "Heretics" were provocative because they regarded pure artistic quality as the obvious salvation for all in the midst of the chaos. Literature and art ought not to be a political instrument, but something entirely separate. Art for art's sake, poetry before politics and almost religious hopes of the poet. Therefore, the writers who didn't feel like writing in *Heretica* or were not invited to do so often became political and for the main part Communists. The found the journal mystical, aloof from the world and hard to understand. Young Jørgen Nash described the magazine as "reactionary Christian spirituality" and "the smokescreen of reaction", whereupon Ole Wivel accused him of being a partisan in underpants and of belonging to the elite of the day before yesterday – the reactionary Communists. Another critic called Wivel a "cultural pessimist with kid gloves" and so on. The time was characterised by tough ideological disputes and merciless battles between the groupings that easily separated old friends.

In 1949 the journal's own big name Martin A. Hansen criticised the apple of his eye for having become the mouthpiece for one particular contemporary trend, anti-modernism. Thus, what was partially Knud W. Jensen's project was hostile to modernism, which would later form the basis for Louisiana. The "Heretics" feared that modernism dissolved meaningfulness and coherence in people's lives. They looked back in European tradition for sustainable positions and were not afraid of being called old-fashioned or nostalgic. Their wish was to renew the tradition, not to destroy it.

At Louisiana a decade later, Knud W. Jensen developed his taste and his collection in a direction that proved too much for the Norse Wivel, who reacted by resisting the sale of the good figurative Danish painters at the museum as long as possible. He preferred their "uninsistent greatness" to Knud W. Jensen's journey into "the flickering light of avantgarde art". While Knud W. felt more and more attracted by the advanced and the global, Wivel clung to the local and regional.

Without Knud W. Jensen's money it is unlikely that the publishing house or the journal would have seen the light of day. The first year he put 60,000 kroner in Wivel's Publishing House, the following year 30,000, then 45,000, 30,000 and so on in the same style. In return he had access to artistic material that he had dreamed about ever since he had studied art history and written a little treatise in Switzerland in 1937.

In his apartment in Skt. Thomas Allé in Frederiksberg the editors knocked down the wall between two of the rooms and allowed Knud W. Jensen to have the third room to himself. Late in the afternoon the anonymous financier came home from the office and took part in the night life on an equal footing with the others. And next morning he got up, shaved and went to the office again. To put it crudely, he was the provider. They represented intellect, he found the money. He got into bed with his face to the wall and back to the noise and paid the price for sublime entertainment and having amusing people around him. He *refused* to be bored, a fly in a bottle. He was capable of getting up at two o'clock in the morning and asking to be driven to Jutland.

Karen Blixen at Louisiana
together with the sculp-
tor Robert Jacobsen
in front of one of his
dolls in 1959. Modern
art was not her thing.

When the young poet Jørgen Gustava Brandt visited the editorial office in 1948, he found – in addition to exhausting intellectuality and spirituality and only male company – that Ole Wivel was affable and schoolboyish and Knud was full of initiative and extremely hospitable, inviting all and sundry to a concert in his mother's big white summer villa by the Sound.

The Communists at *Land og Folk* couldn't take it:

"While other millionaires keep race horses or, in all discretion, beauty queens, he keeps a stable of poets. He houses them, looks after their material needs, publishes their poems. And the poets are very willing to be kept, just like the well-groomed horses and the manicured beauty queens, and he has really succeeded in producing a litter of beaux-esprits, who have locked themselves hermetically into poetry's ivory tower, where they chant their verses, which do not have the least relevance for people outside the tower."

Knud W. Jensen regarded himself as a necessary intermediary between two worlds – the bourgeois life of action and the artistic world. He was at home in both and could therefore be useful. In the beginning, he was most involved in literature and friends with Karen Blixen, Martin A. Hansen, Poul La Cour, Thorkild Bjørnvig, Ole Wivel and Frank Jæger:

"For me it was the *poet* who had the key to the mystery, and who was somehow just something I could be glad about – well, perhaps if I could do some good or create an environment around his work or create the conditions in which it could prosper – that was my task."

Money creates dependence, and Knud W. Jensen created dependence, but he also created hope. He himself modestly described his role among the writers as "the chap who brought the beers in". He created the framework discreetly, but in reality he drove things forward very dynamically, first by acquiring Gyldendal and shortly after by inventing Louisiana. The framework grew super-large because that was what he wanted and could bring about. He underwent a real metamorphosis from upper-class youth through anonymous financier to a central figure in Danish cultural life.

"It is an irony of fate that he became the most famous of them all, and that his name will be remembered. He actually developed into a cultural personality. He didn't just pay – he filled out Louisiana, took part in the debate and became a person many were prepared to listen to. If anyone had predicted this development, people would not have believed it. He has only himself to thank that the picture has changed. He had success and discovered that he too had something to say. But he kept his mouth shut at that time and didn't make a strong impression on me. One thought most about his money," says Werner Svendsen.

The patron's typecasting of himself as the happy donor is too modest. In a long letter to Knud W. Jensen from Martin A. Hansen, dated 2nd November 1950 it appears that he was a sparring partner for the writer in the entire discussion about *Heretica*, not merely at a practical but also just much at an artistic level. The businessman had views that the writer heard and respected. Whether the latter knew of Knud W. Jensen's carefully concealed dark spot in his life is not known, but it is almost impossible to imagine that Martin A. Hansen, who had been deeply involved in the resistance movement and in a famous article had legitimised the liquidation of stool-pigeons, could have swallowed so bitter a pill.

The secret

In 1928 a charming and gifted seducer arrived in Denmark from Vienna. Fritz Waschnitius was 27 years old and only on an exploratory visit to the country, he said, but with the exception of a break just after the war he stayed in Denmark until his death in 1981. He succeeded in ruining two people's lives and spreading sorrow and guilt around him, insofar as it was all his work, which it wasn't.

Propagandists can only make an impact on those who are ready to receive them. Others turn around and leave.

Waschnitius soon sought to contact Danes with the same interest in classical, high-flown and grandiose literature. And art of course. Extrovert and eloquent, he found it easy to acquire friends. He visited the exhibitions put on by most of the Copenhagen artists' associations and already in the year following his arrival he met the young painter Ole Wiedemann Høst, son of the great landscape painter Oluf Høst on the island of Bornholm. Waschnitius became a close friend of both father and son, and later his circle of admirers was extended as people were bowled over like skittles by him and his "world spirit".

In the summer of 1932, the then 16-year-old Knud W. Jensen was on a biking holiday on Bornholm with his friend Ib Wiedemann, a nephew of Oluf Høst, and the two schoolboys stayed for a couple of days at the painter's open and lively red-plastered houses Norresân, which nestles up to Bokul, the cliff above the town of Gudhjem. Later Knud W. Jensen wrote of the pleasure he experienced in making his first acquaintance with a real painter:

"It is a world by itself, a large and seen from the outside rather inaccessible house, the façade of which is broken by a deep-lying stone stairway. But once one has entered, one is enveloped by a warm, intimate homeliness that is under-scored by the family's hospitality. Paintings, furniture and articles for everyday use merge into a whole, an expression of a simple, but artistically sophisticated bourgeois culture that I have met only a few times in my life."

Next summer, Fritz Waschnitius moved into the house as a guest of the Høst family, who always extended a welcome to the friends of their children. But already the following summer the German-speaking Austrian was the object of discussion in the small fishing town. It was not everywhere that he was *so* welcome. The young painter Sven Havsteen-Mikkelsen's stepfather was at any rate sceptical of his son's acquaintance with the stranger, and this was rumoured in the small town. The rumour also reached Waschnitius, who wrote angrily to Havsteen's stepfather that he would not accept being talked about in that way, for he had nothing else on his conscience than that as a German he had not con-cealed his sympathies for the National-Socialist government in Germany. With this letter Waschnitius made it clear that his sympathies lay with the Nazis.

Also Ole Lippmann came to Vedbæk Tennis Club in the fatal summer of 1939. The later resistance fighter, English major and parachute chief in Denmark heard the two new friends Wivel and Jensen raving about something they called "Neueuropa", that is to say the Third Reich's dream of an Arian continent under German leadership. From that day and all his life Lippmann distanced himself for political reasons from the two, also when summer after summer they ran into each other at Skagen. They merely nodded.

The same autumn Ole Wivel got to know a number of aspiring young painters through Knud W. Jensen. He met Sven Havsteen-Mikkelsen and Erik Johansen, son of the proprietor of Café Kronborg in the centre of town, where Knud lunched every day with his father. But neither Jensen nor Wivel mention with a single word their memories of the third young painter in the circle, Ole Høst, even though he became one of their best friends. One evening in September, Fritz Waschnitius turned up at the café and the ring was closed:

"The circle, the Ring, developed an interest in cultivating heroic masculine ideals. They read books, were occupied by discussing, translating and working on German, French and English literature, the old heroic poetry: Homer and Dante, Goethe, Nietzsche, Hölderlin, Schiller, Rilke, Stefan George and Vilhelm Grønbech, and these were works the stranger knew well," writes Hansaage Bøggild in "Ringen omkring Ole" [The Ring Around Ole].

Knud W. Jensen brought cheese and red wine; they smoked and talked and cultivated the aristocratic aesthetic ideals of the literature, now and again slipping into a homoerotic enthusiasm for great men. Possibly they did not see themselves as Nazis, but felt attracted by the pathos with which Nazi ideas could be presented.

"They were inspired by the will for *action* and the will for *change* that permeated the totalitarian ideologies," writes Bo Lidegaard in "Kampen om Danmark1933-45" [The Fight for Denmark] – the first scholarly work to place Knud W. Jensen's name in connection with Nazism. Like other young men in the 1930s he was captivated by the cult of the biggest and purest practised by charismatic leaders of the period and by the dream of a masculine community under strong leaders. With the German occupation of Denmark in 1940 it all became more concrete. In that year, the painters Helge Bertram and Sven Havsteen-Mikkelsen broke absolutely with Waschnitius, while Ole Høst and Erik Johansen, Ole Wivel and Knud W. Jensen remained absolutely connected with him. The two first volunteered for a work camp in Germany in order to get to know the powerful, promising country, and afterwards they wanted to go to the Eastern Front to fight against Communism on Germany's side. Wivel and Jensen supported them. In August 1941 expressing his recognition of the decision Ole Wivel sent a poem to Erik Johansen, in which one of the stanzas runs:

> Against all that will make no sacrifice
> Greater Germany's song rises
> On the wingspan of the eagle of victory
> To the sky

Members of the Ring.
From left: Knud W.
Jensen, Ole Wivel,
Fritz Waschnitius, Erik
Johansen, Ole Høst.

The poem is about a "mighty leader, strict and warm", about "blond children", "the beliefs and violence of alien races", "the shame of cowardice" and more of that sort of thing. The two parlour combatants themselves had no thoughts of setting off for the front. They planned to open publishing firms, they needed to think – and the business had to be looked after. Ole Høst stayed with his best friend Knud in Skt. Thomas Allé in the last week before the departure from Copenhagen Main Station on 22 August 1942, when Wivel, Knud W. Jensen and Waschnitius in German uniform waved goodbye, surrounded by Nazi banners and music.

Afterwards Erik Johansen hesitated. The idea was that he would follow Ole Høst to the front later, but he changed his mind and backed out because he had made a woman pregnant. Wivel wrote immediately and angrily: "Your defeat is irrevocable. In this fall, you know well, you tear down everything that has been between us. My contempt for you is great and I am inconsolable." Knud W. Jensen offered to pay for a protective equipment, but Johansen stayed at home, and 50 years later came after them with his blackmailing letters.

Ole Høst was 28 years old when he was killed on the Eastern Front in the Soviet Union in 1943. His mother and father received a letter from Berlin, which briefly announced that their son had fallen for Greater Germany. Then the conspiracy of silence began. Knud W. Jensen neither spoke nor wrote about his role in the Ring or about his friendship with Ole Høst, Erik Johansen and Fritz Waschnitius, not even when he was ready to write his memoirs in "Mit Louisiana-liv" [My Louisiana Life], which appeared in 1985. He was not interested in the story becoming known, but as always interest focuses on the very things one is trying to conceal.

The story slowly began to surface in 1999, when the doctor and writer Tage Voss was the first to write publicly that Ole Wivel, Knud W. Jensen and several others "once marched through the streets of Gudhjem with their arms outstretched in a taut Nazi salute" and added: "Boyish pranks, of course, also that Ole Høst volunteered for the Eastern Front, but just see if he didn't die of it!"

The artist Jørgen Nash confirmed the story, but nothing happened. On the contrary, aspersions were cast on Tage Voss in the large circle of sympathisers around Ole Wivel and Knud W. Jensen. As victors they had written history, and their version was accepted. The following year, in December 2000, the literary critic Jørgen Hunosøe analysed Ole Wivel's poems from the beginning of the 1940s and found Nazi ideas in them plus a "misconceived longing for perfection". Then came the rumpus, for the article appeared in the serious journal *Nordica*, and the charges had moved up to a higher level. Many people were indignant that anyone could think of writing that sort of thing about Wivel, including himself. He rejected all the charges in the piece "En ondskabsfuld klodsmajor" [A Malicious Bull in a China Shop] the year after.

The next development was the newspaper *Jyllands-Posten's* publication of the eulogising poem "Korset" [The Cross] from 1941, which had not been printed anywhere, but as mentioned above sent privately to Erik Johansen to support his decision to volunteer for the Eastern Front. The poem is so glowingly Nazi that that Wivel's last defenders surrendered to the idea that in his thinking at any rate the man had lost his way. Ole Wivel did not react to the publication of the poem. He died in 2004, and his reputation had suffered a blow.

Strangely enough Knud W. Jensen's reputation was not correspondingly damaged despite a number of sensitive spots: in the first place, Tage Voss mentions him as one of those giving the Nazi salute in the streets of Gudhjem: second, he was a member of the Ring, which was headed by a man who since 1933 at any rate had been enthusiastic about Hitler, and who during the Occupation made propaganda for German culture on the Danish radio; third, together with Ole Wivel he encouraged both Ole Høst and Erik Johansen to volunteer for the Eastern Front, and fourth he kept silent when it was all over.

Nor is Ole Høst's fate mentioned in the book on Oluf Høst published on the occasion of the opening of the Høst Museum in Gudhjem in 1998, which Knud W. Jensen had worked hard for. He sent a copy to the old painter and resistance fighter Sven Havsteen-Mikkelsen, who answered: "Thanks for the Høst book. One thing I can't accept, and that is that Ole's fate is dealt with so superficially. It was of course something Waschnitius got him to do – he could just as well have been on the other side, and one can't imagine what he went through before he fell."

Also the writer and journalist Hansaage Bøggild took part in the work for the museum in Gudhjem. When they had almost finished hanging the paintings, he heard Knud W. Jensen say: "Well, now, none of us owe Oluf Høst any longer". The remark made such an impression on Bøggild that he went straight home and wrote it down. He had expected more talk and memories from a man who had known the Høst family when he was young, had been the son's best friend and had frequented their home, but there was nothing. This made Bøggild wonder whether Knud W. Jensen felt a guilt in relation to Høst that was now being expiated through the one-artist museum. Bøggild sensed a line from this dark spot to the hard work of establishing the Høst Museum.

Critics of this explanation believe that Knud W. Jensen's "none of us owe Oluf Høst any longer" may have been a tired little remark after a hard day, and that that kind of motive analysis is unfruitful because it can only be pure speculation. But the idea arose in the discussion after the revelation that his indispensable and committed contribution to Danish cultural life should be understood as an expiation in which he tried to make things all right again, to repay society and to repent. Some people thought and think that Knud W. Jensen's irreparable sense of guilt was a central driving force in his patronage of the arts, and that never has a country profited so much from one man's bad conscience. It is not certain that this is the case, but it is possible. Knud W. Jensen himself always said it was pure and unadulterated egoism that made him want to have artistic material in his hands, and that he wanted to have fun, which may also be the full explanation.

Young Ole Høst himself wanted to go to the Eastern Front – no doubt about that. He defied both his family and his fiancée by doing so just as Erik Johansen defied the anger of his friends by not leaving. Both acted of their own free will. And "Korset" was Ole Wivel's pompous poem, not Knud W. Jensen's. But he ought to have said something about his errors irrespective of whether the fascistoid and dangerous ideals were decisive or not for the rest of his life. "It would have been a good story," as Torben Brostrøm says, in the sense that it would have been instructive. Their silence reflected their belief that one can control one's public image oneself. They were both among the most important and respected figures in Danish cultural life after the War, but their settlement of accounts came hesitantly and "in a form that never permitted an honest and self-critical confrontation with the way of thinking and the community that had so fascinating an effect," writes the historian Bo Lidegaard. Even though Ole Wivel tried to address the problem and in his memoirs called it "our heroic misunderstanding", it has set its mark on the assessment of posterity "that he and other members of the Ring did not dare openly face the demon that seems to have survived in the dark for a long time."

The difference between the two men was that Knud W. Jensen was extremely popular, and Ole Wivel had a number of enemies. When the story broke out, Knud W. Jensen was not drawn into the debate, for "everyone loves Knud", as Bo Bjørnvig wrote in *Weekendavisen*.

"The explanation seems to have been the respect that surrounded Knud W. Jensen as one of the really great museum creators and patron of the arts in Denmark – he was not be dragged through the mud as well. The people who knew him thought that he did too much good for that to happen. He really expiated. So no one urged him to explain himself, and he kept silent until his death. Some people asked him privately, but nothing came out of it."

Professor of literature Hans Hertel knew something about the story and as early as in 1995 asked Knud W. Jensen, who replied: "It's a dark point in my past that I'm not at all proud of, but I will tell you about it honestly and show you the letters I have." But it never got that far. He did not manage to do so before his death five years later. The writer Tage Skou-Hansen knew all those who were involved from his time as editor of *Heretica*. He related how in the 1990s Ole Wivel gave Knud W. Jensen's niece Hanne Engberg access to his archive when she was working on a book about the journal, but resolutely closed the door when he discovered that she wanted to go right back to the early 1940s.

"That was the end of my relationship to Ole Wivel. I tried to say to him: listen here: now that story from your past is beginning to leak out. Right now at this moment you can have it told. I understood all right that it was impossible for them to bring it out as long as Martin A. Hansen was alive. But now it was possible. I said so, and I wrote it to him. That led to our losing contact forever. In fact, he threatened to sue me if I revealed anything. On the other hand, I was friends with Knud W. Jensen to the end. But we never said a word about the past. They were very different people, those two. Everything was more innocent with Knud W. Jensen – he was born under a lucky star."

When Hanne Engberg asked about her uncle's acquaintance with Waschnitius, he answered the same as to the few others who approached the subject: "They are the darkest years of my life." And then people didn't go any further – they were too fond of him to press him.

"The adjective 'dark' is so difficult to apply to Knud, whose life was so light," says Engberg. "Our family has a great ability to repress things. He was not the kind of person who dug in his past or the shadow side of his life in public. But there was also the aspect that one ought to move on with other things, with life. If one had problems, one had to deal with them oneself. They weren't something one talked about."

He did, however, talk with his secretary Hanne Skydsgaard when the black-mailing letters from Erik Johansen began to arrive in the 1990s, initiating a conflict that lasted for several years and from time to time keeping Knud W. Jensen sleepless at night. Until then, the friend of his youth Erik Johansen had visited Louisiana a couple of times a year, had been friendliness itself and had brought flowers for Hanne Skydsgaard. Knud W. Jensen felt sorry for him because his health was bad and his economic situation miserable. He lent him a little money but became upset when Johansen began to talk about the old days and say that now the truth had to come out.

"Knud became afraid, but especially on Ole's behalf because he was apparently more involved. Even though they were no longer friends, he rang Ole and suggested that they lay their cards on the table. Ole didn't want to. Then Knud suggested that they should pay Erik Johansen, but Ole didn't want to do that either. He didn't want anything to come out at all."

Like most other sources, Hanne Skydsgaard sees Knud W. Jensen as a spectator rather than a participant. When they are to find excuses for him – and they very much wish to do that – they say that he was interested in art and literature and by chance also in some people who were interested in Nazism. And that he allowed himself to be carried along. Later at Louisiana, he proved not to be interested in politics, but only concerned as to who was minister of culture and whether he had any political clout. Otherwise, the level of his political analysis was low. Of a left-wing politician he could say to his niece Hanne Engberg, "Gert Petersen is really nice," and that was that. Friends and acquaintances of the two men describe them as essentially different and always compare the strength of their commitment to Knud W. Jensen's advantage. He was the questioner and seeker, and there was something of the camp follower about him, while Ole Wivel was assured in his ideology. "Knud was much more fluid and changeable and did not seek control like Ole, who was an anchorman for those involved and their ideology," says Niels Barfoed. Werner Svendsen, who like Barfoed and most of the other friends had equally little idea before the story broke out, thinks that at that fatal time in his life Knud W. Jensen had very little intellectual ballast. "To be candid, I think he was a very banal young man. He became mature very late, was immature and thought that it was fun to keep up with the latest fashion all the time."

In October 1943, Herbert Pundik was hiding together with his family in a large white villa some hundred meters south of Louisiana. They had fled from their home and were tensely waiting for a chance to cross the Sound by night. On the planned night, the man who was to row them across came and showed them the bleeding blisters on his hands. He was exhausted, so they did not leave. The next night, the boat they were waiting for sailed past them and picked up some other refugees. When on the third day there was a knock on the door of the villa and a man's voice asked if the Pundik family was there, Herbert Pundik's father thought he recognised the voice of a business colleague, risked everything and revealed their presence. The man helped them to Ålsgårde further up the coast, from where they were sailed to Sweden and safety.

Knud W. Jensen knew that story well. The two men had been friends since 1970, when Herbert Pundik was appointed chief editor of *Politiken*. Every Sunday they conducted hour-long telephone conversations, Pundik in his office, Knud W. Jensen at home in Sletten. They spoke about Louisiana and literature, about art and travel, about the Middle East and about everything that was going on. But there was one subject they never touched on.

"We never spoke about the War and the period of the Occupation. Not even though he knew my story. I was really surprised that he never talked about his work in the resistance movement because so many from that generation and his circle of friends had participated, for instance Martin A. Hansen and Tage Skou-Hansen. There was an unspoken fear of touching on the subject. I thought that he had been one of the those who had been passive in Denmark, but it never occurred to me that he had been on the way to the wrong side."

During a big Picasso exhibition that filled the whole of Louisiana, Knud W. Jensen lent his lifework at Pundik's suggestion to the Museum of Modern Art in Tel Aviv. He sent the collection, including the beloved sculptures by Giacometti, across the Mediterranean and placed them in the midst of a centre of disturbance. When after Knud W. Jensen's death Pundik heard about his friend's involvement on the wrong side, he could not escape from the idea that the generous gesture at that time had been an act of expiation.

"His entire relationship to me must in some way have been conditioned by what my reaction would have been if it had all come out. He must have been terribly anxious about what he would have to explain to me as a refugee and a Jew. He must have had the same anxiety in relation to other friends of his and must have lived on the brink of revelation. It is not inconceivable that his entire driving force was conditioned by his wish to make amends. To give Denmark something."

Rite of transition

The 1950s formed themselves as one long rite of transition for Knud W. Jensen, in which he placed his old life behind him and took hold of all the strings leading to the new life. Everything was defined for him in that decade, which began with his wedding, soon to be followed by his unwished-for divorce from Benedicte Hergel. After a year and a half's marriage, she fell head over heels in love with her husband's close friend, Thorkild Bjørnvig, and left him.

One day immediately after their return home from their long trip to Greece and Italy Knud W. Jensen and Karen Blixen had found out that Thorkild Bjørnvig was bored in Bonn, where he was on a study stay in the summer of 1951. They sent Benedicte off to cheer him up. It had not been Knud W. Jensen's intention to send his wife into the arms of another man – it just happened. Karen Blixen, on the other hand, openly moved the figures around on the stage to keep the plot going. The young woman's feelings were reciprocated, but Martin A. Hansen, whom the Heretics admired and respected, urged Bjørnvig to take the responsibility for his wife and child, which he did. The two lovers renounced one another, but Benedicte never got over Bjørnvig – she took her own life just at the moment when in the beginning of, the 1970s he was sitting in the green room at Rungstedlund writing his book "Pagten" [The Pact] about his deep fascination with and passion for the now deceased Blixen.

The friendship between Knud W. Jensen and Thorkild Bjørnvig stood the test without much trouble, which suggests that Knud W. Jensen had more feelings invested in the friendship than in the marriage. The friendship held so well that when in the same year Bjørnvig discovered an old summer cottage with a view situated high above Sletten Harbour, he "gave" it to the newly divorced Knud W. Jensen, who was happy to buy it and moved in in 1952. Bjørnvig was at one and the same time his protégé and confidential adviser in an affair that Bjørnvig himself had triggered by seducing his friend's wife. The two men often met and went for walks together with their dogs. "Knud's was a big Airedale Terrier called Trofast; mine was a black Alsatian called Grif, and even though they were both males, they got along fine," Bjørnvig wrote as an old man. Karen Blixen had directly encouraged Bjørnvig to fall in love in spite of the fact that she was passionately taken by the man. She too remained in Knud W. Jensen's circle of acquaintances afterwards. At Rungstedlund, she passed the time making anagrams of people's names. The three main characters in the drama became Vridbor kling højt [Gimlet ring loudly] (Thorkild Bjørnvig), Den eneste bikini [The only bikini] (Benedicte Jensen) and Du min sande eunuk [You my true eunuch] (Knud W. Jensen).

Martin A. Hansen wrote in his diary that the abandoned Knud seemed very tired and almost ill. That he was weakened and was having a nervous breakdown.

Nevertheless the divorce did not in any way paralyse him outwardly, but drove him further, further, further. The same year he expanded his cheese firm and moved it from the city centre to Sydhavn, where he had built a new factory with Marshall Aid funding. But what about the old premises in Hestemøllestræde? He discussed with Otto B. Lindhardt from Wivel's Publishing House, whether they should move the little firm in there. The story goes that while Otto B. Lindhardt was measuring up the rooms in Hestemøllestræde, the telephone rang and an eager Knud W. Jensen asked if it wouldn't be much easier to buy Gyldendal?

"Excellent!" answered the young publisher. Jensen bought a controlling interest in dusty old Gyldendal and put three young men – Otto B. Lindhardt, Ole Wivel and Jokum Smith – with an average age of 31 in charge. It was immediately christened the Danish Boys' Publishing House. The appointment was sensational and front-page news everywhere. Knud W. Jensen's task was to explain to Gyldendal's venerable and conservative board that it was a good idea. A masterpiece in the art of persuasion. He guaranteed that he would be the arbiter if the three equally ranked directors could not agree, but otherwise he would give them complete freedom. Decades later, Otto B. Lindhardt had the feeling that the three men may have been stand-offish towards Knud W. Jensen. That he may have been disappointed at not being involved in the literary work. That they didn't *use* him for anything and were self-sufficient. Perhaps Louisiana became a compensation for him.

Most of his friends had tried to dissuade him from buying just as two years later they tried to get him to give up the crazy idea of Louisiana. Better to keep hold of the territory that had been gained – Wivel's Publishing House and *Heretica*. They feared that both would be swallowed up by Gyldendal, which is what happened. They knew what they had, but not what they would get. Of course the same thing applied to Knud W. Jensen, but throughout his life he had constant expectations of something different and more. His ambitious idea was to translate all the classics, but there the boys had to disappoint him for they had taken over a run-down enterprise and were solemnly resolved first to straighten out the financial situation. He thought that they should just jump in at the deep end.

Martin A. Hansen felt convinced that Knud W. Jensen could run a "fresher and more effective" publishing business and rescue the distinguished firm from unrest and unhealthy speculation in its shares. And then Knud W. Jensen had a suitable platform from which he could exercise his own private cultural support for poets and writers. "My understanding was that in the first place Knud sensed that with Gyldendal he could realise his great idea, namely that his big cheese firm could gradually slip in as a permanent support for cultural work, especially in literature – but probably art in general. I believe that without his having said it directly to me he has a similar idea to that Brewer Jacobsen had in his day, but

Berlingske Aftenavis

Torsdag 14. August 1952

UNG GROSSERER BLIVER EJER AF GYLDENDAL

Har overtaget Erik Wibergs, Hjalmar Joensens og Kresten Krestensens store Aktieposter

The sensation is out. Placard for *Berlingske Aftenavis* on 14 August 1952. Louisiana owns Gyldendal. According to its statutes the objective of the Museum's Foundation is to support Louisiana and be the majority shareholder in the stock exchange listed publishing house. The shares cannot be sold.

that he wanted to make this cultural work essentially practical – which he could do by getting Gyldendal."

Many years and disappointments later Ole Wivel called Knud W. Jensen "a gambler, reckless as few", but Wivel forgot or didn't wish to see that his friend was primarily a winner type whose dreams were fulfilled and were thus transformed into realities.

From the 1950s and on to his death in 2000 most of Knud W. Jensen's advisers tried to do the same thing: to restrain him, to cut down his plans a little, to postpone them, to wait until the money had come, to get him to be realistic, etc. He asked them all for advice the whole time – and didn't listen to them. He didn't hear the word "no", and as the lawyer Allan Philip later admitted it was hard to be realistic when Knud W. Jensen was unrealistic all the time and nevertheless succeeded in carrying out the wildest art purchases, expansions and arrangements. Of all arguments, he found economic arguments the most meaningless. Money was there to be spent, not to be hoarded, and if one didn't have any, it had to be procured. When he had spent his own, he proved to be fantastically good at persuading others to spend theirs.

After the purchase of Gyldendal in August 1952, everyone was sure that he had had enough, and that things would be calm around him for a time. Thorkild Bjørnvig believed that his friend had reached his material and human limit, "your real wedding with destiny", but he was wrong. Destiny was still waiting in a quite different place.

That year Knud W. Jensen had also had time, in between all his other affairs, to appear on the radio and discuss the future of *Statens Museum for Kunst*, which was about to exchange one director of many years' service with another. Would it now at last be possible to do something for contemporary art? Should it have its own museum? It surprised Knud W. Jensen that his opinion was sought, but he turned up and suggested building a low, open pavilion for the most recent art in a Copenhagen park called Østre Anlæg. And nobody paid the slightest attention. But now a little idea had been planted at the back of his mind, a little wish to just do it himself one day.

"Of course it might sound a little ambitious, and I didn't talk about it, but it didn't seem utopian to me. In the offices and canteens of my firm there had gradually come to hang a quite respectable Danish collection from the Funen artists to the abstractionists. As chairman of the newly founded Art in the Workplace, I learned that art purchases didn't necessarily require big investments."

And there *he* was wrong.

Here it is!

In the autumn of 1954, Knud W. Jensen ventured into a forbidden area with Trofast by his side as a cheery Danish parallel to Tintin and Terry. They discovered an unknown paradise with chasms and mountains, a woodland lake and a stream, a jungle-like wilderness under beautiful trees. The site was bounded like an island with the sea at the end of the lawn. Abandoned by people and expectant, it was perfect for a genesis myth.

They crossed to and fro between an overgrown rose garden and overgrown tennis courts, passing an orchard and some stables, a beach and a pheasant warren. That this fertile relic of the past still existed among the well-trimmed villa gardens of Humlebæk! He *had* to have Louisiana, the crucial chance of his life. He was not in doubt for a moment. This was his hour, this was his place and he knew it.

Louisiana from the air, when it was still only a private villa. The founder had to assure the mortgage institution that if the museum went bankrupt, the buildings could be converted into a hotel in no time. Only then did he get his mortgage.

"A gambler, reckless as few"

At this point he had no idea that the excavators had already been ordered and a few months later were planned to eat their way into the bracken gully to make room for the municipality's 90-meter-long sewage farm. The main building itself had been designated to become an old people's home, and the rear part of the plot, where the museum is placed today, had, rather tactlessly, been reserved for extensions to the graveyard. The bridge from the old part of the graveyard to the new territory already rose high above the lake, and that bridge had been expensive. Paradise crumbled before Knud W. Jensen's eyes – now he could imagine a big, gloomy memento mori. That he now rolled up as a private person begging to be allowed to spend his money on a new museum did not make a decisive impression on the authorities.

It can't be right that Louisiana should end up as a *shit boiling plant,* Knud W. Jensen's attorney Erik Pontoppidan exclaimed indignantly, after which they started month-long negotiations with and creative processing of the other party. In the period just after the war, Knud W. Jensen had demonstrated his superior abilities as a businessman by capturing the American market and increasing his firm's sales and personnel by a factor of five. Now he bought a nearby property, offered it to the municipality at an absurdly low price, and that was the end of the shit boiling plant. Afterwards he drank coffee and ate mountains of cookies with the parochial church council of Humlebæk Kirke, who in the end proved to be good neighbours – or couldn't be bothered any longer – and surrendered. But then the whole plan ran aground in, of all places, the Ministry of Ecclesiastical Affairs, which had spent taxpayer money on the bridge. It would of course be completely wasted if it didn't lead to the planned graves on Louisiana's land. Knud W. Jensen was desperate.

"At this point the minister, Bodil Koch, came into the room, sat down, lit a cheroot and listened attentively to the explanations of the parties. For a long time she said nothing. Then suddenly she hammered her fist on the table, the cheroot bobbed up in the corner of her mouth, her glasses flashed and her decision fell like a canon shot: "Now I'll tell you something, friends: when there comes a man who wants to do something for the living, then we can take care of the dead in here all right." With this the last obstacle to using Louisiana for a museum had been overcome. A huge sense of relief overwhelmed me."

Now he began to look around for an architect. The choice was just as much a matter of chance and just as fortunate as the finding of Louisiana. He reached out for most frequently used tool – the telephone.

There was a result: "We have a young man here who has been on a study trip to Italy. Maybe you can use him," explained Mogens Gjødesen from his office at *Glyptotektet*. He was a member of the Carlsberg Foundation's board and was an

Knud W. Jensen inspects the building site in Humlebæk. He took so much part in everything that Jørgen Bo always said that in reality there were three architects to do the job.

old friend of Knud W. Jensen, who soon after anchored up in front of the building in his big Mercedes with Erno at the wheel. Inside to meet 35-year-old Vilhelm Wohlert, who was helping the museum's permanent architects with an assignment. At this point, Knud W. had already asked Jørn Utzon whether he would look at Louisiana, but he pleaded that he was too busy. Later it turned out that he had been immersed in drawings for a new opera house in Sidney.

So Knud W. Jensen got into Wohlert's little Citroen and together they slithered up the ice-covered coast road to Humlebæk followed by Erno, who was deeply concerned for his employer's life. Now began a rare relationship between architect and client, the result of which found a natural place in Denmark's *Arkitekturkanon* [Architectural Canon] (2005), and already shortly after the opening in 1958 was declared by Kaare Klint to be *the monument* to Danish modernism. Wohlert soon drew the architect Jørgen Bo into the enterprise, because he himself thought that he lacked building experience, and in the course of the years they jointly laid a famous ring of buildings around the periphery of the park. Above and below ground. When Jørgen Bo died, and Vilhelm Wohlert' strength ran out, his son Claus Wohlert took over and continued his father's life work.

The winter day when Vilhelm Wohlert entered by the white garden gate in Humlebæk, the scope of the project was still easy to grasp. "You shouldn't expect

Architect Jørgen Bo, client Knud W. Jensen and architect Vilhelm Wohlert in front of the museum, which proved to be a lifelong task for all three of them.

anything special", he quickly told Jørgen Bo. Knud W. Jensen was still a cheese wholesaler, still bound by his duties and well on the way to over-straining and ruining his health with his demanding double life. In December 1954, his doctor diagnosed a nervous breakdown and ordered him to go on a month-long cruise. Before that there had been other trips to the south or to Danish islands to convalesce. Knud W. Jensen suffered from a heart condition occasioned by stress and nervousness that brought cold sweat, faintness, anxiety and weakness and only got worse if he was busy, which he always was. He did not like sleeping on his right side, a position in which he could hear his heartbeat, but he succeeded in living to the age of 84 without slowing down.

To begin with Wohlert worked on the original buildings around the courtyard. A little had to be done in the old garage, something in the stables, where the Larsen Stevns cartoons, which the Carlsberg Foundation had promised to lend, could be exhibited. There was not enough money for anything more until one day it was suddenly there in a large enough amount to forget about the frugality of the postwar period, and Wohlert sensed that something big was on the way:

"He stood there in the wind at Amagertorv in his light raincoat, when I happened to run into him, and told me that he had sold his firm to Kraft Foods. It must have been like jumping into 70 fathoms of water. All this is more or less well-known history, but it is hard not to recall it because it was so fairytale-like and different from the realities of the day, which are formed by unimaginative money policies and leaden administration. Here came this young businessman, who with his intelligent blue eyes tore through all sour scepticism and habitual thinking. His infectious eagerness, humour and cheerfulness drove Jørgen and me to "give it all we had", to use one of his expressions."

The architects moved in on the first floor in the main building for some weeks and examined the terrain minutely. They liked all that they saw. They studied the passage of the sun over the park and discovered its best features – the bracken gully, the woodland lake, the tall sculptural trees and the view from the high bastion at the edge of the Sound. The remains of a cannon could still be seen from part of a defence installation, and the woodland lake had originally been excavated to form a secret harbour, where Danish privateers could hide between attacks on solitary members of the English fleet in the Sound. Never used, the

▶ "Here in these rooms, which are so clearly modelled on a family house, people understood that art was not merely a remote thing quite apart from their daily lives. In the almost home-like surroundings it affected its public in a quite different way," wrote the newspaper *B.T.* on Louisiana's fifth birthday in 1963.

The grand piano in the
cafeteria. As far from the
economies and modesty of the
1950s as can be imagined.

"Is there a modern art?"

narrow channel had sanded up, and the harbour now lay as a deep-lying innocent lake surrounded by beech trees.

The terrain itself contained great beauty and variety and was permitted to determine the ground plan of the new museum. Louisiana was and is a composition inspired by the site – it would not have looked as it does on a different plot, for instance on the flat field in Rungsted that Knud W. Jensen originally tried to persuade its owner, Karen Blixen, to part with. It was at that time that the idea of an out-of-town museum had formed once and for all in his mind. But she just looked at him and said wonderingly: "Is there a modern art?" They did not return to the subject.

In Humlebæk the three men were deeply occupied with the park itself, which they wished to spare as much as possible. In fact it determined the position of the museum, which was placed carefully and lightly around the perimeter and not as a compact and heavy building in the middle. They further developed Jensen's old idea of low pavilions for *Statens Museum for Kunst*. Now it was realised here. It was the I'll-damn-well-do-it-myself idea at full throttle. But first yet another heavy obstacle had to be overcome. Knud W. Jensen applied to a mortgage company for a loan of 350,000 kroner and received a flat refusal. The company's man wrote in an internal memorandum from April 1957 that the property Louisiana would directly fall in value by being given a modern museum building – for what could one do with it if the museum went bankrupt? – and "with the very large annual expenses and very season-dependent visits I regard the mortgage as extremely risky!" He rounded off with a crushing verdict: "On the basis of the information we have on the matter at the present moment I do not think we should make an offer."

The rejection echoed Landmandsbanken's "no" five years earlier, when Knud W. Jensen wanted to borrow in order to buy Gyldendal. The bank had stood behind the Jensen family's firm for more than half a century and knew that Knud W. Jensen had an outstanding business talent, but the director declared self-assuredly that "the sun has never shone on Gyldendal" and stuck to his "no". Knud W. Jensen immediately moved all his business to a competitor, Privatbanken, which received him with open arms. So he naturally did not regard the anxious refusal from Østifternes Kreditforening as final either. It had to be changed. He knew a man whose son was an executive in the mortgage company, and they sat down together and drew up an emergency plan so that the project could be accepted: Louisiana could, if necessary, be converted into a hotel! Once again Knud W. Jensen wrote a letter to the mortgage company at Jarmers Plads in Copenhagen:

"The proposal envisages converting the museum buildings into a holiday hotel with a total of 51 rooms and also presupposes the construction of a motel with 14 rooms. By the extension of the connecting passage between the buildings

The famous glass corridor,
which zigzags through the
park, was built because
there was not enough money
to erect real buildings all the
way down to the seashore.

Vilhelm Wohlert
(1920-2007) and Jørgen
Bo (1919-99) in front of
Louisiana's character-
istic wall and their own
breakthrough work.

space can be created for a further number of rooms over and above the already mentioned 51. There is also the possibility of converting the museum buildings into residences, and this will probably be cheaper than the conversion into a hotel."

The loan went through.

Knud W. Jensen appreciated atmosphere and views and set three conditions that the architects had to fulfil and which determined the shape of the ground plan. The original main building was to form the entrance to the museum because it reminded him of a delightful private home and supported the relaxed atmosphere he was seeking. The passage through the extension could have only one logical climax – a pavilion with a view over the Sound. And on the way there visitors ought to be able to see the atmospheric woodland lake, which therefore had to have a room with a full window devoted to the view.

So they built a chain of buildings and glass passages from the house to the sea. Louisiana's underlying idea is the covered walk in which one zigzags through the park alternately looking at art and nature. One is not shut up with the art as in the old museums' high windowless rooms, but is offered emergency exits and variety for the eyes, for Knud W. Jensen recognised that the concept of museum fatigue very much exists and must be combated. He knew it from his own experience and was not afraid to admit his thirst, his sore feet and exhaustion, even though it was more comme il faut to grin and bear it. His goal was to free his visitors from the implicit and rigorous demands made by a classical museum visit, and the means were air, light and variety. As they pass through the museum, visitors sees the climaxes of the park as clearly framed nature pictures. At some points the vegetation is on the point of assaulting the museum and devouring it, elsewhere nicely and aristocratically trimmed as in Busky-Neergaard's day it keeps a distance.

Louisiana is built out into a landscape – it is a museum in the countryside as opposed to the majority in the cities. Its interconnectedness with nature is its special feature, immediately recognised by the critics' descriptive labels like "the hidden museum", "the natural museum" or "the museum on the grass". Photographers found and find it difficult to identify a centre because the museum discreetly distributes itself in the landscape without fuss and monumental pretensions.

When Vilhelm Wohlert and Jørgen Bo stayed there in order to gather inspiration and draw the first sketches, they knocked pegs into the ground and tied string between them in order to maintain a constant idea of the relationship between the rooms and the natural attractions outside. They edged around the 200-year-old beech tree with nine trunks by putting two angles into the line of the corridor, and they discovered the perfect placing for the room looking out

The high-ceilinged room looking out on the woodland lake. "The house was quite simply designed on the spot. We staggered around in wellies with wide open arms," Jørgen Bo explained.

on the woodland lake. There wasn't enough money to build all the way from the main building to the sea, so they had to find another solution. The glass corridors were one way of progressing. They were cheaper than exhibition rooms of brick, and their transparent lightness permits the landscape to push its way in on both sides. The spaces between the pavilions are totally without art.

From two sides the architects found themselves under agreeable pressure: from the luxuriance of the landscape outside and from the richness of the art collection inside. Both aspects were taken into consideration when they built the 1958 version of Louisiana. They were almost puritanically restrained, ready to compromise, to balance. The buildings are low so that in some places they remind one of a large one-family house. They are not theatrical and pompous, but informal and quiet and far from what architects call with disgust "an external urge to make a show".

Bo and Wohlert combined the same simple materials – brick, tiles, wood – with great variation in the rooms. We are as far as humanly possible from the classical museum's ruler-straight sequence of identical rooms. Louisiana is laby-rinthine in comparison. "In terms of museum psychology this was a wise move. It counteracts fatigue and stimulates curiosity," Wohlert said. One goes from a nar-

Louisiana's controver-sial cafeteria in 1950s colours. Knud W. Jensen got the idea from the Museum of Modern Art in New York and had it squeezed into the library at the last moment The narrow kitchen was no bigger than that in a one-family house.

row to a broad space, from high to low, from simple to complex, from closed to open, from light to dark, from intimate to imposing. Monotony has little chance – one just wants to see what there is around the next corner. Louisiana's ground plan is based on the principle of surprise, and the tour through the museum reminds people of all sorts of things, for instance of going through a town with streets and alleys, large and small open squares. Or: "When I was a kid, Louisiana always reminded me of a zoo," says a young gallery-owner from New York, who often visited the museum with his art dealer parents. All those glass panes, the flickering light through the trees, that one went inside and outside, that dark rooms were reminiscent of elephant houses and light rooms of aviaries.

Louisiana resembles Danish architects' experimental houses from the 1950s, which they built with cheap state loans and a maximum of 110 square meters. The era did not permit extravagances. Everything was small and rationalised, so their houses became simple, but elegant and innovative. The style was international modernism, inspired by American architecture with Japanese features. The architects moved into their oblong boxes with flat roofs, raw brick walls and glass panes from floor to ceiling. They fitted out their living space airily with bare floors of wood or tile, rice paper lampshades, Hardoy chairs and Guernica above the sofa. Cool. Louisiana followed suit, but on a far bigger scale.

For two years Vilhelm Wohlert had taught at Berkeley University in California, where Jørgen Bo visited him, and together they travelled around to look at the delectable architecture of San Francisco Bay. "It was akin to our Scandinavian approach, used wood and tiles like us and preferred the informal. Because of the climate they devote a lot of attention to the interplay between interior and exterior. The outside is drawn into the house and vice-versa," said Wohlert.

When the two friends were staying in California, some of the most admired houses were actually being put up by Japanese craftsmen, so closely was modernism fused with Japanese simplicity. And both things can be seen at Louisiana, which irradiates Nordic coolness, America and Zen.

Gone were all casement windows, pointed roofs, colours and ornamentation. The modernists simplified their buildings to white walls, thin flat roofs and large glass surfaces. They looked graphic, almost like abstract compositions. Even though Professor of Art History Christian Elling said to his students that Louisiana was the beginning of the end for architecture, most other people were crazy about it. After Louisiana Vilhelm Wohlert and Jørgen Bo were *en vogue* and received lots of commissions. They built small Louisiana clones for North Zealanders. In postwar Europe Scandinavian architecture was admired for its simplicity and modesty in contrast to Hitler and Mussolini's grandiose manifestations of power, from which everyone wanted to distance themselves as quickly as possible. The era wanted a "democratic" architecture that didn't push people around, so it was impossible to imagine anything much better than a combination of Danish and American.

When the two young architects were close to completing their work on Louisiana, Knud W. Jensen came rushing home from a business trip to the USA and changed things at the last moment, as he would do so many times later. He had visited the Museum of Modern Art in New York, the world's first museum for modern art, founded in 1929 by a handful of millionaires, including Rockefeller. And now Knud. W. Jensen also wanted a cafeteria. The architects pressed it into the library and stuck a diminutive kitchen plus a serving hatch onto it, and that was that problem solved: Louisiana was on the way to becoming a Danish MoMA. For the rest of his life Knud W. Jensen remained at his castle, extending it and reinforcing it. He loved putting up buildings. As soon as one extension had been inaugurated, he began planning a new one. On, on, on! "Everyone believes I'm a compulsive builder," he complained to his successor Poul Erik Tøjner at the end of the 1990s. "Well, you are," answered Tøjner, "but there are only a few of us who know it for sure."

Louisiana is a cathedral building in Humlebæk. It begins on a small scale, but it grows and grows and ends by determining the town, making it a place of pilgrimage for an eternal stream of visitors. Shortly after the museum's opening in 1958 the Social-Democratic Minister of Ecclesiastical Affairs Bodil Koch did not find that Humlebæk Church fitted into the modernist whole any longer. She suggested that the church be pulled down and a new one be built by a modern architect that could measure up to the position next to Louisiana. She would get the money from various art foundations because her idea had more of an aesthetic than a religious aim. She received 300 proposals and awarded the first prize to one of Jørn Utzon's former associates, the Norwegian Helge Hjertholm, for a church formed as a 30-meter-tall sculpture or flower made of large leaves of reinforced concrete. The locals met the plan with protests, and finally oblivion descended on Bodil Koch's idea.

Fortunately, Knud W. Jensen did not have enough money to build the whole museum in one go. It has come in stages that clearly reflect his and his architects' growing age and experience. Already in Louisiana's first decade art came down from the walls and began to move, to make noises and to sway, to spread out across the floor, to rise in the air. As a compulsive builder Knud W. Jensen could only follow it.

They looked graphic

Louisiana sparked a huge demand for its two architects,
and they built beautiful Louisiana clones in North Zealand.
Here is their demonstration villa "The House in the Garden"
erected in Forum for an architecture exhibition in 1959.

lmost like abstract compositions

1960s

ROBERT INDIANA

documenta

Værker fra documenta: grafik og multikunst·23/11·68-12/1·69

LOUISIANA

In the 1960s a typical Louisiana type – one could call him Louisiana Man – is sitting at home in his Børge Mogensen full-grain leather safari chair softly embedded in a handwoven shag carpet. He gets up and draws the light flax curtains across the window opening onto his patio, lights a cigarette and the Louisiana pendant lamp, designed by the museum's architects. His age and his mood at this moment decide whether he puts the Frank Jæger record on the gramophone or "Martin A. Hansen fortæller" [Martin A. Hansen Relates] or "Hva' skal vi lave" [What shall We Do?] by the country's two newest provocateurs, Klaus Rifbjerg and Jesper Jensen. All are safe, approved products published by the museum itself.

On the coffee table next to the negro sculpture lie a couple of issues of *Louisiana Revy*, one of the 1960s' most important organs for the few. From this magazine he has absorbed deep inside his middle-class gut that jazz is free and lifegiving music, while pop is a term of abuse, that it is brainwashing and inescapable brain death. From *Louisiana Revy* – and *Politiken* of course – he knows that there is a mixed misuse of TV and transistor radio that he should stay far away from if he wishes to be a modern man. His house looks as it should, for he has happily abandoned the "pretentious middle class style" of his childhood home, which is the name that Louisiana's founder gave to the shiny furniture in fake rococo that ravaged the country before the modern style of interior decoration took over. The room is simple, free of knick-knacks and resembles a moderate suburban version of the museum in Humlebæk, where the cream of Danish design stands freely around. He knows very well that a *sideboard* is a term of abuse, something one simply can't have in one's home.

From Poul Henningsen he knows how dangerous it can be to allow a cosy tassel to come into the house. PH hates all "retrospective sentimentality" and warns against an idealising, petit bourgeois taste. It is more dangerous than the Communists in the Danish Communist party, which is after all only a little sect, while the other phenomenon is an organised campaign to make people stupid. And it can get worse yet, writes the culture hero in *Louisiana Revy* in January 1962: consumption, advertising and the press constitute a greater danger than Hitler. So the crucial thing is to keep one's balance.

Louisiana Man is an excellent, hard-working reader and gets through even the heaviest of Gyldendal's intellectual publications and Professor Løgstrup's essay on art and ethics in the magazine. For a moment he allows his eyes to rest on his Minerva reproduction (a Legér composition). He strokes his beard. One man in twelve in Denmark has a beard, and he is one of them. If everyone was just like him, the passionately discussed cultural gap would be bridged, and Danish workers would embrace art. Then the country's intelligentsia would not have to lie sleepless at the prospect of a 30-hour-week, aghast at the thought

In the beginning the villa looked old-fashioned, with high panelling, oriental carpets and chairs upholstered in black horsehair from the museum director's childhood home.

A sideboard is a term of abuse

of all the drooling pop and quizzes the lower classes will be able contaminate themselves with in all that suddenly acquired leisure time?

But everyone is not like Louisiana Man. It is not him the philosopher Villy Sørensen is criticising in *Louisiana Revy* of January 1962:

"That the people are unwilling to occupy themselves with art does not prove that there is a crisis in art, but rather that there is a crisis in the people, and this is not due to the fact that the artists have not taken sufficient account of the people, but that the cultural politicians have not done so."

The leading writers for *Louisiana Revy* hate "journalism" and find the hostility to art of the day directly anti-democratic. They are working to change all this and are of the opinion that they have an effective weapon: modern art. It must be thrown down among a self-satisfied but unhappy population like a bomb, a cleansing acid bath. At one and the same time it must shake people in their sense of prosperity and save them. This point of view is quite generally held, also by Knud W. Jensen:

"If democracy wants to have culture, if it does not wish to leave the battle-ground to the advancing steamroller of the entertainment industry, which the majority of the population find it hard to resist, if leisure time is not to become a vacuum, in which passivity and boredom flourish, momentarily expelled by cheap, sensational diversions, society must both support the artists we have (while they are alive) and also create a new and better framework for cultural life. What art is created and to what extent the offer of popularisation is accepted and used is immaterial in this connection. One should simply close one's ears to counter-arguments based on the exclusiveness of contemporary art or on responsibility for the taxpayer's money."

The writers believe to the utmost extent of their good will that modern art is strong enough to liberate the unfortunate Danes from of the claws of pop music and all the other stuff they themselves don't know is not good for them. Art just has to be explained sufficiently, be shown well and have more money. Its function as medicine is used as *the argument* for it. It is not until the 1980s that art is re-leased from utilitarian thinking and can just be enjoyed or ignored for what it is.

While an enthusiastic public overruns Louisiana and in record time wears out the Arne Jacobsen cutlery in the cafeteria, trend-setting circles can never-theless find something to worry about. Never have so many Danes listened to music, bought paperbacks, looked at art or read poetry. Nevertheless, Louisiana Man has to work his way through one jeremiad after the other in his magazine. On the TV culture and the passivity of the citizens. On the anaesthetising power of advertising and man's isolation in a world of machines. On the anti-life of the petit bourgeois in a society of superabundance. The writers *know* that the oth-ers are in a bad state and seek refuge in an irrelevant dream world. That their

"It is the very idea of art tha

Gentlemen for tea on the lawn.
Whereas immediately after the War
you were either robustly left- or
right-wing, in the 1960s you were
either for or against modern art.

eople shouldn't have what they like"

No one has promised that it will b

The museum was furnished with the cream of Danish design, so people could sit and relax in small groups. Fresh flowers on the coffee tables – and ashtrays. In time, as Louisiana grew, some of the domestic atmosphere disappeared.

easy to be saved

need for genuine commitment is fulfilled by hobbies and entertainment, but is "crippled, perverted or masked", as Erik Aalbæk Jensen writes in 1962. In other words: Come over to our side! We have deep and committing experiences. We know best – we have art while the others have only the falsification of values, etc.

Art bears a colossal burden. It has to fulfil the hope of new, better human beings and give the finishing touch to those who are already good. Why not teach *everybody* the wonderful language of art? It is like a lesson that must be learned and understood – and then one will immediately feel better. The buzzword in the 1960s is self-realisation. Know thyself. Freud and Jung were translated into Danish a moment ago and Louisiana Man knows the best instrument on the shelf when it is a matter of lightening repressions and developing personality: to look modern art straight in the eye. The uglier, the better. As Villy Sørensen asks: "What is the reason why it is often the most valuable works that are the most unpleasant?"

Critical researchers from a later period call modernism "a holistic theory", because its standard-bearers with Torben Brostrøm and Villy Sørensen at their head advertise its healing effect. Modern art unhesitatingly locates the anxiety and the unwanted in the individual's psyche, sets it free and unites him with society. Modernists love analyses of one's soul and sex life. Once one has recognised one's repressions, one can live peacefully with them. "Failure to recognise reality" and "conventional thinking" are the next worst thing they know. Tradition is the worst. Modernism's requirement of itself is constant renewal – no looking back.

The expectations of art as a super-drug grow sky-high during the decade, and Knud W. Jensen was speaking for many when he said "Despite our apparent materialism art must be one of the highest values we possess, placed right at the top where religious norms were previously located."

Where immediately after the War people were decidedly either right-wing or left-wing, now they were for or against modern art. Louisiana Man was for. And this rescued him from a fate as a conformist, moderate, nostalgic citizen, frightened of the future and with an inhibited sex life. Instead he drinks wine from his Holmegaard glass and takes provocation and confrontation with pleasure just like PH: "It is the very idea of art that people shouldn't have what they like "

Now and then the editorial board in the shape of Knud W. Jensen allows a contrary voice to enter the jubilant *Louisiana Revy* chorus. This may be old Jacob Paludan, who speaks of painting monkeys and mundane modernism. It may be Tørk Haxthausen's dig at the bearers of the culture who cannot get themselves to believe that the people can manage without them and their incessant enlightenment and instruction. And it may be the novelist Anders Bodelsen, who has spent a wearisome weekend in company with the high priests of culture and reports back to *Louisiana Revy*:

"One can become lowbrow and hostile to culture after a whole weekend in which everyone except for a couple of unpopular and querulous types, confirms each other in the view that *we can't live without art*. The thought quickly arose in my mind that the minority in the population, who give up a whole weekend in order to allow themselves to be scolded for cultural (read: artistic) laziness are on the whole fond of being scolded, also in art. The others spend the weekend in other ways. Perhaps they go to the pub or fly kites." Bodelsen expected that just one single person would say that he read for pleasure and not just for edification, but that is too easy. "We carry a heavy responsibility for having insisted on the necessity and difficulty of art. That art is necessary for society is not the same as that it is necessary for everyone all the time."

Personally Knud W. Jensen can't stand admonitions, arrogant attendants, instructions and compulsion. The whole of Louisiana is a breach with that kind of thing, but he cannot escape from his own educational and cultural background and expects so much of his readers that he excludes some of them.

Louisiana Man gets through Karen Blixen's speech to the American Academy of Arts and Letters, printed in English in *Louisiana Årbogen* [Louisiana Year Book] 1959. Perhaps he also manages the quote on Henry Moore – *l'art ne commence qu'avec la vérité intérieure* – which is placed side by side with a tribute to Europe's best modern museum, the Stedelijk in Amsterdam, because it tries to attract people from the street, more or less like a department store. Its exhibitions are intended for everyone and are not reserved for a narrow circle of friends of art. But Louisiana hopes for the best and assumes that as a minimum the man on the street knows English and French.

But the question is whether Louisiana Man is able to decode the abstract language of art theory for which the museum generously provides pages. Does he understand why the artist of our day "will no longer impose on us his egocentric vision of an inner world at the expense of the near and the real. With the help of science and technology he has regained confidence in man and wishes to participate organically in the ever progressing formation of a new world order."

No one has promised that it will be easy to be saved.

The 1960s are the period of the utopias and the big debates, and Knud W. Jensen has not yet encountered the wall in 1968 and the subsequent hatred of elite culture that would put an end to his desire to participate in public debate and send him into the camp of pure art. He feels the ground shake beneath his feet. All fixed positions are up for redistribution, and he is quite right when he puts his sense of what is happening into words: "the new society that is developing". He is passionately interested in creating a forum for debate in *Louisiana Revy* rather than an art journal. "So much is written about art in the daily press," he says in 1964 and allows the magazine to embrace the whole spectrum from space travel and television (in particular!) to the pop radio programme, motor traffic, dormitory towns and self-deception. His faith in experts and specialist knowledge is strong. A favourite phrase of his is that it is a matter of "presenting a material" so that people can decide for themselves. And it requires a maximum of concentration for Louisiana Man to understand complicated sociological figures like "Communicative process between two persons" or "Number of TV licences in Denmark year by year depicted respectively linearly and logarithmically."

When he phones Mrs Kirsten Strømstad, tel. Humlebæk 719, and asks for membership of the Louisiana Club, he is at the same time joining a the winning side. In the course of the 1960s modernism takes firm control of emergent Danish cultural policy and slips painlessly into upper and lower secondary schools. It becomes the benchmark for all that is good and modern.

Many writers and artists depart from the straight and narrow – especially those who look back – but Knud W. Jensen and his debaters Torben Brostrøm, Villy Sørensen, Klaus Rifbjerg, Elsa Gress, Uffe Harder and Ole Wivel keep a grip on the wheel. Also when they overtake storekeeper Peter Rindal in 1965. The man appears as the culmination of the growing irritation between the modernists and the general public. But he disappears again.

U-turn

Louisiana lay in its park, sunning itself in the attention of a constant stream of visitors. Only a few advanced enthusiasts felt surprise that Knud W. Jensen had one kind of taste when building and another kind when he chose paintings: the museum was ultra-modern – the paintings not quite. The founder's sympathies clearly lay back in time and around artists that had died, but he was not alone in preferring art that in most cases made it possible to see what it represented. Critics and public also liked Poul S. Christiansen, Larsen Stevns, Carl Kylberg, Astrid Noack and Lundstrøm, so Knud W. Jensen could lean back comfortably and enjoy the fruit of his passion, his toil and his fortune. Success is the best revenge, and that is what he had achieved.

Instead he travelled abroad and changed everything. Despite his at times extreme irresoluteness he had the remarkable courage to make a new departure in his life. In August 1959, exactly a year after the opening he took the train to the heavily bombed industrial town of Kassel in Germany and had a shock. With rolled up sleeves and a note block in his hand he worked his way through

A shocked Knud
W. Jensen at
Documenta II in
Kassel. He was
obliged to return
home and change
everything.

93

the hot exhibition Documenta II and noted that 685 out of 700 pictures were non-figurative, and that naturalism had completely vanished. By naturalism he meant depictions of the external recognisable world, in fact what he had hanging at home on Louisiana's white walls, his youth's painter-heroes from the 1920s and 30s.

Documenta II was a requiem – nothing in the world seemed whole any longer. Among the ruined baroque palaces with blackened walls and empty windows he discovered that he had not kept up with the new art, and what was worse, he had been wrong about Louisiana's content and meaning. All this revolutionary new art had passed him by – and the rest of Denmark, where one stuck to the security of the national tradition but forgot international art. Knud W. Jensen described his abrupt entry onto the world stage as like coming from the peaceful provinces to a hectic, fascinating, almost scary metropolis. But he preferred the latter even though the troublesome consequence was that he could not go on living with the art he had just used all his strength to collect. In Humlebæk, furthermore, he had on the actual inauguration day declared his love for Danish art and said that "it is true that we do not possess the artistic mastery of French art, but there is a mindset and a human authenticity in our art that gives those who are personally occupied with it a just as big an experience and as much pleasure as the art of any other country or epoch."

And now this. So much stronger and freer than Danish art. And as Louisiana was his own private museum, he did not feel that there was anything else to do but to abandon his sure-fire success. He began to draw the foreign art in via a stream of exhibitions and decided later that he would also build the collection up around it. In Kassel the rug was pulled out from under his feet, without his having wanted it, but the works were irresistible.

"It was suddenly up in a quite different format, artistically, expressionally. New, new for me. I was really shocked and felt that I simply had to change my life. We thought we were so happily self-sufficient. But we had no idea what was going on elsewhere in the world."

At the colossal exhibition with 700 paintings and 200 sculptures, he saw not only well-known names like Picasso, Calder and Henry Moore, but also Antonio Tàpies, Jean Dubuffet, Wols, Miró, Vasarely and all the intense Americans – Jackson Pollock, de Kooning, Kline and Rothko – who effectively and remorselessly were ousting France as the centre of art and replacing it with New York. As the trend-setting metropolis of art Paris's days were numbered – this also applied to the motif. The victory of "objectless" art was so absolute that Knud W. Jensen feared its "self-constituted censorship and inquisitorial attitude". Nevertheless he could recognise something in the pictures. Perhaps naturalism had just been

reshaped and transformed. Nature entered in another way into the new painting: as an intimation, hint of a landscape or a light, as vague contours of human
figures, he thought.

Documenta had immediate consequences at Louisiana, for Knud W. Jensen
went straight to the exhibition's control centre and asked to speak with the man
behind the exhibition. At once. In the architect and painter Arnold Bode he met a
stubborn and visionary type life like himself, *ein Macher*. After the War, Bode had
become a professor at the academy in Kassel and arranged the first Documenta
exhibition in 1954 to open Germany again, to rescind the artists' Nazi-paralysis
and bring them together with international art. In a letter Knud W. Jensen sent in
advance in order to obtain help at Documenta, he respectfully addressed Arnold
Bode as "sehr geehrter Herr Professor". In the next letter he used the intimate
"lieber Arnold". The two men became friends for life, and the incredible happened.
Only two months later "Works from Documenta" opened at Louisiana, and the
Danes got to see the Americans & Co. for the first time.

Slowly Denmark opened itself to the surrounding world and saw a somewhat
mortifying image in the mirror. Art-interested people travelled abroad, became
envious, felt provincial and wrote thirstily home about the new art. And always
with a direct or indirect criticism of the Danish museum world, which neither
bought nor exhibited modern art. In 1959, the painter Albert Mertz got off the
train in Paris. He was the Danish artist who first drew attention to what was
happening in the USA. He went straight to see "Jackson Pollock et la nouvelle
peinture americaine".

"I went into the exhibition and fell to my knees from an enormous knockout
blow. The myth Jackson Pollock, the beat, the swindler, the destructive per-
former, the squeaking balloon inflated by the capitalist art dealer environment,
the desperado Pollock, the James Dean of painting, all these designations and
accusations whirled in my head. Here then one could see for oneself – what was
this Pollock? My answer was without hesitation – a great painter," Mertz writes
in *Louisiana Årbog* 1959, which also contains Knud W. Jensen's travel letter from
Kassel. They were both explorers who had been taken unawares and now wanted
to bring some of what they had discovered home with them.

It began to dawn on Knud W. Jensen that there was a larger vacuum than
that which he was trying to fill with his museum. The Danes were even more
hopelessly undernourished with international modern art than with their own.
There was a hole in their cultural background, and as an attentive businessman
he couldn't bear to see a need without meeting it.

In art circles there prevailed an almost automatic anger at the one-sidedness
of Danish museums, the Academy and all official art organs and "the special

Alexander Calder's
mobiles in play in 1961.
After the Documenta
exhibition Louisiana
began to show inter-
national art. The initial
caution was gone.

Danish view that nothing is happening around us, and that we can calmly turn our backs and rely on it that our own deeply inherited tradition and sense of quality will undoubtedly take care of the rest," as sculptor Bent Sørensen writes in *Louisiana Årbog* 1960.

"Where are Arp, Brancusi, Gonzales, Lipchitz, Zadkine, Archipenko, Giacometti, Moore, Vantongerloo and so on? All these became classics long ago. Where were the museum people then? How are Danish sculptors supposed to be able to find their orientation when this entire development is absent? It is fifty years of acquisitions that are missing," he fumes after having visited Mittelheim sculpture park in Antwerp and the Stedelijk in Amsterdam. The profoundly enviable Stedelijk is not a museum in the normal sense of the word, he writes. It is "a museum machine", in which there are continuously changing exhibitions from the whole world; only now and again do they have room for their own collections. This museum is a working museum, whose director is constantly travelling around Europe in order to arrange exhibitions and procure things for the museum.

It is as if the angry Danish sculptor is speaking directly to Knud W. Jensen's new awareness. We lack something; the others have it and we should too. In a very short space of time the museum goes the whole way and invites provocative international art into the country in three rapid, scandalous steps: Works from

Knud W. Jensen and Pontus Hultén from Moderna Museet in Stockholm. Hultén too was unable to resist Louisiana's dynamic founder, who wanted to learn everything in no time and therefore placed himself in the slipstream of Europe's two most rebellious and interesting museum directors.

Documenta 1959, Vitality in Art 1960 and Movement in Art 1961. In a country in which the highest expertise despises exhibitions, Louisiana becomes a "museum machine" like the Stedelijk, and the Dutch museum's energetic director Willem Sandberg virtually adopts the new boy in the class. Knud writes to him: "Denmark is certainly an underdeveloped country as to exhibitions of foreign modern art!" and Sandberg sends one epoch-making exhibition after the other to the north on loan. "Thanks for Malevitch," writes Knud. "It had a good and calming effect after Vitality in Art, which evoked lots of discussion and criticism to the very end."

Then the third figure in the North European axis appears, Pontus Hultén from Moderna Museet in Stockholm. The three inspire one another, lend each other works and send exhibitions to and fro among each other – also in the coming decades. The Danish beginner starts an apprenticeship as museum director with the best teachers to be found, and what is more they have the territory for themselves.

"Around 1960 it became known in the world of art that two museums in Scandinavia – one in Stockholm and the other in Humlebæk – were on the way to developing a lively activity in the field of modern art. Up to that point the Stedelijk Museum in Amsterdam had been the northernmost institution in Europe that had made contemporary art the central object of its activity. It looked as if the two

Scandinavian museums were working in the same spirit as the Stedelijk," says Edy de Wilde, director of the Stedelijk from 1963.

The three wild museum leaders went in for the same idea of a vital and extrovert museum free of hollow solemnity, and they added music, film, dance, debate, guided tours, readings and food (clearly the worst thing of all in the eyes of some critics). Sandberg wrote a kind of love poem to the new kind of museum, which he was absolutely the first to introduce in postwar Europe:

today they're looking for museum directors
everywhere
is that so difficult a task then
yes
because they'd prefer to appoint people who are
dead
– that is to say those whose opinions have rigidified

as long as man lives, really lives,
he develops over time
constantly changes his viewpoint
in his eyes the true value of
the museum's collections changes from day to day
he would prefer to put certain works,
certain artists in store
because they don't say anything to him any longer
replace them with others that the museum does not
possess – yet

people who think they are competent prefer
the permanent museum
where things always have their own places
those who are competent write in the papers
speak fierily to assemblies of the
overlooked figurative art
the museums that are arranged in accordance with the taste of the competent have few visitors
but the museum that moves has visitors
in their thousands
among them the young, leather jackets.
girls with pony tails!

In Sandberg's eyes "the competent" were a death-bringing crowd of stiff museum men who loved the past, figurative art, few visitors and things in permanent places, so in that way none of the three were competent in the old sense but became so in the new sense.

The time of scandals

The 28-year-old composer Nam June Paik arrived in Copenhagen one evening in October 1961 on the ferry from Oslo, where he had made trouble. A short, slender man, smiling and with a nervous twitch. During his overbooked concert next evening at Louisiana the quiet artist hurled fried eggs at the wall, smashed a grand piano and disappeared into a barrel of water. To the accompaniment of extreme noise he wrote on the blackboard he had brought along "are you a gentleman?", poured flour over his head and strolled to and fro across the floor, now with his hand under his chin, now thoughtfully staring into the air.

"It was like seeing grown-up people behave like children in a sandbox," wrote B.T.'s reviewer, but the shocked audience reacted as it was supposed to: it booed, laughed and protested at the crazy noise, and in that way the "contact" between artist and audience had been secured. Information's music critic Hans Georg Lenz participated involuntarily in the session as artistic raw material, since Paik sprayed foam on his hair, cut his tie in two, tore his vest into pieces and ruined his shirt. Lenz responded by judging the show to be "kitsch" and calling the artist "the avantgarde's old gardener" in his review.

Later in his life Nam June Paik (1932-2006) became "the father of video art" and was the first video artist ever to sell a work to a museum. This was to Louisiana in 1974. But that Saturday in October he was hugely scandalous and the culmination of a series of wild incidents at the museum, which was rapidly moving away from its placing as a harmonious, Elysian spot.

Paik was the last straw. The week before his concert one of the biggest scandals in the museum's history took place when Jean Tinguely's self-destructive sculpture "Study for the End of the World" accidentally took the life of an encased white dove, which as a symbol of hope was supposed to have risen above the smoking ruins, but instead lay blown up and very dead in a bucket on the front page of Politiken the following day: "Macabre prelude to art exhibition". But there was more than that. The dove was the starting signal for a collective burst of fury with front-page stories, leading articles and readers' letters like: "How can civilised people accept such a macabre firework display as that held at Louisiana?"

In fact, the civilised prime minister Viggo Kampmann and his wife were present on the balcony that evening, both members of a society, Svalen, for the

Nam June Paik pours flour over himself during the concert at Louisiana in October 1961. The reviewers foamed at the mouth, the audience booed, so everything was as it should be.

"It was like seeing grown-u

eople behave like children in a sandbox"

The public and Knud
W. Jensen in tense
anticipation on oppo-
site sides of the tape.

prevention of cruelty to animals, which accused Louisiana and Tinguely of cruelty to animals and took the case to the public prosecutor. A post mortem of the dove at the Royal Veterinary and Agricultural University's poultry laboratory showed that it had died of a broken pelvis and internal bleeding. What would it look like, wondered *Politiken*, when English TV shows its documentary film from the event with the subtitle: "Danish Prime Minister Viggo Kampmann witnessed peace dove's demise."

Ugly and incomprehensible art had come to Denmark. A lot of it and all at once. People actually discussed it. At that time they dared to ask *stupid* questions and demand an explanation. Art no longer resembled itself – what had happened to its beauty, its elevating effect and recognisability? What was the meaning of Paik's meaninglessness? What conceivable use was there for art now that it dismantled and destroyed rather than giving pleasure and building up?

"I was very surprised to read that you have to understand modern art in order to derive pleasure from it. I thought that art was something that you hung on the wall, and which was intended to please the eye by its beauty, but apparently that is not the case any longer. Now you have to have spent ten years at university to be able to understand art," goes a typical letter, in which a humanities student Kresten Bruun is clearly looking for what art could do before. He wants the old art back.

People are afraid of being ridiculous and therefore ask one and the same question throughout most of the 20th century: "Is that supposed to be art?" A host of successful painting apes appear not only in cartoons but also in literature, as in Hans Scherfig's novel "Den fortabte abe" [The Lost Ape] (1964), in which the capuchin ape Primus's aesthetic experiments "must be regarded as ground-breaking within the infra-human school in art", and in which the ape's painting "in its fan-shaped division of the surface into darker and lighter zones in accordance with the additive method as if through an invisible white handwriting communicate the colour as an afterthought in the universe." Deeply satirical and as if taken from an art review – or *Louisiana Revy*. Scherfig was inspired by an exhibition in Oslo Art Society in 1962, which had evoked a storm of protest. Here the arrangers had hung Klee and Kandinsky together with drawings by people with Down's syndrome, children and apes. 26 abstract painters boycotted the exhibition.

For fear of being fooled many people in the 1960s talked about the emperor's new clothes and demanded guarantees. For this reason, *Information*'s critic Ejner Johansson had to explain his enthusiasm for Robert Jacobsen's dolls at Louisiana in 1959 to readers who were more likely to see "rusty scissors and handlebars". One reader after the other asked the reviewer – who boasted of 10 years of university studies – to argue better and to answer clearly: Why are Robert Jacobsen's

Jean Tinguely building his self-destroying sculpture on the lawn. "White dove burnt and windows broken during art explosions at Louisiana", ran the headline on *Ekstra Bladet's* front page the next day.

iron dolls art? Is it the material? Is it because they are amusing? Is it because it is impressive that they are made of scrap metal, or what is it? Come on!

He answered that art can be described with subjective words, but never fixed in a definition that can be produced on demand when the ticket collector asks to see the ticket. Johansson consoled himself with the thought that no one else from Antiquity to that day had been able to give a tenable explanation of what art is. The only thing he and the other reviewers were certain of was their uncertainty.

Louisiana received no complaints from the four people who had been hurt in the five minutes it took the firework sculpture to destroy itself and spread its components over the public, but as *Politiken* wrote, feelings "ranging from the bitterest pity to the most hardened cynicism" had come to expression afterwards. The newspaper was happy to print an open letter to Knud W. Jensen from a *prominent* member of the Louisiana club, retired judge Sven Hiorth-Lorenzen, who resigned in protest. He was disappointed at the transformation of the beautiful Louisiana's into something hideous:

"In time as I saw how the sterling little collection of good modern art by names such as Isakson, Agger, Hoppe and Høst were swamped and pushed aside by an increasingly sensationalist art and extremely advanced modernism, my interest cooled considerably. Only the considerable charm of the place and individual pleasurable art experiences like the recent glass exhibition have kept me there.

The unhappy dove that found its painful death at the top of the idiotic, dilettantish, life-threatening firework arrangement, which was the high spot of the evening, this victim of a puerile sadistic prank, which is now deplored so deeply by all animal friends, should not have been the only contribution from the animal world to this ill-reputed ceremony. A sack full of rats emptied among the legs of the festive audience would have been extremely appropriate and quite in agreement with the basic mood of the exhibition."

Furthermore, Hiort-Lorenzen was angry at the scandal's coincidence with the Berlin Crisis and Dag Hammarskjöld's plane crash. That Knud W. Jensen in this summer of destiny 1961, perhaps to be civilisation's last, could think of transforming his lovely dream into a reeking rubbish dump! "Whose purposes do you actually think you are fulfilling by doing that?"

The simple answer on the part of the modernists was that the strife in the world and the nuclear arms race could scarcely be better illustrated than by an exploding sculpture. Ugly art for an ugly time. In all probability the expression "hardened cynicism" was aimed at Klaus Rifbjerg, PH and other writers of

Politiken was most indignant and covered the affair intensively.

MAGASINET I DAG · SEKTION II — weekend læsning

POLITIKEN

Lyt — RADIO OG FJERNSYN I DAG SEKTION II

Tlf. C. 8511 . Døgnet rundt . »Oplysningen« hverdage 10—22. C. 4088   KØBENHAVN, LØRDAG 23. SEPTEMBER 1961   77. årgang . Nummer 354 . Løssalg over hele landet 50 øre

Krav om ny stærk FN-generalsekretær

USA foreslår international lederskikkelse udpeget til midlertidigt at tage ansvaret

NEW YORK, fredag POLITIKEN PRIVAT

DEN amerikanske udenrigsminister Dean Rusk udtalte i dag, at USA anså det for nødvendigt, at FN-forsamlingen umiddelbart udpeger „en fremstående international lederskikkelse" til provisorisk at tage sig af generalsekretærembedets funktioner.

Fra anden side i FN taler man om, at generalforsamlingen bør stille Sikkerhedsrådet over for et „ultimatum", der kræver, at rådet inden for en bestemt og snævert tilmålt tidsfrist udpeger Dag Hammarskjölds efterfølger, hvis man ikke vil risikere at forsamlingen selv finder en midlertidig generalsekretær.

Rusks udtalelse, som blev fremsat under en frokost arrangeret af FN-korrespondenterne, vidnede klart om, at han ikke mente at være kommet nogen vegne i FN-spørgsmålet under sin fire timer lange samtale med udenrigsminister Gromyko dagen før. Han udtalte sin beklagelse over, at der tydeligvis ikke kan forudses nogen umiddelbar enighed om udnævnelsen af en permanent generalsekretær.

FN på skillevej

Men med FN ved en „afgørende skillevej" som følge af Hammarskjölds pludselige bortgang, er det uomgængeligt nødvendigt, at det vidtomfattende virksomhed uden af brud får en kraftig administrativ ledelse, sagde Rusk. Man måtte derfor omgående gå til aktion og sørge for, at embedets funktioner bliver varetaget effektivt og fuldt ud, medens man forsøger at nå til enighed om udnævnelse af en ny efterfølger.

Rusk vendte sig bestemt mod det sovjetiske forslag om en tredelt „trojka"-ledelse eller nogen form for komitéstyre inden for sekretariatet „på hvilket niveau det end måtte være"

Dette var klar besked om, at USA nu modsatte sig projektet om at supplere en tilfældig eller permanent indehaver af posten som FN-chef med et trumvirat af underseketkretærer, således at nogle inden for den afrosiatiske lejr var begyndt at tale om. Rusk hævdede, at FN-statutterne giver generalforsamlingen klar befajelse til at oprette provisorium på mindre sandsynligt, at en europæiske som f. eks den afgående FN-præsident Boland fra Irland ikke kunne samle den store afronasiatiske stemmegruppe. Et nyopdukket navn i diskussionen er Indiens Washington-ambassadør B. K. Nehru, som dog ikke lanceres af sit eget land.

S. A.

Svært at finde en kandidat

Med Norge og Irland i ledende roller arbejder en gruppe på en halv snes mindre FN-stater stadig for at fremskaffe en kandidat til posten som generalsekretær, men endnu har anstrengelserne ikke ført til noget egentligt forslag.

Hvis ikke FN-præsidenten Mongi Slim fravier sin uvillighed til selv at stille sig til rådighed, ser det i øjeblikket nærmest ud til, at man forsøger at få Burmas FN-delegat U. Thant udpeget af forsamlingen på provisorisk basis.

Den kendsgerning, som alle har kunnet blive meget langvarigt, gør den mindre sandsynligt, at en europæiske...

Fortsættes side 2, sp. 6.

På det store billede ses fyrværkeriet, mens det knaldede på sit højeste. Det var i kassen oven på stigen til venstre, duen var anbragt, mens den ifølge kunstneren var tiltænkt, da forestillingen begyndte, og som øjenvidner fortæller blafrede med vingerne, få minutter før forestillingen begyndte. Tinguelys version fortæller, at det blafrede, man kunne se, må være et stykke lineret stanniol.

Tipskroner redder havn

Nyt perspektiv for de små havne: Tips-penge af hensyn til friluftslivet på søen

Hele den vestlige badestrand ved Hornbæk bliver reddet, fordi havnemolen sættes i stand for 15.000 tipskroner.

Med denne bevilling har Friluftsrådet knæsat et nyt princip, der åbner vide perspektiver for de små havnes bevarelser og udbygning med henblik på friluftslivet til søs.

Rådet gav sin indstilling i går.

— Det sker sid fra to bevægingar-de, oplyser kontorchef Hornten fra Friluftsrådet. Hvis ikke havnemolen udbedres, vil stranden i løbet af nogle få år være skyllet væk, og desuden har vi en naturlig interesse i at støtte friluftslivet på vandet ved at hjælpe til med at bevare de små hyggelige havne for lystsejlerne.

Et havnerednings-program

— Vi er klar over, at denne principielle afgørelse let kan afføde mange ansøgninger, hvorfor vi må nøge på, at vore midler er begrænset, og at vi derfor i gjort fald må foretage en nøje sortering og lægge et program for eventuelle havneilskud over en årrække. Vi må naturligvis ikke svigte andre friluftsinteresser som f. eks vandrer-bevægelsen til fordel for havnene.

Hornbæk havn har været i den fortvivlede situation ikke at kunne skaffe midler til vedligeholdelsen, skønt havnens betydning som lystudelsvætn er stærkt voksende. Som erhvervshavn er den ikke vigtig nok til at opnå statstilskud, men nu består man, at tidligere tilslager om støtte fra amt og kommune indfries.

— Jeg var uvilligt indstillet på, at tipspræmiens maksimumregel blev...

Fortsættes side 2, sp. 6.

EG

Makaber optakt til kunst-udstilling

Due skulle affyres som fyrværkerisensation

Den franske kunstner Jean Tinguely holdt som led i udstillingen „Bevægelse i kunsten" generalprøve på jordens undergang foran Louisiana i aftes, på plænen i Humlebæk var fuld af interesserede tilskuere, mens statsminister Kampmann stod på husets balkon. Sjældent har en fernisering fået et sådant punktum.

På Tinguelys signal sluttedes de elektriske kontakter og udløste først en blid røgsky, hvorefter en rød legetøjsbørnevogn rullede hen over plænen mod den opstillede skulptur. Men komikken gik snart over til dramatik, det lynede, det bragede og det tordnede, atomskyer reiste sig over skulpturen, raketterne løb tilskuerne ov faldt, at den var lydt og meget tryk af, en langsomt sank skulpturen et pur, og langsomt sank skulpturen i grus. Da den lå sønderknust, udløstes nogle kampekbrag, og til slut dalede en tynd silkefaldskærm med en tricolore ned fra den stille aftenhimmel.

Hvordan man nogen sinde får plæne ud af Louisians afvedne græs, vil ingen vise.

Men mere uhyggeligt virkede det på mange af de tilstedeværende, da det gik op for dem, at „skulpturen" der blev brændt af — øverst havde en kassen øverst på den besynderlige stykke fyrværkeri. Man påstod, at duen havde været syg og var død en time før fyrværkeriet var brændt af. Han havde selv følt, at den var kold og tung, da han så til den en time før fyrværkeriet.

Hvis publikum har bemærket noget levende, så siger Tinguely, at det må have været noget staniol, der blafrede op af kassen.

Kunstneren mente i øvrigt, nummere plejede at lykkes for ham.

Fortsættes side 2, sp. 6.

Den franske kunstner Jean Tinguely, om duen var død før eller efter skyderiet står endnu klart. Men meningen var under alle omstændigheder, duen skulle have været indejtakt i forestillingen som brænde.

Kunstnerens version af historien

Politikens møding i løbet af aftenen flere henvendelser fra forargede tilskuere, der var oprørte over at have overværet dette stykke dyrplageri.

Duen som den så ud efter den makabre forestilling. Blev den dræbt ved fyrværkeriet eller af sårene, den kan have pådraget sig derved eller var den død, da forestillingen begyndte. Hele denne historie med anbringelse af en due på toppen af fyrværkeriet er mere end besynderlig.

EG

Barnevogn med lille pige røvet

Dyb mystik om spædbarns forsvinden

En fortvivlet ung mor henvendte sig sent i aftes til politiet i Gladsaxe og fortalte, at hendes fire måneder gamle datter var blevet bortført i barnevogn, der stod parkeret ved trafikkiltdegbladene i Gladsaxe.

Den unge kvinde var opsøgt fod før blevet ringet op af sin mand, der bad hende træffe sig på holdepladsen. Hun forlod hjemmet og tog sin datter med i barnevognen.

Da hun ved knap 23-tiden kom hen til 'holdepladsen, stillede hun barnevognen på fortovet og gik ind i ventesalen for at afvente mandens ankomst.

Nogle minutter senere gik hun ud for at se til barnet, men opdagede, at både det og barnevognen var fjernet. Hun gennemsøgte den nærmeste omegn uden resultat og henvendte sig derefter til politiet, som straks iværksatte en eftersøgning.

Man undersøgte sig om at finde frem til øgemanden, idet moderen mente, det muligvis kunne være ham, der havde fjernet barnet. Han forklarede, at han havde ventet forgæves og at bortkørslen af datteren kunne være nået meget senere end den sidste tidskunst, samtidens kunst frem i for nogen.

Jakob.

Film som fag foreslår næste del af Den blå

Læseplanudvalget færdig til at underskrive betænkningen

Folkeskolens Læseplanudvalg vil forleden samlet til det korrektursstilingsmøde, der i realiteten betyder, at film som et af de vigtige blik henvisninger og tryksopprevelser, men mens man i skolens brugen af de trykte sprøge ABC, grammatik, syntaks og stil, giver man og kun i de færreste tilfælde af mod det audio-visuelle sprog, hvis udformninger volter ud over os, ikke mindst når vi sen volte har forladt skolen.

Dette påpeger Saxtorphs pjece og giver samtidig pædagogerne anvisninger på, hvor i skemaet filmkundskab kan placeres, hvilket undervisningsmateriale, der forrligger, osv.

Undervisningsministeriet har i øvrigt med den ny skoleordning godt kendt esperanto som valgfrit fag i 8. og 9. klassetrin samt i alternkolen. Men hvor skaffer man lærerne?

For at råde bod på dette, sætter to ministeriet nu i disse mistbrug — har sagt det, at åbne og skarpe elevernes sind og sanser for den storslåede bergelse, der er at hente i den bedste filmkunst, samtidens kunst frem i for nogen.

Fortsættes side 2, sp. 6.

Norden sammen om Hammarskjöld-minde

Dansk forslag om at de nordiske lande skænker portrætbuste til opstilling i FN-hovedkvarteret

NEW YORK, fredag. POLITIKEN PRIVAT

DANMARK har foreslået de øvrige nordiske regeringer, at alle fem lande går sammen om at rejse Dag Hammarskjöld et mindesmærke i De forenede Nationer.

Udenrigsminister Jens Otto Krag meddelte i dag i en samtale med Deres korrespondent, at han har fremført forslaget over for Sverige, Norge, Finlands og Islands FN-ambassadører. Det er Krags tanke, at mindesmærket skal have form af en portrætbuste af Hammarskjöld, og at placeres enten i det parkanlæg der omgiver FN-bygningen i New York, eller inde i selve hovedkvarteret.

— Jeg mener, at dette ville være en naturlig hyldest fra Norden til Hammarskjölds minde, siger udenrigsminister Krag.

De øvrige nordiske FN-delegationer...

Fortsættes side 2, sp. 2.

An apparently paralysed audience regarding a work at the exhibition Movement in Art, which the exploded dove was part of.

"The reason why people are so upset is that the

readers' letters who were surprised at all the sentimental dove nonsense, and that the creature's friends did not criticise the mass killing that major cities were performing all the time to keep streets and squares free of droppings.

The department store Anva in Copenhagen reacted with a huge Tinguely-inspired window exhibition called "Hososianva – but where is art going?". Mannequins demonstrated piquant underwear next to figures made of junk, and under a kettle on a stand there was the text: "Manno Fraud. 1924 born in Hungary. 1948 discharged from hospital in TSHJFK as 'good-naturedly crazy'. "I sleep with flour in my mouth... it is so dough-lightful", a strongly naturalist action. In 1961 clearly affected by the tooth of time he will exhibit in the spring "The right-off-the handle kettle steam."

The reason why people are so upset is that they are hopelessly behind in their taste, asserted Torben Brostrøm cheerfully in *Louisiana Revy*, which in a number of issues ran its large-scale poll "Taking the bearings of modernism" in 1962. There is no prospect of reconciliation between free art and the broader public; there must still be a gap because "the majority with their more sporadic concern with artistic problems, indeed with art at all, will be attached to antiquated ideas about what art is, inherited concepts that are as a rule two to four generations behind contemporary art. This is what one has experienced in connection with the exhibition "Movement in Art" at Louisiana. The war was waged mercilessly from both sides because for several of the attackers it was a matter of traumatic experiences and for the defenders and the few interpreters it was about matters of principle."

In other words, the attackers are tied up in a kind of loop that points back to themselves all the time: If they do not like modern art including Tinguely, it is because they are behind the times. If they directly attack it, they are driven by a trauma. Thus, there is no such thing as ordinary criticism, only one's own unacknowledged problems. The adherent of modern art on the other hand is impelled by principles. And it is at any rate quite clear that "only a few people have an artistic, objective relationship to art – something that modernism has only now made evident, as more traditional art can be perceived in many inoffensive ways."

Then they can learn! And that was in reality what was attempted at Louisiana in the 1960s and everywhere else where the temptation grew too strong, and the art specialists marched forth under the banner: If you don't like modern art, it's because you don't understand it. They were sent into the field to fill the gap between artists and public – with knowledge. Also, Knud W. Jensen was looking for a formula. He found it difficult to explain and defend modernism for the public and even for his old literary friends. In particular, he wanted to know what the artist himself thought about his work, and how one should try to get it to make sense for other people.

Woman on one of Tinguely's rubbish sculptures. "If you feel lost in the daily round, go to Louisiana. Here there is art everyone can understand even though it is not what most people would understand to be art. But the exhibition contains what one can demand of good art. It is fun, cheeky, provocative and unorthodox," wrote *Ekstra Bladet*.

Kontakt med kunsten

– „Færdelsulykke?"
– „Nej, 'Louisiana'..."

For him modernism was to want to create a new language: "One might say that there is something of an Oedipal showdown, something of an aggression towards what had gone before in that attitude. A kind of anarchism. For Christ's sake, let's begin all over again and make something new, something that suits our time." No doubt that Louisiana effectively disseminated modernism in Denmark. It was an educational project they were engaged in. A comprehensive demonstration of international modernism from Picasso and Braque to the new names that arrived later.

"Modern art is a liberation from the old bonds and authorities, but then in many people's eyes becomes an elitist authority itself. Modernism was an elitist concept, but not meant like that. We thought we were propagating a gospel," says Brostrøm today.

For modernism there was only one right way forward, forward in constant renewal. The motif was gone, and soon the painting itself was in danger of disappearing. In the middle of the1960s, the iconoclastic revolt began in earnest, and *easel painting* had suddenly become a term of abuse. The avantgarde considered it to be bourgeois and as dead as the dodo because it was a capitalist sales

Bo Bojesen's drawing from *Politiken*, 26 September 1961.

article, and because it didn't impact politically. One had to *live* art, act, begin all over again.

Young Per Kirkeby wished to paint paintings, but mentally this was too closely connected with the preceding generation. Out with it. "It wasn't so good that Per was painting," as the even younger revolutionary Bjørn Nørgaard explained. It was unacceptable to insist on producing one's own egoistical art, when one was faced by a rotten society calling for change. So Kirkeby chose square masonite boards, where "all four sides are equally valid" and used enamel paint instead of oils, but that was not always enough, for "there was always a reproach in the air that I wasn't living in a commune and screwing the seven feminists that were to be found in such places," Kirkeby felt. One couldn't permit oneself to make pictures. At the alternative Eks-school in Copenhagen, he learnt that style was the worst thing of all – nothing but a banal trademark by which to sell oneself. The important thing was to have an attitude, not to serve one's own narrow purposes.

The task for the mediators of art was to break down the public's massive resistance to "ugly", non-figurative art. It was typical of the period that the adult education movement Folkevirke issued a package of books entitled "Hvorfor maler de sådan?" [Why Do They Paint Like That?]. The package was to be leased to study groups in order to counteract "the general lamentation that usually accompanies all conversation about contemporary art." They little suspected what lay just around the corner. Not lamentation, but loud, angry protest.

Rindal comes

Towards the end of February 1965 853 slaughterhouse workers from Vejle sent an open letter to the government. Their attack was directed at the brand-new State Art Foundation:

"In the light of the fact that the Minister of Culture intends to disburse 3½ million kroner, and more later, as marks of the State's recognition, to artists among whom there are to be found practitioners of so-called modern art, we hereby send our sharpest protest.

We are, with the income we have, and the burden of taxation imposed on us, obliged to have our wives work in order to manage our commitments, and we think that the State should economise rather than waste.

We do not wish to pay for "the emperor's new clothes" "at a time when workers are being urged by both the government and the Folketing to exhibit moderation in connection with the collective wage negotiations."

And then letters poured in to the almost equally new Ministry of Culture, established in 1961, and its second minister, the Social-Democrat Hans Sølvhøj. The protests came from his core voters, not from the prissy bourgeoisie artists love to hate. It was workers against artists: "A diligent worker is not rewarded, not even when a widow brings up a number of children on her own. If artists cannot sell their production, it seems reasonable that they must do the same as workers when their labour is not needed," wrote 200 workers from Hjørring. "How long is this wastefulness going to continue, to the benefit of all the mummery that ordinary people do not understand?" asked 34 others.

Storekeeper Peter Rindal from Kolding got a total of 20,447 people to sign a protest in the course of five inflamed weeks: "We find that this is a misuse of the State's money, and if these people cannot live from their art, there are good opportunities for finding employment in the productive occupations."

People were dissatisfied with three things: that they had to pay money; that they had to pay money for a modern art they neither liked nor understood; and that the State awards were lifelong so that certain artists could live the rest of their days in comfort without lifting a finger. A Mr Knud Krusdorff was watching a television programme one evening from "the stronghold of art and culture Louisiana", in which he was presented with a large number of pictures by Asger Jorn, while the commentator tried to explain to the viewers what they were seeing. "It is modern to be able to understand modern art, it is said. Some people try to persuade themselves and others that they can, but dare one believe them?" he asked in the Danish paper *Vestjysk Aktuelt*. "Those who do so are in my view the more or less intellectual types, who lack contact with the reality of the life that is lived around us."

After the programme, he studied with pleasure the drawings his children had made, for he saw in them reflected an immediacy that he would not wish to call art, but which on the other hand was not artificial or provided with titles like "Stupid Pigs", "Fool" or "Quite Ridiculous".

The postman continued to unload children's drawings in Sølvhøj's ministry from parents who asked him to have their kids included in the annual grants list. He visited Ålborg Shipbuilding Yard to explain the policy, and he mounted the Folketing's rostrum eighty days in succession to defend the State Art Foundation established by law the previous year. In fact, however, he did not himself understand modern art either, he said. When the names of the first award recipients ticked into the newspapers from Ritzau's News Service, the storm broke. But the civil servants couldn't find the Minister until later in the evening. He had been to the cinema with his family to see Morten Korch's hugely popular family film "The Red Horses". In the dispute, Sølvhøj chose the standpoint that as a taxpayer one can very well pay for something one does not use oneself. For him that would be the municipality's football pitches.

"The workers' movement's mistake was that it confused the interest in art of narrow, elitist circles with popular support," he admitted many years later. Already

before Rindal appeared, the Social-Democrat Minister of Education K. B. Andersen warned against a self-appointed cultural elite that wanted to tell the people what art was. And also his party colleague Ivar Nørgaard understood the protest from worn out slaughterhouse workers, whose every movement was subjected to time and motion studies to ensure that they could work faster and generate more profit.

All talk of the working class's own culture had fallen silent. The Social Democrats supported the avantgarde and the art of the upper classes. In the Party's self-view, of course, there was no longer any difference between people. At any rate that is what they believed until the revolt.

In the counter-attack, the front of writers, painters and sympathisers did not hold back either. The worst of them regarded *the others* as being cultureless. In *Information* Leif Blædel set his teeth in the man in the street's "pure cultural fascism", and in *Politiken* Jess Ørnsbo attacked "the philistine petit bourgeois" who in all their provincial anarchism were in reality merely complaining that it had all become too complicated. Mankind back to the hunter-collector stage.

One evening in Ribe upper-secondary school, student Hans Edvard Nørregård-Nielsen heard a lecture by a testy Elsa Gress, in which she consistently and deliberately called the slaughterhouse workers *swinery workers*. In a distorted voice she outlined her opponents' views as if Rindal (a sewer of ignorance) was

Peter Rindal liked art. He just could not see why it should be paid for via our taxes. Rindalism was an attack on all that Knud W. Jensen worked for in his ten long and boring years in the Folketing's Culture Committee.

g is this wastefulness going to continue"

not even able to speak properly. *The swinery workers* were not only hindering all cultural development in Denmark, but in their stupidity they were dragging the country towards fascist conditions and book burnings. On their way to the lecture most of the audience had eaten their supper in a sitting-room with a couple of pseudo-paintings on the wall, lowbrow Danish trivial literature in the bookcase and the TV set as an altar.

"Now one was sitting there on the way over into the camp of the elite but felt in this transitional situation a little uncomfortable at taking part in scorning decent people who didn't think that the State Art Foundation was relevant for them. These were people who worked in cold and constantly wet rooms; they moved around under an infinity of truncated porcine carcasses that had to be transported from one place to the next, and in order to make ends meet many of them were out at farms in the weekends to slaughter pigs there. It was heavy and wearing work, which Elsa Gress perhaps understood less about than the rest of us sitting listening to her."

At the heat of battle, Knud W. Jensen quietly expressed his opinion to the Social Democrat paper *Aktuelt*: Because artists are indispensable for making society human, they should be supported. Because in a democratic society there should be respect for the minority constituted by artists and people interested in art, they should be supported. And because the hostility to art is so great, efforts must be made to initiate every possible form of popularisation of art.

The vehemence of Rindalism and the bitterness against "the culture clan in Copenhagen" were a direct blow to his ideas. This was depressing for a man who in the first place had taken the initiative for Art in the Workplace already in 1954, in the second place had assumed the task of opening a museum for all, and in the third place regarded Louisiana's activities as an important interpretive intermediary between public and artists now that art had become so difficult and intellectual. He who had always insisted on "presenting a material" so everybody could form their own views and become wiser. On the day in August when Louisiana was inaugurated by the minister of education Jørgen Jørgensen, called "the peasant from Lejre" and often photographed in wooden clogs, the minister praised his idea of creating links with "the man in the street". Today his efforts seemed to have been in vain.

And in the fourth place he himself was deeply involved in the invention of the State Art Foundation.

It had begun five years previously with what was probably Denmark's only prime minister to have read all sixteen volumes of Søren Kierkegaard's collected works. Viggo Kampmann was interested in artists; he wished to chase them out of their critical isolation and into politics, to hear their opinions and receive guidance,

Denmark's second minister of culture, the Social Democrat
Hans Sølvhøj, defends the party's culture policy at Aalborg
Shipbuilding Yard. A hard struggle against his core voters.

preferably in an affectionate and understanding way. If they couldn't be bothered, they would be the ones who would suffer most. In an interview he underlined the obvious point: "They can of course withdraw, but they must realise that the country will be governed nevertheless."

The next step was that the two otherwise irreconcilable parties talked together, which took place at the so-called Louisiana-Krogerup meeting in the autumn of 1960. Afterwards, it became fashionable for politicians to meet with artists, intellectuals and critics. In time with inspiration from the Louisiana-Krogerup meeting this became something that every respectable political party arranged because the enthusiasm at the possibilities of art to "tell man who he is" rose to enormous heights in the 1960s. There was so much hope in the air that Minister of Culture Bomholt was asked whether the Social Democrats were considering becoming an artistic movement instead of a political party. All parties wrote culture programmes and were loath to be outdone by the others.

The journalist Ejvind Larsen was present in Humlebæk and afterwards thought that the meeting became one of the first expressions of the fact that the paralysis following the Occupation was diminishing. Modernism had never been more strongly placed because the efforts of the first 15 years to give art and cultural work in general a raison d'être in the wake of the World War, Occupation and Resistance struggle were now completed. "One was now conscious of one's own value, and the politicians gave way," he concluded. The meeting had important consequences for the rest of the 1960s: Denmark acquired a Ministry of Culture and an Arts Foundation.

From the beginning, Knud W. Jensen took part in the building up of the welfare state's first slender cultural policy. In the winter of 1961 Kampmann repeated the success and invited hundreds of cultural representatives to Christiansborg, including Knud W. Jensen, who arrived somewhat concerned. He knew how bad-tempered and unconstructive ("critical") artists could be and feared that the prime minister would merely hear reproaches about the decline of standards, that is about pop music, advertising, consumption, but no affectionate and understanding guidance. He was right: the architect PH and the writer Elsa Gress joined in the general indignation at full volume. He himself suggested not particularly emotionally but practically that a committee should immediately be set up to form an overview of the economic needs of cultural life and then to draw up a long-term budget for investments. The manuscript was printed in *Verdens Gang*, and then there was quiet for a year or so. Kampmann established his ministry of culture, made Julius Bomholt its minister, and Bomholt invited Knud W. Jensen in 1962, placed him in a deep armchair and circled around it. There was something he needed to say. Bomholt wished to make use of Jensen's idea for a

Louisiana visits Århus in 1964. The exhibition was shown in Arne Jacobsen's City Hall.

The Århus public saw Louisiana's own collection, which at that time consisted only of Danish art.

Louisiana became an institution in the course of just a few years. "Knud W. Jensen has in a way created his own ministry of culture, which can easily compare with the real one. He has created an apparatus with an enormous influence that can simply not be explained away," opined *Berlingske Aftenavis*.

Kulturpave Julius den Første i funktion.

culture committee, but there was a problem: he couldn't become chairman of the committee because he owned both Gyldendal and Louisiana. This norm-setting alliance would acquire great power and people would talk.

Instead he became an ordinary member of the new culture committee containing 19 persons, but one of Gyldendal's directors, Ole Wivel, also came in, so the power concentration was at least just as great. The press immediately drew attention to it: Knud W. Jensen's possessions were really a major power centre in the cultural life of a little country and could easily become an autocracy. The cultural committee was dominated by the very same private circle that already had most influence. At this time, Louisiana was only four years old – it was a small museum in the countryside with a minimal collection in comparison with its competitors, but was nevertheless regarded as fully grown:

"Knud W. Jensen has in a way his own ministry of culture, which can easily compare with the real one. He has created an apparatus, whose enormous influence on Danish cultural life should in no way be underestimated and thereby he has likewise and quite naturally provided cause for irritation in the artistic circles that are neither directly or indirectly linked to the Gyldendal-Louisiana concern," wrote Henning Fonsmark in *Berlingske Aftenavis* and added that all tendencies

Among the culture boss's subjects there were also representatives of Louisiana. Julius Bomholt was Denmark's first minister of culture. Knud W. Jensen was discussed internally among Social Democrats as a possible successor. Drawing by Herluf Jensenius in the satirical magazine *Blæksprutten*.

towards monopolies are dangerous even though they are administered with the best will in the world, and even though the sulking that surrounds the monopoly can perhaps be interpreted as ingratitude and envy.

Besides the economic advantages Knud W. Jensen might derive from leading Louisiana and Gyldendal directly into the political life, there were also ideological gains: to make his own taste that of the whole country and to give modernism the top position. Critics said then as now that the welfare state comprises the whole population while modernism is only a narrow sect in literature and art. Nevertheless it won. Modernism in its special Danish distillation became the welfare state's official artistic ideology.

For more than ten years Knud W. Jensen was a member of the culture committee, the most important result of which was the State Arts Foundation. He left the meetings with an aching head because it was so demanding both to follow what was going on and to think of something else. He was therefore glad *not* to be invited to join boards all that often and guessed that people refrained because they knew that his interest in his own place was too obsessive for him to be able to become deeply involved elsewhere.

"It is as if life is slipping away between one's fingers while one is at a meeting. Boredom sets in and become physical discomfort. While with half an ear I followed the slow process, I drew little sketches of Louisiana projects and hoped that one of them would be as brilliant as that Lord Paxton drew on a piece of blotting paper for the Crystal Palace during a meeting."

"The Social Democrat politician suggested to Prime Minister Krag that he should invite Knud W. Jensen to be their second minister of culture. But it was Hans Sølvhøj who received the offer and took over from the deeply disappointed Bomholt, who had no wish to be replaced. Knud W. Jensen remained at Louisiana, as he preferred to do right through his life. Louisiana before anything else. His wife Vivi participated in the celebrations in the first years as a kind of First Lady, but then opted out once and for all. She hoped his condition would pass, but it never did.

The Americans come

In 1949 Jackson Pollock appeared on the front page of *Life* with a cigarette in his mouth and folded arms. "Is He The Greatest Living Painter In The United States?" the headline asked rhetorically. Yes, of course. He was the brilliant new phenomenon in American art, and he was in the process of ousting the ancient European monopoly on art to make room for the New World. For the first time the Americans meant something at all in international art, also in their own eyes. They came with unique contributions, not pale imitations of European masters. They were not disciples of any school, did not paint to change or save the world – they painted just to paint. In the mid-1950s, the American State Department began to work closely together with MoMA to promote American art in the world. The official USA wished to ally itself with the painters from *downtown* in order to counter Soviet propaganda and social realism with living examples of American individualism and cultural strength.

In 1959 Documenta showed some of Pollock's pictures, which continued to Denmark and Louisiana for the first time. Few people took serious note of him. The sculptor Erik Thommesen did not like Pollock's "blind spontaneity, which is just as little artistic originality as reflexes are dance". Two years later, Pollock came again with a few pictures at "The Stedelijk Museum Visits Louisiana" and in 1963 with a comprehensive retrospective exhibition. Now he was dead and more mythical than ever. With three times Pollock in only five years Louisiana had followed the path of art history really closely and documented the postwar shift from European to American dominance in art and culture. Since then the museum has had a soft spot for American artists – they became a speciality, particularly from 1970 and onwards. Knud W. Jensen suffered almost physically from not being able to afford to buy a Jackson Pollock.

Pollock placed his enormous canvases on the floor and dripped or sprayed paint on them. At the same time as Pollock, a sequence of other Americans broke through, and they could all be seen over the years in Humlebæk: Franz Kline, Willem de Kooning, Mark Tobey. And when these old monarchs of the canvas were pushed off the throne at a fairly youthful age by the next generation – the pop artists – the latter appeared on the placards for "American Pop Art" in 1964. And suddenly all that the Danish intelligentsia detested and combated became art: banal pop, consumption, vulgar surface, coarseness. Again a provocation direct from the USA.

"It's a hard nut to crack: comic strip pictures in big formats with texts painted on them: I know how you must feel, Brad! Patisseries, raw meat and ladies' underclothes made of plaster and coloured in revolting enamel colours. Advertising boards for cigarettes and American soups. An imitation wall of a room with a telephone hung on it, a radiator, a red ladies' coat and in the middle of the work a painted nude girl. *By Jove*, that's the worst slap in the face that we have been dealt so far!" wrote Leo Estvad from *Berlingske Aftenavis* in dismay when he had examined the horrible works. "There lay art ... flat on its face in the ditch."

At Louisiana they just sat waiting for trouble, well knowing that pop art was a provocation. "We'll probably get it in the neck," said Knud W. Jensen, "but one grows tired of being the careful and responsible guarantor for quality." The reviewers had now understood that there was no reason to shoot the messenger. They admitted that it was Louisiana's task to show the public what was going on

Vital, mythical, world famous Jackson Pollock on the front cover of *Louisiana Revy*, which also contained articles like "Themes in modern Polish literature" and "The poet as Tupilak".

NR. 1 · SEPTEMBER 1963 · 4. ÅRGANG

LOUISIANA REVY

KUNST · ARKITEKTUR · BRUGSKUNST · LITTERATUR · MUSIK · TEATER · FILM

**Jackson Pollock i sit atelier. 1946.
Fot. Hans Namuth.**

Pollock in Humlebæk 1963. He had only been shown twice
before in Denmark. At Louisiana in 1959 and again in 1961.

"I was too cautious, too modest an

in art, whether they liked it or not, and this exhibition was absolutely up to date. More so than they suspected at the time. The seven artists in the exhibition – Jim Dine, Roy Lichtenstein, Claes Oldenburg, James Rosenquist, Georg Segal, Andy Warhol and Tom Wesselman – had not brought great works of art with them, but loudly presented an idea that, to put it crudely, aimed at throwing the rawness and vulgarity of everyday life into the faces of the public. It was at any rate just as real as the obscure poetry, absurd drama and abstract art of the day, perhaps even more real. But it meant that the 1960s' leading arbiters of taste had rejected reality when they had cast scorn on pop music, comic strips and advertisements and had seriously proposed a linguistic analysis of the texts of ten hits from the jukebox. They believed they could make it disappear. In *Louisiana Revy* the French sociologist Edgar Morin touched on the paradox: "Mass culture is the only form of culture that is on the level of reality and is in contact with the majority," he said. "You can't take up a position for or against – it *is* there. The intellectuals who oppose mass culture *en bloc* are way out."

Later the same year, Robert Rauschenberg was given the major award at the Venice Biennale as shocking proof that the Americans had penetrated right into the heart of the international art scene. This caused pain for elderly connoisseurs in Europe, but not at the museum in Humlebæk, which together with Moderna Museet and the Stedelijk had been among the first museums in Europe to allow pop art entry to good society. It never left the building again. At this time, the museum was only five years old but had already witnessed a number of revolutions and new departures in art and in its own history.

Goodbye Danish art

By a strange chance the first foreign art work ever bought by Louisiana quite quietly became the museum's most important work. After a proposal and pressure from the Danish painter Albert Mertz Louisiana took the plunge and acquired Yves Klein's triptych "Monopink, Monogold and Monoblue" from 1960. Not everyone was equally enthusiastic. The painter Ejler Bille called it "an altar in a brothel" and in general opposed the international development threatening Louisiana. Others did so too. Two letters between friends who disagreed tell the story of the decisive choice Knud W. Jensen made in 1966, when he transformed Louisiana into a museum for international modern art. Once again, he was alone with his decision and carried it out despite the opposition of friends and Danish artists, and once again it proved to be the right decision. Later he would always call it the biggest mistake of his life that he had hesitated so long. Seven years passed after the Documenta shock. Seven years in which the prices for Picasso, Pollock and the others rose to unattainable heights. Seven years in which he bought lots of

Vincent van Gogh queue,
1963. With picnic basket.

▶ People couldn't get enough
of van Gogh. Louisiana
borrowed 106 invaluable
works from the Stedelijk
Museum and showed them
in 1963 right after Jackson
Pollock, thus establish-
ing peace in the ranks.

works by good Danish artists, while his heart was elsewhere. "I was too cautious, too modest and provincial," he explained. "Documenta made him more restless than ever," thought Ole Wivel. Already at that time, things were beginning to go wrong between the two.

In 1966 Knud W. Jensen self-confidently turned 50. *Politiken*'s readers were on first-name terms with him and now he dared to make the attempt. The statutes of the Louisiana Foundation had to be changed, but he encountered resistance on Louisiana's board. Ole Wivel, who was called "the bailiff" and "the lord of the manor" behind his back at Gyldendal's, was directly opposed. He regarded a breach with naturalism as a personal breach with what they had together. He was accustomed to getting his way, and until then Knud W. Jensen had scarcely bought a picture without asking his opinion. Wivel now wrote:

"We know that, if we want to, we can create a first-class collection of contemporary Danish art – we already have the foundation and it is economically attainable. A Danish collection of modern art must be measured by a Danish yardstick, and that is a goal we can live up to. A collection of contemporary art that includes foreign works must in all justice be measured by a foreign yardstick. I don't think we can live up to that."

Wivel was afraid of ending with a conventional and incomplete accumulation of art that would at all times be outdone by the Stedelijk and Moderna Museet. "And will it not then be the source of constant annoyance and envy?" and then there was also the national viewpoint:

"It is true that all national art is bad, but just as true that all good art is national, a fact the greatest artists in the major cultural countries are also aware of today. The provincial consists not of acknowledging one's own specialness and giving it expression, but on the contrary of aping the foreign in order to resemble something that is 'higher class'."

The following day Knud W. Jensen replied: "Our task must first and foremost be to do what no one else will or can. As neither the State, the municipalities, the Carlsberg Foundation or others can carry out the specific task of creating an international modern museum, I simply regard it as our duty to do so."

He acknowledged that he was facing a very serious decision, but at the same he saw a dangerous adventure ahead, perhaps with defeats, criticism and disappointments, but this is what made the task attractive to Knud W. Jensen. It was precisely the demands the task posed, all the challenges to his awareness, will, insight and endurance that tempted him and gave him "an insuperable desire to carry it out." Louisiana was not a static, completed museum, so why not go the whole way when already a year after its opening the museum nevertheless became something different from the harmonious place it had been conceived as:

"Louisiana assumed a task that no one else could perform, became a window to the world. Through this work my own horizon was extended because of both an inner and an outer necessity and I actually believe that I have acquired better expert qualifications for carrying out my work, so that my contribution can become increasingly significant. It is therefore not as you may think just parrotry or influence from outside that are the reason why I now wish to spend the rest of my life on creating a museum of modern art, but a consequence of the development I have been through."

In the future, Louisiana would not only show foreign art, but also buy it. Its quality was to be just as high, preferably higher, as that which could be acquired in Danish art. Already in ten years' time, he thought, the decision would be seen to have been right. "If during this period we have merely been able to buy two important art works a year + 2-3 chancy acquisitions, some of which will perhaps stand up to the wear and tear of time, there will be a couple of rooms with good foreign art next to the Danish collection ... The purchase of the two Calders, the two Arps and of Giacometti's major work show that it can be done."

Knud W. Jensen wrote to his friend that his dream of Louisiana was to create a place where one could spend a whole day and could leave filled with impressions of good, not to say great art and lovely natural surroundings. The place was to be a work of art itself. "A voluntary limitation to Danish art might perhaps make this work of art more complete, but limited in its effect on the mind, not opening up the same perspective as a confrontation between the best Danish and foreign art."

And that is what happened. Once again he followed his own enthusiasm, even though it was tremendously expensive and apparently impossible to attain. In time the collection of Astrid Noack sculptures was sold to Holstebro Museum, Niels Larsen Stevns went to Hjørring Art Museum, and a large number of domestic Danish divinities left the building. It hurt, but the international Louisiana had acquired its first important and wealthy ally. Ill-disposed Thorlacius Ussing vacated the chairmanship of the Carlsberg Foundation in favour of Jørgen Sthyr, who was far more favourably inclined. And then something more radical happened. When the museum obtained state recognition in 1968 and received a small allocation in the Budget, the Foundation donated the works it had loaned to the now ten-year-old Louisiana and continued to support and buy.

"It took a little time to get used to the provo Knud W. Jensen," Jørgen Sthyr admitted in his speech on 18 August 1968. After ten years the museum was no longer *just* a museum, but a concept. "A couple of times a year we read in the papers that now a town or a municipality wishes to have its Louisiana, and to this one can only answer that even if one has been able to create a building,

Together with Rotraut Klein,
Knud W. Jensen puts on an
exhibition of Yves Klein's
works in 1968. Here they
stand in front of Louisiana's
first foreign acquisition: Yves
Klein's Triptychon from 1960.

It must be seen in colour...

"An altar in a brothel"

one cannot create a Knud W. Jensen. For first and last the active person is the decisive factor." And the Fund – now in the person of Hans Edvard Nørregård-Nielsen – is still of the opinion that the museum's departure from the somewhat self-sufficient Danish tradition, which one could see in many other places in the period, can quite simply be characterised as "the most important input that has affected the Danish museal world in living human memory."

Up through the 1960s the museum was under pressure from three widely different fronts: from the renowned old museums, from the Rindalists and from the young anti-artists. The old art institutions could not get the word Louisiana past their lips without also saying "exhibitions" and "entertainment". They were still discussing *whether* exhibitions should be arranged at all when *Statens Museum for Kunst* reopened in the summer of 1969 after three years' reconstruction and noted with concern that the Minister of Culture had lost patience with them and their rooms empty of visitors. In fact, they were faced by a political demand for exhibitions and life in their buildings. They were justifiably afraid that they would be confronted with Louisiana's brilliant visitor figures and already ten years after the museum's opening were tired to the bone of being compared with the upstart from Humlebæk.

The problem with Louisiana in the 1960s is that the museum gives the public "stones for bread by contributing to the general entertainment with artistic pseudoevents," writes Erik Fischer, senior curator at *Statens Museum for Kunst*. His own angle is, in contrast, "the coherence and wholeness of art", which is of course something quite different and better. Fischer knows very well what goes on in people's minds: "Louisiana appears. Isn't it what happens there that those that hunger for exhibitions believe they will get sustenance from? Ever-changing art, often just to be new and for general orientation."

But *Statens Museum for Kunst* has neither time nor the wish to comply with the politicians' *peculiar* attempts at changing it. "They probably think they are doing it for the sake of the public," another museum curator speculates in the press. "Perhaps they are thinking more of the great mass of consumers than of the more special users such as artists, art historians, aestheticians of many kinds."

No doubt that the museum in Sølvgade itself feels at home among the chosen few who know how to approach art with "calm, respect, indeed humility," as curator Bente Skovgaard prefers, directly inspired by the Louvre, where you lower your voice. "Denmark does not have quite so grand a style, but we are familiar with it, respect it and have successfully imitated it in the course of the years."

Statens Museum for Kunst fears that the suitable calm and grand style will evaporate if the museum allows itself to be inspired by Louisiana and condescends to becoming an exhibition house that *incessantly* puts on exhibitions. If one has given the devil a finger and recognised the obligation to hold changing exhibitions the whole time, the museum will enter into "a hectic work tempo that is unnatural for a museum", and a chain of unpleasant working tasks commences. Now the management will have to consider the enormous range of international exhibitions on offer and try to fend off the worst of them. Now a catalogue must be produced and insurance and transport arranged. Other members of staff will have to unpack, conservators repair transport damage and the hanging personnel mount the whole thing, not to speak of the deep inconvenience arising from the fact that the museum will feel obliged in return to loan out more of its own works than before, which will involve the same staff in reverse order and so on and so forth. Even with a couple of extra posts the museum will not be able to cope with the enormous work. Curator Bente Skovgaard is sure. It will be impossible to avoid the distinguished museum's "complicated, but well oiled and well adjusted mechanism suffering fatally from having to function in step with both a hectic and a harmonious form of art life." The reference is to Louisiana as the supplier of the hectic and Sølvgade of the harmonious.

At Louisiana, a handful of people are fulfilling this impossible task. None of them are art historians. In the year of the debate, 1969, they manage to open nine exhibitions: Works from Documenta, Van Gogh drawings, Pierre Alechinsky, Carl-Henning Pedersen, George Braque & Henri Laurens, Alexander Calder, Finland at Louisiana, Arman and Italian art. Our local art historians hold the view that people can themselves travel and see the art where it belongs. They fear that the works will be damaged from being continually moved around from exhibition to exhibition and are otherwise of the opinion that the most important duty of the museums is to preserve and do research.

An angry Kirsten Strømstad, financial director at Louisiana, participates in the debate and answers the old institutions' direct or indirect accusations. She rejects as exclusive and arrogant the idea that people can afford to travel around the world to see art in its original surroundings and prefers that art works should be seen rather than remain in the same place forever for reasons of caution. But then there is one somewhat more intangible thing. It is as if the old museums "are fighting with a phantom, which it must be possible to do away with: there is no *respect* attached to arranging exhibitions – it doesn't *count* in the same way as doing research and publishing academic works. It is therefore only very occasionally that there is an exhibition."

At this point, the museum in Humlebæk had held 80 exhibitions and received 200,000 visitors a year, actually 280,000 in 1968, on a basis of a high entrance fee and a ridiculously low state subsidy of 100,000 kroner per annum, and

Curator and painter
Knud Mühlhausen
at work. "The great
pop fraud, a horrible
exhibition," wrote *B.T.*

Woman and figure at the
Giacometti exhibition in 1965.
The artist himself came to
Denmark. He wrote to Knud
W. Jensen that he would like
to visit Denmark, because his
favourite author when he was
young, was J.P. Jacobsen.

nevertheless it was for the most part met with scorn on Parnassus, where the bigwigs restricted themselves to enjoying each other's congenial company.

"Nor should it be concealed that now after having proved its viability for ten years Louisiana must soon be recognised as worthy of 'admission to the guild' – as we have long been among leading foreign museums." She finds it wearisome to be singled out as an inferior institution that acts from 'commercial', 'entertainment' or other in this context doubtful motives." She cannot see why on earth it is not acceptable to contribute to the general entertainment of the public.

The criticism from the young anti-artists and ascetic Marxists is aimed in the opposite direction. They accuse Louisiana of being so horribly posh and pompous that it makes ordinary folk long for the funfair. It makes its founder weak at the knees to hear that kind of thing – for instance from Erik Clausen, a young student at Krogerup Højskole down the road – for that is exactly what he himself criticises the established museums for. Knud W. Jensen can't see himself in company with them. His own youth revolt consisted of selling his father's fantastic and valuable book collection and spending all the money on bricks in Humlebæk.

Erik Clausen's criticism comes only seven years after the opening of the museum, but Louisiana is already an institution, a national jewel, like the Royal Theatre and Frederiksborg Palace, and at the end of the 1960s institutions are there to be combated. Jørgen Nash cuts the head off the little mermaid in 1964 and many years later justifies the murder as a protest against "the art snobs, the Gyldendal-Louisiana gramophones and the campaign started up by the Danish cultural elite to erect another national symbol."

Knud W. Jensen sighs. Among his opponents he is least fond of the rebels and their hatred of "elite culture", a term that covers everything he loves and will not allow to be lumped together. He withdraws somewhat, drops the social debate in *Louisiana Revy* and turns his concentration inward. But first he will stick his hand into a wasps' nest and once and for all experience that he has had enough.

Alberto Giacometti in Louisiana's park. The two persons in the background resemble his sculptures.

Louisiana's 10th anni-
versary party in 1968.
The man in sunglasses
is author and critic Poul
Borum. On his right graphic
artist Austin Grandjean.

"It took a little time to get use

Guests at the anniversary party to celebrate that Louisiana had now been given the works the Carlsberg Foundation had loaned the museum.

o the provo Knud W. Jensen"

Acquisitions meeting.
From the left: Ole Wivel,
Knud W. Jensen, Vivi
Jensen, architect Vilhelm
Wohlert and with back
turned Erik Gyldenkrone.

7. SEPT. – 3. NOV. 1974

JAPAN
PÅ LOUISIANA

In the 1970s Louisiana Man relaxes with a lager and a feminist novel (obligatory reading, of course), but he is somewhat confused about the state of things. Everywhere you can sense this voracious appetite for revolution. A man like Knud W. Jensen has in a few years transformed himself from being the generous founder of a museum into a custodian of a moribund elite culture, which according to *Information* does nothing but admit one hundred percent reactionary "up-the-ladder art" into its la-di-da arty-farty museum instead of placing itself at the service of "down-to-earth" art. Louisiana Man himself is ranked lower down on the scale of villains. He cannot extend his list of sins further than to have a bad conscience about having been born in a suburb. Oh yes, he also keeps quiet about his love of great art, great painters. He knows very well what he should do: sing himself, write poems himself, compose his own music! Better hopeless and homemade than capitalist, but he finds it so difficult to become weaned from *the real artist*. His mother is aware of her son's dilemma so she goes with him to Humlebæk as a chaperone in case they meet one of his colleagues up there engaged in enthusiastic, respectful and thoroughly embarrassing worship of Chagall or Giacometti. Then he can always say that he's just there to keep her company.

Louisiana Man reads in *Vindrosen* (yet another Knud W. Jensen publication) that art is in reality merely a court jester, who bears the ideology of the powers that be. It may well be that the artist thinks differently, but then we have a perfect example of false consciousness in one of the success boys of oil painting. Where "pop" was the worst term of abuse in the 1960s, "elite culture" has that role in the 1970s. The Marxists in the neighbourhood are united in their efforts to destroy the language, table manners and what his mother calls ordinary politeness, but the worst thing is their rejection of a special artistic language. Art shouldn't think that it is something special. It is not, unchallengeable, autonomous, but perhaps suitable for use in the struggle for a new and better world. Art with a capital "A" is suspect and discardable, because it revolves around itself and may not be at all interested in reforming society. Now!

Louisiana Man stretches his long, thin, corduroy-clad body in his creaking basket chair and regards a hand-painted cardboard plate on the wall. The female porcelain decorators on strike at the Royal Copenhagen Factory are represented in all the communes he knows. It's OK to have that sort thing on one's walls. Otherwise he is having difficulty in finding out what is correct, for the new art – action art, minimal art, concept art, country art – is not for sale, nor can it be hung or placed anywhere in the room. He know from his guide, *Louisiana Revy*, that "a regular post-object art" has arisen as a settlement of accounts with the one-sided idea that art must manifest itself tangibly in paintings or sculptures.

An idea is enough – one doesn't necessarily have to carry it out. It is no longer a matter of how something is said, but of *what* is said.

He has also understood his own transformation from traditional art viewer (together with his mother) into a receiver "whose spiritual collaboration" is a central component in the conceptual art strategies. He has to be part of the process, he does. Every one does. Everyone's got to take part in everything. The cultural heritage is being demolished around him. There's revolution in the air, and female German terrorists have star status in certain circles. At the universities, more than half the students vote for the far left. There are only three parties in the world for them; the Danish Communist Party, the Communist Workers' Party and the Left Socialists. A moderate left-wing party like the Socialist People's Party simply doesn't come into consideration.

In *Louisiana Revy* Susan Sontag is in love with the Cuban Revolution, whose beautiful propaganda posters are being exhibited in Humlebæk. One can certainly have them on one's walls even though the American critic deeply regrets that counter-revolutionary countries are turning the revolutionary posters into articles of trade. She ends her tribute with a Viva Fidel, New York 1970. Cuba is making wonderful progress and is en route to becoming a highly developed socialist society, Louisiana Man reads in the journal, where Che Guevara and Fidel Castro are cited for their high hopes of the artist, who must help to create the totally aware and perfect new man. The Danish collector and lender of posters Jens Lohmann announces with pleasure that the Cuban artists' contact with the population has become more extensive because they have been sent into the fields where they harvest sugar peas and plant coffee.

A new bluntness of language creeps into the museum's texts. Louisiana Man is slightly shocked when journalist Erik Thygesen admits that his memory has always been "arse-terrible", and that he is "piss-disappointed" at his visits in the homes of Robert Smithson and the other new stars in the USA. In the first place, Smithson lives far too nicely for a difficult avantgarde theorist, and secondly the Dane is repelled by the man because he is not political enough. Thygesen has always seen minimalism as social art, indeed as an almost ur-Communist history, and the American artist has the nerve to live a petit bourgeois existence and pronounce such enormities as: "I don't think that it is primarily a matter of attacking money value as such."

Thygesen is furious: "Gradually I think the man is naïve. It turns out, you see, that the big bananas' impressive manifestos are just something they wipe their arses on. Their social commitment extends to donating a drawing to the next Vietnam collection. They have placed a bomb under conventional art with their non-object art, and then they are not prepared to draw the political consequences."

From all this one point is crystal clear for Louisiana Man. How you live matters. Robert Smithson makes himself vulnerable from the first second by having mirrors in the ceiling and on the tables and in the walls, "which is irritating and slightly perverse" according to Erik Thygesen. What would Thygesen say if he saw Louisiana Man's suburban home?

A very dead horse

A sharp winter sun shone down on Bjørn Nørgaard as he led the horse across the snow-covered fields of Hornsherred. Tulle was no longer called Tulle, but Red Banner. She was twelve years old, had been mistreated by her former owner and was on the way to the slaughterhouse, when Nørgaard gave it a place in history as "the Horse Offering". A fire had been lit in the field and a local butcher stood ready with his instruments. He stunned the horse with a captive bolt pistol and severed its carotid artery so that the blood flowed onto the ground and coloured the snow red. Meanwhile Henning Christiansen played the violin, and Lene Adler Petersen recited the poem "My dear dead horse/ only you I think of/ my dead horse, my beloved dead horse." Then Nørgaard separated the head from the body and set it on a stake. The animal's tongue hung long and palely yellow out of its mouth when he began to dismember the rest of the large body and place the pieces in jam jars. Because the frost was working against the artist and the formalin froze, he managed to fill only 199 of 400 glasses, but this was more than enough to create a huge scandal. Afterwards, Bjørn Nørgaard opined that people might not have become quite so furious, if the slaughtering had taken place at Louisiana as planned since it would then have been placed in an artistic frame of perception.

The idea had been that the horse should stand in its stable at the museum in the first week of the exhibition 'Tabernakel' in January/February 1970, while the 400 jam jars waited out back. After the slaughtering, the glasses were to be exhibited in the stable together with the horse's bit, hay and droppings. As a metaphor of transformation. And a protest against the Vietnam War. And a social criticism of the materialistic mindset of the Western world. And a criticism of how we see the world in fragments and not as wholes. And as an ancient sacrificial ritual. The Horse Offering lived up to what art historians call "a new sculptural idiom". Red Banner's demise as a thoroughly thought out and planned piece of work, just as one models a sculpture. Bye-bye marble and bronze. The artists now operated with sand, horsemeat, wood, margarine, acid, felt, gauze and their own shit.

But Louisiana said no and placed itself "on the side of reaction", as the young artists said. At first the museum (and Elsinore's chief constable) rejected the stabling of the horse, and when the slaughtering had taken place in Hornsherred, Knud W. Jensen asked Bjørn Nørgaard not to set the jars up until he

Ekstra Bladet's front page on 31 January 1970. For the second time a dead animal was at the centre of a Louisiana scandal – Tinguely's dove in 1961, Bjørn Nørgaard's horse in 1970.

Ekstra Bladet

tør - hvor andre tier

LØRDAG 31. JANUAR 1970
Nr. 293 — 66. årgang — 1 kr.

Bjørn Nørgård med hestens hoved.

OFREDE HESTEN SOM PROTEST MOD VOLD

Som en protest mod vold og lemlæstelse i Vietnam, Biafra, og hvor krigen ellers kræver ofre, gennemførte antikunstneren Bjørn Nørgård i går et eller andet sted i Hornsherred den hesteofring, som han i første omgang ville have lavet i forbindelse med sin udstilling på Louisiana i Humlebæk. Hesten blev slagtet af en fagmand, under udfoldelse af stort ceremoniel og dyrkelse af gamle ritualer, og i disse dage er Bjørn Nørgård i færd med at dissekere den. Det er meningen, at den skal vende tilbage til Louisiana, „sat på" fire hundrede syltetøjsglas. Læs om ofringen på midtersiderne i LØRDAGS-EKSTRA.

POLITIKERNE HAR SAT SIG PÅ DE BEDSTE LEJLIGHEDER

Boligpolitik på afveje

Vi bruger for lidt til at bo for — og for meget til alt muligt andet. Det er filosofien bag den nye boligpolitik, regeringen ønsker gennemført. En politik, som vil betyde, at det bliver dyrt at skifte bolig. Statsminister Hilmar Baunsgaard udbredte sig i sin nytårstale om folk, der ikke vil betale 600 kr. om måneden for en lejlighed, mens de gladeligt ofrer 600 kr. på en bil, der står ubenyttet de 22 timer i døgnet. På denne baggrund har Ekstra Bladet undersøgt, hvor politikerne selv bor — og hvad de betaler i husleje. Det viser sig, at 600 kr. om måneden er et slags magisk tal. Københavns boligborgmester Edel Saunte bor i en lejlighed på 178 kva-

dratmeter — som efter yderligere fire års lejeforhøjelser koster 585 kr. Finansminister Poul Møller råder over 531 kvadratmeter. Lejen er godt en tredjedel af lejen i nyt privat byggeri, hvortil mange unge er henvist. Også statsminister Hilmar Baunsgaard og mange andre prominente personer har deres på det tørre.

LÆS SIDERNE 4 OG 5

LO TAVS MENS STREJKE-BØLGEN RULLER

VIGGO KAMPMANN
OM SPILLETS REGLER OG
STREJKESITUATIONEN
LÆS VINDUET SIDE 10

På virksomheder landet over drøftede man i går den største politiske strejke siden „Situationens Generalstab" i 1956. Tusinder besluttede at strejke mandag. Tusinder følger formentlig beslutningerne op mandag morgen.

Medens arbejderne holdt møder i går, samledes LO's øverste ledelse på Højstrupgård ved Helsingør til konference med Socialdemokratiets ledelse. Men ikke ét ord kom der fra mødet.

Thomas Nielsen har stillet et udspil i udsigt. Han havde intet udspil. Han havde ingen vejledning til de mange, der drøftede strejke — ud over meddelelsen fra forretnings-

udvalget, hvori det hed: „Vi opfordrer til øget politisk aktivitet for at fremkalde et regeringsskifte".

Aktioner er i gang for at få standset færgerne og rutebådene på mandag — og på Benzinøen i København drøftes en politisk benzinstrejke.

LÆS REPORTAGEN SIDE 7, 8 OG 9

had come home from a short business trip to Paris. The museum director was nervous because he could remember another animal that died in scandalous circumstances at Louisiana, Tinguely's blown up dove from 1961. But he had not intended to refuse admission to the jam jars – that would be censorship. He just wanted to be there when the animal welfare societies and the writers of letters to the press got all excited as was to be expected. But while he was away, the young Danish 'Tabernakel' artists did the same. After hour-long discussions sitting in a circle on Louisiana's floor tiles Bjørn Nørgaard, Per Kirkeby, Poul Gernes and Peter Louis-Jensen decided to pack up their works and leave Humlebæk in protest. "There was a lot of rhetorical posing on our part," says Kirkeby. They tried to get the main attraction of the show, Joseph Beuys, to join them, but without success. Nor did Richard Long or Panamarenko accompany them.

The Danes were denied far too much: Kirkeby wasn't allowed to take tame rabbits, guinea pigs and turtles with him into the nomad landscape he had built of several tons of sand in a room at the museum, where he moved in with a tent and a sewing machine. Gernes wasn't allowed to fill the park with Citroens in wild colours and was asked to move his functioning boat-building workshop out of the museum itself and into an outhouse, because the poisonous stench was unbearable – especially mixed with Red Banner's droppings, which were transported every day from Stensbjerggaard outside Humlebæk. So they left, slamming the door behind them, which suited them very well, since they had both exhibited at Louisiana, which was without doubt the most important institution in Danish artistic life, and had at the same time rejected the place. A pretty fantastic solution for the radical avantgardists, who in Kirkeby's words arrived "honoured, covered with soot and with split minds." They wanted to, and they didn't want to.

The public defiled past Kirkeby with long hair and wearing a neckerchief, while he lived in the sand: "I slept in a sleeping bag – it was in fact surprisingly cold, and then I had a little primus, on which I made tea, and sat there. It's amazing that that sort of thing was accepted at a museum in those days." While Joseph Beuys participated with 200 works, Per Kirkeby built his one and only work on site. Nørgaard also showed only one work or as much of it as he was permitted to execute. In the catalogue, it is simply called "Stable (or dissection)". At a distance of 30 years the artist regrets that he himself and the other Danes decided to leave the exhibition:

"Seen in retrospect, we undoubtedly behaved completely without inhibitions towards the museum. If we had been bright like the young people today we would have of course merely made a powerplay, as they call it, and used Louisiana to elbow our way forward in the world and achieve 'recognition.' It is clear that career-wise such an exhibition at such a museum would have been a big opportunity for us."

"There was

The painter Per Kirkeby in his nomad landscape in a room at Louisiana. He found the nights chilly.

ot of rhetorical posing on our part"

10. ÅRGANG · NR. 3 · JANUAR 1970

TABERNAKEL

Beuys · Dibbets · Gernes · Kirkeby · Køpcke ·
Long · Louis-Jensen · Nørgård · Panamarenko

UDGIVET AF LOUISIANA · HUMLEBÆK

In 1970 Knud W. Jensen felt unfairly treated by the 'Tabernakel' flock. Louisiana put itself out for them, gave them a free hand with *Louisiana Revy*, cooperated with much effort and energy with them, and then they misused the disagreement about what he interpreted as some details to get an established institution on shaky ground. But twenty years later he said to Bjørn Nørgaard during a lunch: "You were right", after which Nørgaard answered that Knud was too. A number of people were right at the same time. If the artists hadn't been so impatient and Louisiana had had been a little less nervous, 'Tabernakel' could have gone out into the world. For it was a good exhibition, Nørgaard admitted:

'Tabernakel' at Louisiana. The Danish artists left the exhibition in protest because Louisiana had placed itself on the side of reaction".

STØT
USA's
KRIG
I
VIETNAM

SEND DIN SØN

"When one looks at the circle of both foreign and Danish artists who were in the exhibition, one has to say that, seen in retrospect, it was an initiative at a high level and actually a quite grandly conceived exhibition, just as it was a radical new departure for a Danish museum to invite young Danish artists equally together with foreign artists and in that way do what is necessary if Danish 'Tabernakel artists are to measure themselves against foreign artists, namely that our own established museums and established critics and established art historians should lead the way and arrange exhibitions and criticism in which the things are opposed to one another."

In general, an anarchistic approach like 'Tabernakel' demanded distance. In the 1970s the rebels focused on the fact that Louisiana did not go the *whole* way towards a blood-soaked lawn, but posterity is amazed at how far the museum actually went. In the catalogue for the exhibition on Danish art scandals at Aarhus Art Museum in 1999, art historians Lennart Gottlieb writes that it required a will of iron for Knud W. Jensen to maintain his own direction and faith in an environment that despised the capitalist Cheese-Jensen and his so-called modern museum:

"Would you, for instance, invite a 22-year-old artist who had published a drawing with an Uncle Sam-like person who says 'No-o-o! You, death is beautiful, life is empty and love is dead', and who masturbates into your eye, while you as a caricature of Uncle Scrooge are represented thinking: 'Perhaps I should begin to sell cheese again?' Wouldn't you be a tiny bit concerned at inviting an artist who had had a work censored in which a named member of the royal family is called 'a piece of standing shit'? This was nonetheless what Knud W. Jensen did when

The sculptor Bjørn Nørgaard has a political errand in *Louisiana Revy* 1970. Later he called the 1970s "that dark, monkish decade".

in 1969 with John Hunov as consultant he asked Bjørn Nørgaard (born 1947) to take part in an exhibition in his museum."

And to make matters worse the critics hated 'Tabernakel'. They were bored: "waste of effort, not an eyebrow raised" (*Politiken*); they felt nausea at wading through the slum of anti-art (*Berlingske Aftenavis*); or they had seen it all before (*Information*). But the exhibition became a historical landmark, a classic, because already at the beginning of the decade and in an important setting it opened the public's eyes to the political art that would determine the 1970s. It was Beuys who became the big leading figure of the decade. Louisiana proved right in its warning in the catalogue: "We realise that the exhibition 'Tabernakel' will evoke intense discussion and perhaps trigger attacks on Louisiana. Despite this we have felt a sincere urge to present this material, and we believe that it contains some significant pointers to the art of the Seventies."

The Danish Broadcasting Corporation covered the horse offering. Jesus Christ, the trouble I ran into. The Corporation's board went amok!" says Werner Svendsen, who was head of programmes at that time. "It was us who created the attention around Louisiana, but it was Louisiana that did the necessary. If one was invited to something at Louisiana and *Statens Museum for Kunst* at the same time, all the journalists wanted to choose Louisiana. There was always a little uncertainty, an element of madness, while *Statens Museum for Kunst* was guaranteed safe. Louisiana has never ever lacked media awareness. There was man-to-man marking at every single exhibition. They got preferential treatment, one must admit, but it was reasonable because there were stories to be fetched up there – and they weren't exposed to the toughest conceivable competition."

When decades later Bjørn Nørgaard reached Gobelin number nine in the sequence he was weaving for the Queen, he wove one of his own actions into the picture of his own time. He chose "The Female Christ" at Copenhagen's Stock Exchange from 1969, not the horse offering. His explanation was that the population had never really accepted it. As for Louisiana, almost 30 years would pass before the museum again collected a large flock of young Danish artists under its roof. But then it was under a new director, who was a child, when 'Tabernakel' took place.

In Stockholm the battles between the fractions on the left wing soured life so much for Pontus Hultén that he felt pressed out of Moderna Museet. He applied for leave and was quickly chosen to head Centre Pompidou in Paris, which was under construction. The major shareholder in Gyldendal, Knud W. Jensen, could see himself on the front cover of the firm's own magazine MAK, drawn by Bjørn Nørgaard with his trousers down around his ankles. The management laid down a ban on this level of expression "of an especially coarse nature", and the issue

Joseph Beuys with a model of the room that was built at Louisiana specially for his work "Honey Pump". But it was never installed.

was never published. Jensen was in a special situation in the 1970s because he had a chauffeur, had grown up in one of the wealthiest families in the country and had a business background. All very suspect. But many people loved him for his personal commitment. He made good use of his silver spoon.

Knud W. Jensen could not take the trend-setting Marxists and their unbending demands for a rejection of "capitalist and art dealer art" in favour of art that elevated revolutionary consciousness. There was no pleasure or experience to be found where social and political analysis dominated. All power to the imagination, my foot! Where was sensibility, where was joy, where was pluralism? He found it much easier to catch sight of their unpleasant intolerance and rejection of all other forms of expression than their own. For instance, of everything he liked.

"Using a peculiar Germanic terminology, littered with loan words and phrases from Marx and Marcuse, they demanded that art should be mobilised in the service of the new holy cause. But if there is anything that the art of our day is not suited for, it is to be harnessed in the service of collectivism. It's no good as a draught animal, not even for the realisation of the most beautiful dreams."

The trendsetting neo-Marxists called him a custodian of dead elite culture. They hated the great art that he loved.

162

It was not only the artists the critics aimed to turn into draught animals, but of course also the museums. Especially the daily newspaper *Information* headed the crusade for the new orthodoxy. The newspaper was not merely angry, but disappointed that Louisiana was suffering from the ultra-modern and very widespread disease of *false consciousness* (no one knew who they were in reality in the 1970s). The museum itself believed that it was modern, but it was in fact backward-looking and dead. A disappointment since despite everything Louisiana "is and has been the best museum of contemporary art in Denmark," as art historian Jane Pedersen writes in 1972. She is saddened by 'Tabernakel', which showed that that after all Louisiana didn't have room for modern art – it had to be disgorged again – and by the fact that the museum "turns its back on revolutionary art and exhibits it only when it is not dangerous any longer, when it is no longer experienced on its own premises, but on those of the class society, where it merely serves as innocuous entertainment."

When, for instance Louisiana shows the Ny Carlsberg Foundation's new acquisitions under the title "Young Danish Art", it is of course *ripping off* the public by giving the impression that this is new art, while everybody knows of course how *reactionary* the foundation's acquisition policy is, and how passé the purchased artists are, because they are stuck in an "ego trip and fail to set up new social models".

At the beginning of the decade, Knud W. Jensen tried to chase the remorseless Marxists away from the domain of art and into their own domain. If an artist wanted to change society, he should join the army or go into politics instead of making art suffer, he said to the court organ of the revolutionaries *Information*. He thought that artists had a pompously overrated view of themselves, when they believed that they possessed the key to the mysteries of life and were able to show others the true state of things, not to mention how they could be changed radically. Political thinkers and utopian theorists were better at that. "It can never be a central political instrument to paint paintings with themes from Castro's Cuba," he said. "Art has never changed society much."

The difference between Pontus Hultén and Knud W. Jensen was that the Dane could close the door to his own museum and show all the elite culture he wished. Outwardly he kept his mouth shut, but inside he trod on the accelerator. The others could stand outside with their hand-printed revolutionary posters and unbecoming short-sightedness.

"In that term (elite culture) there was so much resentment towards and hate of everything that I believed in that I felt it was more fruitful to cultivate the purely aesthetic than to yield to the demands of those years," Knud W. Jensen felt.

Palace revolution

Surprisingly the revolt at Louisiana came from his own team. Ole Wivel headed the attack together with the museum's financial director Kirsten Strømstad, because they regarded Knud W. Jensen as hopelessly irresponsible and uncontrollable with respect to money. It was necessary to have him declared incapable of managing his affairs. In a shroud of secrecy Kirsten Strømstad contacted the members of the board in order to persuade them to relieve him of his powers. She was profoundly concerned about Louisiana's future in the hands of its founder. Ole Wivel had throughout seen himself as the representative of good sense and restraint, the person who by all means available had to prevent the reckless museum owner from constantly extending his buildings and putting on expensive exhibitions and costly arrangements. In that way, they were well suited to one another. What Knud W. Jensen had in imagination (and yet it was Wivel who was the poet), Ole Wivel had in control. What they had in common was their feeling for art and culture and all the new things taking place while the country was on the verge of a new era after the war. The distribution of roles proved to be fruitful in the first years, but Wivel's lack of generosity towards Knud W. Jensen turned into a millstone around the museum director's neck – the first time in 1966, when his friend tried to block Louisiana's transformation into a museum of international art, the second time now.

In 1969, 1970 and 1971 the deficit crept all the way up to a million kroner annually. Louisiana was devouring its capital, which consisted of all Knud W. Jensen's money placed in two funds. The unsatisfactory accounts clearly reflected the most recent extensions at Louisiana – the cinema from 1966 and the new room from 1971. The work had cost more than calculated – there was no doubt that he had spent too much money. But Knud W. Jensen was of the opinion that there was more where it had come from and continued to allow his expensive and dangerous ideas to rain down over his board. Ole Wivel thought he was exceptionally rash and should be stopped. According to Wivel, it was particularly a matter of 200,000 kroner a year that could nevertheless not be transferred from the founder's private account to the museum for tax reasons.

The plan was initially to cut Louisiana down to a handy little weekend museum that only had its collection to offer, but Knud W. Jensen regarded a peaceful museum enclave of this kind with disgust. It was in opposition to everything that

"Louisiana has been built in a luxuriant natural setting, so that you can meet art here with a positive receptiveness – in something of a holiday mood in which everything becomes fresh and new again," wrote Knud W. Jensen in the first catalogue.

I felt it was more fruitfu

cultivate the purely aesthetic"

a modern art museum should be. From the very start the idea for Louisiana had been that the museum should have a content that extended beyond visual art and should reflect the things that inspire artists – design, music, film, literature. Life whatever the cost. The more volume, the better. He was aiming to continue the museum at full blast and to get the state to provide more than the stingy annual subsidy of 100,000 kroner. He sent a 22-page application to Minister of Culture Knud Helveg Petersen – with a copy to the press – and as a first reaction was awarded seven times the original amount. He managed to get a good price for his shares in the supermarket chain Vime, and at the same time the only remnant of his cheese empire, the powdered milk firm Milco Export, was generating a bigger and bigger profit, which went straight into the Louisiana Museum Foundation. "What could actually go wrong for us?" he asked himself.

After a fateful board meeting in 1973, at which the founder's future at the museum was to be decided, a relieved Knud W. Jensen came into his office and said to his secretary: "It's over. I saved my life!"

His supporter on the board had stymied the plan. Kirsten Strømstad had to leave, and there was cold air between Knud W. Jensen on the one side and Ole Wivel plus rebels on the other. Now they proposed getting a firm of consultants to review the management and finances of the museum. The report recommended that Knud W. Jensen should continue at the head of things but with a commissioner at his side. A kind of superego or an auxiliary arm for the board. The commissioner was to have an office at Louisiana and free access to all information and meetings. Knud W. Jensen said no. The losers began to resign from the board more or less at random. In a short time, two of them left the place along with the highly critical accountant. Ole Wivel calmed down – no one talked about crisis and firings any longer, and Louisiana emerged at full strength ready to make quite unusually vigorous progress during the rest of the 1970s.

Their friendship had received an irreparable blow. They no longer involved themselves in earnest in each other's lives, but nevertheless almost ten years passed before the link between them disintegrated completely to end in direct enmity. In 1982, forty-three years after their meeting at Vedbæk Tennis Club, from which they set out to conquer Danish cultural life with outstanding skill, Knud W. Jensen fired Ole Wivel from Gyldendal because he was forced to choose between

◄ Just after 'Tabernakel' came Chagall to calm everyone down. An illustrative example of the museum's so-called sauna principle – a cold exhibition for the few should be followed by a warm exhibition for the many.

Wivel and Kurt Fromberg, who wanted to have sole power over the publishing house. Fromberg was instrumental in the dismantling of the Ole Wivel era, but Wivel fired himself, say sources from that world. He eroded his own position, made himself impossible with too many complications with women at the publishing house, too much wine, too little control and too much confidence that he had the power of life and death over Gyldendal. That he got his will had been a matter of course, – he seemed to be untouchable. When he failed to obtain approval for a proposal, this was a completely new experience. He sold his shares in protest, and also disappeared from Louisiana's board.

In the 1990s Wivel and Jensen each wrote their version of the breach, which also included disagreement about a number of other decisions at Gyldendal that do not concern Louisiana and perhaps not even the breach. The chief cause was that Knud W. Jensen had at last discovered that he himself could manage things and via his usual gathering of views from his surroundings he liberated himself from his old friend just as he had previously liberated himself from his father and upper-middle class home populated with maiden aunts, servants and corpulent freemasons digesting their lunches in the garden's deckchairs.

The new chairman, Professor Allan Philip, LL.D., had a different view on the economically irresponsible museum director. Philip could see that Louisiana's survival and existence in fact depended on Knud W. Jensen. The museum's success was entirely dependent on his personal qualities, choices and highly charged creativity, which were focused on Louisiana night and day. What might resemble realism in other contexts was not always the case when applied to Knud W. Jensen.

When friends and acquaintances describe Knud W. Jensen, the first word that occurs to them is *generous*. He sent them small tokens of esteem, gave personal and thoughtful presents, pulled books off his own shelves, spent his money freely and did everything in his power to make people feel good. But he was also a businessman. He wanted people to work – preferably a couple of hours extra. "If he could have paid my salary in postcards, that would have suited him fine," says a woman who worked at Louisiana in the 1980s – and liked him. Instead of extra pay for an extra effort, he preferred to give his staff a title. In his supermarket chain Vime it seems that all the buyers were *chief* buyers, and in 1968 when William Hedegaard was working in the firm's reception in an anonymous industrial building in the Copenhagen suburb of Albertslund, he met a respected and popular but "madly parsimonious" boss, who wanted to see the turnover for every single Vime store every single day. There was no art on the walls in Albertslund, where Knud W. Jensen dropped by two or three times a week to keep a careful eye on things.

The daily round

While the storm raged and the poets emitted streams of prose chopped up to resemble verse, there were still reminiscences of the director culture of the old days inside Louisiana. Every morning Knud W. Jensen himself opened the mail behind closed doors. He referred to the office staff as the *girls*, while it was the *ladies* who served Louisiana pastries in the cafeteria, and Knud W. Jensen was the natural centre of it all, deciding everything in a friendly but firm fashion. If one could accept it, he was "a father figure for everyone", as his secretary says. If one couldn't, the management behaved "authoritatively and quite undemocratically", as a museum inspector put it on his way out. "It is Knud who is God," wrote the staff in a birthday song. If one didn't accept him as the uncontested centre of the solar system, it was difficult to be at Louisiana. The best way of taking it was like Hans Erik Wallin, who arranged all the big ethnographical exhibitions and also edited *Louisiana Revy*. His manuscripts always had to pass by the director's desk, and Wallin would come out of the office with all his pages covered with red corrections. "Thank you for your help," he would say with a friendly smile. When late one afternoon the museum realised that a world famous American avantgarde composer, whom it had proved possible to attract to Humlebæk, had sold only three tickets for the concert the same evening, Knud W. Jensen ordered his entire staff and their families to put in overtime as a numerous and enthusiastic audience.

Knud W. Jensen was not a snob, but old-fashioned. He liked things to be in order – that one had a house and a boat. At an architectural arrangement at the museum he made everyone laugh without knowing why. "I think one should always build on a southwest slope leading down to the sea," he said innocently while those who heard burst into laughter at this over-privileged point of view.

He was not characterised by traditional self-importance or pomposity, but rather struck people as charming, odd and absent-minded. He avoided formality and solemnity. Critics and museum people thought they were going to meet a big gun, but found themselves facing a curious and interested little man, who most of all reminded one of an elf or a pixy. He made friends with most people and could nearly always get what he wanted. Despite his modesty and generosity he had an indomitable will and insisted on being in control. A certain brutality came up in him when something or somebody crossed his path.

Louisiana was his home. Even at weekends he strode through it to see whether everything was all right, talked with people and asked their opinions. When his hairdresser told him that the price was too high for pensioners, he took it seriously and considered what he had said. Admission should not cost more than a packet of cigarettes, and eating there wasn't to be expensive. He

went in for plain food, the simple and unpretentious. In the always overcrowded cafeteria he invited people to sit at his table and pumped them. And to find out what was going on among the large group of culture-bearing women, he read a middle-class women's weekly magazines besides a large number of international magazines and journals. One of the attendants at the museum was interested in Romanesque churches and would sit reading about them with passionate interest on his night watches. It was typical of Knud W. Jensen that he asked: "Couldn't you tell me *everything* you know about them?"

Often he would meet the draper Jørgen Nørgaard, who was just as radically alternative in his way of thinking, in the park. "That's a good figure, that one," Knud W. Jensen might say. Then they might talk a bit about the plinth. Perhaps there might be a different one. And then a little about the tree next to it. It was

During the flip 'Alternative Architecture' the usual summer visitor figures rose from 3,000 a week to 12-15,000.

171

time to prune it. "He very much reminded me of an old-fashioned grocer, who himself served in his shop," says Jørgen Nørgaard.

Alongside Knud W. Jensen's foresightedness there was a constant attention to detail and the down-to-earth things. On the first floor in the white main building sat his secretaries at their IBM machines and wrote and rewrote his letters until they were as he wanted them to be. After planning meetings with the architects he would go directly up to his office and dictate his changes to what they had just agreed. The architects didn't even have time to get back to their office before his new and even better proposal arrived as a telefax.

Louisiana was run by him and a little circle of people he knew from the old days and were friends of friends. In the 1970s and 80s a typical Knud team consisted of himself, the painter Hugo Arne Buch and his school friend Hans Erik Wallin, who had read art history for six months but otherwise came from a job as director for Copenhagen's poster pillars. The jurist Steingrim Laursen travelled round the world, visited collectors and museums and created exhibitions of high quality. Then there was the architect Kjeld Kjeldsen. The little group arranged all the eight or nine exhibitions a year and carried the museum together with a telephone operator, a translator, a lady who ran the Louisiana Club, an accounts lady and a financial director. That was that.

"There were very few of us to do what had to be done. We had long, long working days," remembers Hugo Arne Buch, who was fetched from his artists' colony in Hjortekær outside Copenhagen to "give a hand" to the Giacometti exhibition in 1965. He stayed at Louisiana for more than thirty years. Typically, he had been recruited by another painter from the same colony, Knud Mühlhausen, who worked at the museum for a short time, and just as typically another painter from the Hjortekær colony, Flemming Koefoed, was also hired to arrange exhibitions at Louisiana. None of them were art historians, none of them had degrees. When the Ford dealer Børge Hansen was later hired as administering director, he always took time to drive to a wholesaler in Copenhagen, where he could buy mass produced rolls for hot dogs and salami with a maximum of additives for the cafeteria, while another of is duties was to buy cheese in Hillerød, where he lived. At Louisiana, the work was demanding and varied. When Knud W. Jensen took a holiday at his house in Spain, the staff could get their breath back for a brief interval. In the village of Nerja he sat restless and full of ideas and recorded tapes that were sent home to Louisiana and transcribed. Also the street vendor's loud cries in the background: "Sweetstuffs for the weary!"

From his corner office on the first floor Knud W. Jensen cast his net over a broad assemblage of the 1970s' most important painters, musicians, writers, actors, museum directors and film directors. He had a formidable ability to see right

Children touch a Henry Heerup sculpture. Despite the lack of an international status the Danish artist has always had his place at the museum.

and move his focus to where at that moment there was something to be gained, and with every new topic that arose, there immediately appeared a new person who was worth talking to. He could see when someone was passionately engaged, and where there was a story he could mediate and expand. But he was quick – and forgetful. Collected people and ideas, and the people often disappeared to their regret from the warmth of his spotlight once their ideas had been used. He recoiled. There wasn't room for everyone all the time; he had to move on.

"Knud had tons of people he could call – as long as it lasted. That is to say, as long as he needed you. There were periods when you didn't exist, and periods when you were inside again," says Niels Barfoed.

Most people, but not everybody, were aware that when they were invited to dinner at Sletten, it was because Knud W. Jensen needed them for something. Inspiration, advice, support. Bo Bjørnvig takes up the same theme when he says that Knud W. Jensen could turn on and switch off his attention in a way that could at any rate make a child feel uncertain. One moment you were bathed in affectionate interest and being spoiled in all sorts of ways – the next moment it was over.

At one time, he spoke on the phone with Hans Edvard Nørregård-Nielsen every day, at another it was Per Kirkeby, then Kurt Fromberg, then Herbert Pundik, then Peter Augustinus and so on. It could take hours and be tiring. He was a cautious person, whose method was to test his ideas out on many people, tell them what he was planning and hear what they thought. Not only bigwigs, but also secretaries, hairdressers and journalists. It was a matter of having the foundation in order before he took a decision, especially in areas where his own insight was limited.

"God had created Knud in such a way that the ideas just gushed out of him. Every morning, afternoon, evening and night as well he opened up a cornucopia of thoughts and ideas. He needed to create some structure in this enormous pulpy mass, and that was why he rang," says Peter Augustinus.

He involved himself with many people and went a long way with them, which was both good and bad. Because he was so generous and uninhibited and above all wanted to behave nicely and decently, he could be carried away in a moment's enthusiasm to promise too much and have to take it back again. This was the case with the series of men each of whom believed he would be his successor. Or people who were promised his love or attention. This was also the case with the interesting types that he became fascinated by, but who inevitably fell in interest because no one can go on being dazzlingly wonderful. Then he fell in love with something else. He couldn't live without something to be engaged in. The strength in his enthusiasm was that he was able to get other people to go beyond their own limits and even further. *He* discovered what *they* were capable of.

Heerup's small stone sculptures in the garden. He would come by and freshen up the paint now and then.

One day in 1973 he wrote to Ingmar Bergman on the island of Fårö and asked him to consider a film exhibition at Louisiana. The director answered him with a friendly rejection.

"Thank you for your kind letter. At the first moment I of course felt very flattered and looked forward to appearing at your beautiful museum. Later there came a somewhat mixed reaction. You see, I don't always believe in this kind of exhibition, in fact find them a little horrible. I suggest that we wait until I am dead. With cordial greetings. Ingmar Bergman.

A couple of weeks later Knud W. Jensen answered: "Thank you for your letter. I very well understand your reaction. With regard to the last part of your letter I would ask you to inform me in good time!"

Onwards, onwards, onwards. "One does it to make life exciting," he explained the same year. "I suppose one is struggling to achieve a certain self-understanding. After all, it's quite exciting what kind of a person one is – of course we're all on a huge ego trip. And the museum here – that's my ego trip, which forces me to expand my horizons when through exhibitions one is occupied with a huge material that forces one to obtain new knowledge, something that can never be concluded or finished."

He felt that the museum was facing a new start after the unrest of the 1960s' youthful years and the bloody palace revolution. From having been an exhibition place, Louisiana had become an adult museum with a good economic basis and a large new collection of international art. The 1970s became the decade for consolidation and unbroken traffic all the way up the coast road from Copenhagen. The decade in which gifts and art works poured in, and in which the inauguration of the concert hall merely raised the tempo. There was not much oil crisis about it.

To get ideas Knud W. Jensen went to New York in spring 1976 and managed to arrange seven meetings with interesting members of the staff at the Museum of Modern Art (MoMA), the mother of all modern art museums and the biggest in the world. It was from here that he got the idea for the little cafeteria that was pressed into Louisiana's library at the last moment before the opening in 1958, and which virtually became a symbol for how different the place was. And from here once again he flew home with new ideas.

"New York is as always enormously inspiring. One can really learn a lot from these wide-awake, vigorous New Yorkers. The largest number of important artists live here; the museums' exhibitions are outstanding; their publications, membership departments, visitors' services and bookshops compel admiration," he writes in an elated mood. Knud W. Jensen possesses the ability to admire, and it finds plenty of outlets here. He loves this great, energetic country and many years later he sends his new directors over there on lengthy educational tours.

After having dominated all talk about the museum's economy for years the concert hall was completed in 1976.

MoMA is filled with people from morning till evening. On warm spring days they sit on the terrace and eat or relax in the sculpture garden. The American museum directors clearly think more about how their visitors feel than their European colleagues do. At the entrance visitors are offered a wealth of free brochures with information – on the ground plan, on the exhibitions, lectures, films, and members' club. They are better at informing, better at making people interested and what is more the Americans can earn money in new ways that Knud W. Jensen would like to bring back with him across the Atlantic. Some of them have an immediate impact, others not until the 1980s, but practically all of them materialise at Humlebæk. Not only do the Americans have a "for us Europeans almost incomprehensible" sponsorship system from which they derive enormous sums that are paid from the public purse in Europe. But MoMA also publishes a magazine for members with information about exhibitions and arrangements – six months later so does Louisiana. In New York they also earn money from corporate memberships, which means that firms can borrow the museum for evening arrangements for their business connections, a guided tour of the museum and dinner in the restaurant. From time to time MoMA houses business congresses, and the director is considering selling the airspace above the museum and allowing a developer to put up a block of apartments 50 or 80 floors high. The Dane is immediately more interested in the museum's large bookstore even though he thinks it lacks atmosphere. Louisiana also acquires one of these, and from the 1980s onwards sponsors and companies obtain access to and privileges at the museum. "We were thinking American at Louisiana – without knowing. We ended up by taking over many of their museal norms," said Steingrim Laursen.

In the light of brilliant America, where it is a matter of course that a museum arranges exhibitions every year, it appears absurd to Knud W. Jensen that back in Denmark he has to defend himself for arranging exhibitions at all. In the eyes of his Danish critics permanent collections are the genuine thing and exhibitions mummery. They alternately accuse Louisiana's exhibitions of being "ready made" – when they have been arranged by other museums – or "of degrading art to an article for consumption", as the artist Erik Thommesen writes in an article in *Information* in 1977. Knud W. Jensen is good at shaking off the criticism and continuing on his way.

"Why not spend half or a whole day at the place now that one *has* come to Humlebæk?" he tempts his readers in the first issue of the member's magazine *Louisiana-Klubben*. "Perhaps there is a film that you would like to see, a puppet theatre for children, a poetry reading or a concert that you could profitably put into your weekend programme. But of course it is necessary to set aside time for it so that you don't neglect the exhibition!"

He invents the club already one year after the opening and 50 years later it is surprisingly unchanged. Some of the first members are even still paying their subscriptions. Ideologically, the club is *pure Knud,* as they say in the house because he did not wish to discriminate among people. All members are still treated in the same way today; you can't buy a Gold Card or a VIP card, even though all national and international trends point in that direction. The club becomes and remains by far Denmark's and North Europe's largest art club with 30,000 memberships (50,000 people), until Tate Modern in London overtakes Humlebæk at the beginning of the new century. Otherwise, one has to go south, to the Louvre, to find competition.

The weekends overflow with jazz and poetry, piano recitals, round-table discussions, film days, "mixture festivals", folk music and debate meetings. The whole institution is like a handy thermometer for taking the temperature of the 1970s. Suzanne Brøgger reads *Creme fraiche,* Trille sings *Hej Søster,* Laurie Anderson performs, and 18-year-old Michala Petri represents classical music. The political bestseller "Oprør fra midten" [Rebellion from the Middle] is just Louisiana's cup of tea and a good reflection of the gentle, questioning ideology at Humlebæk. The book criticises the prevailing ideas of growth in the West and the East based on pollution, private consumption and the arms race. Rather: a "humane society in balance" and citizen's pay for everyone. The right-wing debaters dismiss the utopia as an "inferno of compulsory well-being", but they are the very people who never get a word in edgewise at Louisiana, where there is a preference for discussing with the like-minded.

Even though it sounds like resonant seventies dialect to speak of Louisiana as a "meeting-place for the Muses and a socially committed environment", this is what Knud W. Jensen has wanted all the time. Also as early as in 1958, when the museum opens as a fusion of social democracy and elite culture, attempting to effect a transformation in "the lives of ordinary people" and not only of the highly educated. (Actually there are not enough of the latter in Denmark to keep a sensible business going.)

He realises that art is not a little enclosed area for aesthetes, but also debates, films and all that jazz. The museum bursts the narrow, classical concept of art, and therefore some critics attack the archaeological exhibitions,

▸ The violinist Anton Kontra.

▸ The Danish debate book "Oprør fra midten" [Rebellion from the Middle] was perfectly suited for progressive Louisiana and its public. From the left: the politician K. Helveg Petersen, Professor Niels I. Meyer and the writer Villy Sørensen.

for what the hell are they doing at an art museum? The concept of art is given maximum space in which to unfold itself long before it becomes modern to talk all the time about art in very broad terms. Nowadays, of course, everything is art. As the representative of an art institution, Knud W. Jensen was a pioneer in the first 25-30 years. He wanted a non-museal museum with other points of entry than knowledge – for instance, feelings and sensibility. The strategy was to pull in a broad public by having other things besides art, something for all tastes, as long as it is of good quality. And then get just some of them to fall for the most essential thing – the art.

Louisiana was created by an amateur in the best sense of the word. By a man who uses his mind, his common sense and the principles of the business world in which he was born, grew up and was trained. Many years later the new director of Louisiana Lars Nittve gives a lecture at the Louvre and says that Louisiana is the first museum in the world to put the customer in the centre and keeps its focus there, while other modern museums that would like to do the same thing can't help getting more and more museal and traditional with the passing of the years. Even the old confederates like the Stedelijk and Moderna Museet. Because Knud W. Jensen was there for so long, the museum stuck to its line and style. Open doors, breaks, food, informal atmosphere.

Free us from art historians

Perhaps it helped that he wasn't an art historian Perhaps that was the very reason for the museum's enormous power of attraction from the first day. The founder of Scandinavia's most successful art museum had *not* taken a lengthy university education, had *not* specialised and was *not* schooled in a particular direction. This meant that his approach to art was different from that of the academics. Louisiana was founded con amore. The approach is not duty or a commitment to cultural education but curiosity, experience and attraction as opposed to the classical academia, which also regards art as a science and a discipline. At Louisiana, he wanted to show art, not all the theory. There was not to be the slightest trace of the school bench.

"We mediate experiences, not knowledge. Let the traditional museums look after that, he said. "We are not running a museum for the sake of art history.

◄ The German writer and Nobel laureate Günter Grass has appeared innumerable times at Louisiana, most recently in 2007, when his surprising and hitherto unreported past in the SS had become known.

◄ The poet Henrik Nordbrandt.

That's what you have scholarly literature for. Nor to exert influence on the artists, for they will always find their inspiration where it suits them. Artists are subjective, they have to be, and they will always pass severe judgement on the museums. The museums are there first and foremost for the public's sake."

He was a curator, even though as far as we know, the word never passed his lips, not even when it became modern in the 1980s and even more so in the 1990s. But he arranged exhibitions, he bought works of art and rejected many others. Behind his choices lay an undogmatic attitude that did not pose specific preconceived demands of the works so that they could fit in with a special definitive interpretation that smoothly accorded with the dominant idea of the exhibition.

"Knud had an intuitive judgement – his choices were always right, always ground-breaking," says the painter Hugo Arne Buch, who worked closely together with Knud W. Jensen on exhibitions and acquisitions. When many years later the Swedish art historian Bo Nilsson was working at Louisiana, he described Knud W. Jensen as the archetype of a generous and open curator who understands that an art work can have meanings at several different levels. He did not allow himself to be bound by the borders between genres, historical periods or the fixed interpretations of the day and instead looked at the artist as a person engaged in something of universal human relevance. His understanding was intuitive rather than intellectual. "Perhaps it is connected with the fact that the academic establishment has never impressed him," says Bo Nilsson.

As a private collector for a private museum he had no other obligations than to his own taste. That is why private collections often have more character than public collections. On Louisiana's walls one can see this view of art, here described by the critic Poul Erik Tøjner before he himself became director of the museum:

"Louisiana is a break with traditional museal institutions; it does not offer compulsory chronological or educational hangings. It is cultural education as a relatively free project that has been the aim. And cultural education in a broad sense – the place's many lectures, concerts, debate days, conferences, ethnographic exhibitions and so on place themselves like rings around a concept of culture whose special feature is to expand. Never to shut anything up in the closed spaces of expertise or the elite."

Because he in general found art historians to be irritating know-alls, Knud W. Jensen rarely allowed them into the building. Some of the youngest staff studied or had studied art history, but it was still he who decided. As late as in 1981 the affairs of the museum were being handled by an ex-cheese wholesaler, and ex-Ford dealer, a retired advertising man, a painter and the tall, elegant man of the world Steingrim Laursen as its foreign minister. This son of a landed proprietor from North Jutland had originally studied law and was "liberated" after nine years in the Ministry for Greenland in 1971 to begin a new life in Louisiana's service, first as a freelance consultant and exhibitor, later as inspector and finally as director of the museum. The relationship was to last for thirty years. His formidable sense for art and diplomacy, his personal friendships and connections, his fluent French, English and Italian brought him and thereby the museum to the high table in the international art world, where Laursen was a member of more international committees and boards than any other Danish museum man of his generation. Laursen was extremely clued up on American art, before it became modern, and besides Andy Warhol and Edward Hopper brought a number of the big blockbusters to Humlebæk from Picasso through Magritte to Monet. He chose themes and works, hung them and wrote catalogues. Entirely without exam certificates.

But the Danish museum world found it odd that Louisiana's administering director came from the automobile trade, and the others came from wherever it was they came from. They regarded the museum as unorthodox and on a sidetrack because the collection was not big yet, and there were no art experts attached. When art historian Øystein Hjort joined the board in 1973, he became *the* specialist at Louisiana and raised its prestige in other people's eyes, but it was Knud W. Jensen who did the things the experts would never think of doing – a shop, a café, a children's section at a museum that, what was more, was situated in the countryside as a destination for excursions (a naughty word). In the beginning, these things were unimaginable anywhere else. Now they are the norm.

The management discovered a simple tactic, which they called the sauna principle. After a warm and "easy" exhibition came the cold shower in the form of uncompromising contemporary art. The warm exhibitions paid for the cold ones. A narrowly visited exhibition like 'Bearings in German Art' had to be compensated for by the popular 'Gold from Peru'. 'Soho, New York' by 'Akhenaton and Nefertiti'. When admission figures plunged at the end of the 1990s, it was because the museum had become too cold and too advanced for too long at a time.

"This policy, which of course largely rests on a tactic for economic survival, will undoubtedly be criticised," Knud W. Jensen writes to the board in 1976, "but it has the advantage that the advanced art is seen by many people and is financed by the large number of visitors to the classical and "archaeological" exhibitions." This solicitous attitude to the public extended all the way into the exhibition rooms: not too much of the hard stuff all at once. In the 1970s Knud W. Jensen considered the new concept art difficult to understand for the uninitiated. They must find it opaque and boring. He had a proposal to make it easier to digest:

"We're in the field of esoteric art, which is concerned with its own artistic means and problems more than with communicating a message to the viewer, and to counteract this trend in the collection, I think it would be a good idea to have a room with Munch's graphic art, which, as it were, compensates the less accustomed museum visitor through something he can understand and derive pleasure from."

In the course of the decade Louisiana showed a large number of modernism's classics – warm exhibitions that people could "understand and derive pleasure from". Just after 'Tabernakel' in 1970 Chagall came and calmed everyone, then Kandinsky and Klee in 1971, Man Ray the year after, Dali in 1973, Miro the year after, Henry Moore in 1976 and Warhol in 1978. And with the exception of

▶ Steingrim Laursen at the planning of a Francis Bacon exhibition.

Kandinsky and Klee they were all still alive. Even in comparison with these superstars the Pompeii exhibition in 1977 was red hot – the largest in the museum's first quarter of a century. Its record of 416,166 visitors was not beaten until Monet seventeen years later.

From the first archaeological exhibition in the museum's history (Gold from Peru 1962) to the most recent (New Finds from Old China 1997) the museum has had to defend the mere idea of exhibiting that kind of thing at an art museum. It has shown great ingenuity in drawing parallels between modern art and other or old cultures, has searched high and low for convincing links and in every single catalogue immediately tackled the expected criticism from specialists who would prefer to have the genres kept distinct and have the alien material sent to cultural-historical museums. Internally at Louisiana the exhibition team had a more ambiguous and sceptical attitude to Pompeii than to any of the other exhibitions because the things the archaeologists found in the buried city are not the best examples of the art of that time. Pompeii was a provincial city, so a parallel would have been if Odense or Skive were struck by a disaster and frozen for posterity. So where was the artistic alibi? But the public couldn't care less. When the Queen opened the exhibition, two of Louisiana's staff were still working feverishly to label the objects. All the way they were barely one room ahead of her. After the Queen came a sea of people, for Pompeii carried a fascinating history, in which the disaster and plaster casts of dead watchdogs and panicked inhabitants were a stronger attraction than the objects as such. The exhibition was visited by thousands of children, who slid around in the corridors and drew on the lavatory doors to the profound indignation of the museum's regular visitors.

One day in 1976 Knud W. Jensen asked the young, newly hired secretary and switchboard operator Lisbeth Ruben to fetch a cup of tea. She answered that this would be the first and last time since she was a redstocking. The 1970s were reflected at Louisiana and moved into the exhibition rooms and the magazine with its alternative spirit and criticism. In the decade in which everybody had the ability and the duty to become an artist, the Louisiana exhibitions typical of the time were about children, outsiders, naive art, anonymous design and alternative architecture. The architect Kjeld Kjeldsen and Knud W. Jensen had a fruitful failure of communication when they planned the enormously successful "Alternative Architecture" for the summer of 1977 at a time when Louisiana was entirely alone in arranging architectural exhibitions. The older man was thinking historically – the "alternative" he wished to show was Gaudi, Mendelsohn and Rudolf Steiner – while the younger man was thinking of the present and Christiania, American hippies and the Thy Camp in North Jutland, where he had stayed in its

188

'Akhnaton and Nefertiti'. The classical or archaeological exhibitions financed the more advanced and less popular exhibitions.

first summer and delivered milk inside the camp on his motorbike with sidecar. Both aspects were represented in "Alternative Architecture", and at the same time one could see Chinese peasant paintings with motifs from the everyday life of the communes under the beloved dictatorship of Chairman Mao – "a genuinely popular art, not only for the people but created by the people itself."

In the park, huge sets were built, an entire street, and Kjeld Kjeldsen borrowed the amusing recycled cathedral, the Opera House, which he had seen at Christiania. "Alternative Architecture" was spectacular and devoted much attention to the physical staging, which became a characteristic feature of a typical cultural-historical Louisiana exhibition. This is a concept, an event. Like ordering a hot dog with *all* the trimmings. Films, art, architecture, design, lectures at the same time. Things were taken to their limits in all directions, so to speak, and greater risks were taken than at the other museums, which were primarily concerned to teach someone something. At Louisiana the idea was that the public should *see*, experience something physically and spatially. The visual always came before the didactic. For this reason also films and slide shows consisted of visual juxtapositions, not of words and objects. The entire presentation tried to keep well away from the written word. Kjeld Kjeldsen had an artistic and experience-oriented approach to the material with less focus on art history, chronology or safety measures. Things were set free, made dramatic and exciting. Rooms one thought one knew ad nauseam were unrecognisable, and Louisiana had no inhibitions about painting them red, blue or black for the occasion, if this could make the objects more visible and look good at a time when other museums wouldn't have dreamt of such extravagances. Kjeldsen was awarded the Academy's N.L. Høyen medal, which is given for extraordinary research, interpretation or mediation of the fine arts. He became an expert in large, spatial stagings and reflections of the epoch, and he made – or built – "The House as a Picture" (1981) on postmodernism and "On the Edge of Chaos" (1993) on deconstructivism. Each of the three draws a clear portrait of its decade.

During "Alternative Architecture" *Louisiana Revy* urged its readers to, for example, "Support the groups of residents" and "Join NOAH, tel.: (01)156052" and "Read the handbook on sun and wind energy published by *Information*". Embedded in the exhibition there was a deep longing to be able to send the children out to play among the chickens and the horse droppings. To wake up at the crowing of the cock and make do with a small, basic home. To be able to make playgrounds superfluous because the kids were busily occupied with the soil and animals. Among trendsetting young people there was a spirit of retreat and regret at everything the country had achieved in the 1960s. "All across the country young people are building sheds and moving into old factories or to Christiania. They live in self-made

Children crawling on one of Henry Moore's recumbent women. "Louisiana must be *used*, be the framework for a piece of life. Something must happen here, for here there are many possibilities," declared the first catalogue.

"Ar

The public for 'Alternative Architecture' in 1977, when Louisiana was quite alone in presenting architectural exhibitions and what is more on a large scale. The elderly gentleman in the middle is the architect Steen Eiler Rasmussen. On his right the poet Uffe Harder.

as never changed society much"

environments meaningfully put together of old crap. They know that if they want to have time to love and to seek, they can't take part in the escalation, the inorganic belief in progress in technology and the power of money," Susanne Ussing and Carsten Hoff write programmatically in *Louisiana Revy*.

The exhibition was an imaginative protest against the functional and conformist low-quality buildings of those years. It was about architecture as a free work of art, as fairy-tale, play, dream and poetry. So of course it was criticised for not being sufficiently critical of society and political, to which Knud W. Jensen answered on the basis of his strong conviction that for Louisiana what was important was to show the multiplicity, imagination and wealth of forms to be found in the alternative architecture. Then people could think for themselves. He did *not*

The Opera House from Christiania built by Anders Thygesen from a sawn across schooner.

194

wish to be harnessed to the correct political carriage, but to show man's urge to create spaces that are different. And anyway he was a social democrat.

Next autumn, as an offshoot of the exhibition, the museum opened the equally grandly conceived and equally flip "Children are a People", which attracted 160,000 parents and children to Louisiana. At Humlebæk Cemetery, just on the other side of the lake, where the children swung through the air on a ropeway and boated, a man asked to have his wife's grave moved, and Knud W. Jensen whispered discreetly to an acquaintance that he personally "would have enjoyed having so much life around him". On the other hand, the exhibition was danger-ous. This was a lake!! Compared with today, when the staff do the rounds almost daily to check the fence, the 1970s were directly unsafe, even at a museum. A typical example of the decade was the exhibition planned as the springboard for debate on "the situation of children in society". Serious and critical. The idea was to do something that would get children to "experience their own situation", and "give parents food for reflection" and then add a series of conferences with well-known experts. Fortunately it proved impossible to present the problem in visual terms, so the museum dropped the conscience-stricken manuscript and began to play. Precisely what the children were dreaming of. They weren't terribly interested in the photo exhibition "Children of the World" or in texts and pictures, but in the physical activities in the Lake Garden and the park. Everything outdoors was enjoyed, used and worn down. They didn't bother to comment on the photo exhibition in "the children's people's wall newspaper", as the museum had expected them to do, but filled it with drawings of houses, animals and Pippi Longstockings. Knud W. Jensen, who as was his custom moved around among the visitors with his ears wide open, did however hear a girl say: "Daddy, come and look. I've drawn a hungry child!"

The inevitable consciousness of crisis and cultural pessimism survives only in the appertaining issue of *Louisiana Revy*, in which a large number of deeply worried adults describe "children's situation in society". It is *not* good. The world is full of neurotics, who enter into neurotic marriages and have neurotic children doomed to be just as neurotic as they are themselves, writes Frederik Dessau and quotes Suzanne Brøgger with approval for having said that "just as one buys a washing machine, one has a baby." Children's lives consist of egoistical parents and fear, not to mention the fact that "they live among concrete in polluted air and eat poi-soned food from plastic plates." And when they get a little older, they stop drawing imaginatively and wonderfully. Their drawings become sad and pale, but they are praised. "They are schooled. They give up their identity. This is called a beginning realism." And so it goes on. When the children are not at home or at school, they drift aimlessly around in society, which stores them in cheap pubs – in shopping

malls, where it is easier to steal than to be permitted to pay, on skating rinks and in sports clubs, where they learn that the strongest wins. That's society.

The only ray of sunshine is Knud W. Jensen's detailed reportage from various theme parks for children, including Legoland in Jutland and Disneyland in Los Angeles, where he had been carrying out research prior to the exhibition at Louisiana. In contrast to the other contributors' wailing and gnashing of teeth he recommends with delight Brændesgårdhave on the island of Bornholm, because its owner Emil Ipsen has in an inexplicable fashion succeeded in giving his beautiful garden a magic, charm and innocence far from spirit the 1970s, in which art and everything else is stripped of its enchantment, and virtually everybody, to be on the safe side, adopts an extremely critical and pessimistic view on existence. This attitude also permeates the book in honour of Knud W. Jensen on the occasion of his 60th birthday in 1976 – "Skete der noget?" [Did Something Happen?] It was written by friends in "these black times" and illustrated with photos of Vietnam demonstrations, shanties in Africa, sludge in streams, oil pollution on the beach, the first ban-the-bomb march, a students' demonstration and so on. Six demonstrations in all plus a variety of miseries. Happy birthday!

At the end of the decade, Knud W. Jensen felt under pressure from his health and his marriage, which suffered from constant absence and manic preoccupation with Louisiana. For the first time, he considered a crown prince who could not only take over some of the hard work, but could really lead the museum and be ready for the day when he simply didn't have the energy and strength any longer. His choice fell on Øystein Hjort, a twenty-year-younger art historian who joined the museum's board in 1973 after having defended the museum in *Information* against the neo-Marxists. The two men had composed a director's contract, agreed a salary, a free car and had set a starting date for 1 January 1980, on which date the founder would at the same time retire. Knud W. Jensen's immediate reaction was one of relief, but when Hjort insisted on having his freedom of action guaranteed on paper – he used the expression that he didn't want anyone breathing down his neck – Knud W. Jensen became frightened and backed out, and the agreement was scrapped. He was not ready to let go of his lifework so absolutely. On the contrary, he took over more and more. It turned out that he had the strength for another fifteen years – and a number of other crown princes, who never acceded to the throne either.

Louisiana fills in holes

Every day at Louisiana was hectic. Every day a new jigsaw puzzle that required a maximum of imagination had to be laid if everything was to find its right place. The problem was always money, of which there was too little in comparison with the museum's excess of building plans and proposals for buying art that it simply *had*

The raft was the big attraction at the exhibition "Children are a People". A man asked to have his wife's grave moved from the other side of the lake.

Grass-clad car from 'Children are a People'. In Humlebæk there was more of a spirit of adventure than in other museums, which aimed first and foremost at teaching people something. At Louisiana the idea was that they should *see* and *experience* something physical and spatial.

▶ 160,000 parents and children occupied Louisiana. Everything outside was enjoyed and worn down.

to own. In the course of the 1970s the museum doubled its collection and opened a series of big and expensive exhibitions, while the plan for a concert hall dominated all talk about finances. The museum produced and sold graphic art in order to save up, but when at last a good sum of money had been collected for the concert hall, the possibility of acquiring a sculpture by Alexander Calder arrived: a stabile-mobile, bright red below and in different colours above. Just what Louisiana needed! Then the museum would have three works by Calder, and precisely three would be the perfect number to have hanging and standing in and around the cafeteria and the concert hall. Knud W. Jensen immediately set about convincing his board:

"We had such sculptures at the Calder exhibition (in 1969), where they looked wonderful, but Galerie Maeght demanded some huge prices for them. Calder was willing to make two for us at a quite special price, which in view of the fact that production costs have risen considerably since then nevertheless amounts to 40,000 dollars or 225,000 kroner. I have asked whether he would place some lithographs at our disposal for free in order to reduce the price of the sculpture, and he is prepared to do that. My calculation is now that we can earn about one-third of the price of the stabile-mobile from the sale of the three lithographs. In that way we really get the Calder sculpture down to a very low price in relation to the world market level."

For years Knud W. Jensen had been negotiating with the American sculptor, and it was typical that things began to fall into place just as a whole lot of other art works began to line up for acquisition. In 1975 he went to France and visited Calder for the third time. The artist was almost ready. He accepted that the sculpture would be cast in Denmark, that is for 30,000 kroner as opposed to about 200,000 in France, and Louisiana's director became so eager that he offered to advance the money himself, since there was no room in the budget and the opportunity had arisen. At the same time, Jean Arp's widow offered to sell her husband's sculpture "Stacked Bowls" at a special price, "and it's been on my Christmas present wishes list for almost 20 years," Knud W. Jensen explained. And then, moreover, the Japanese government wanted to give Louisiana Nobuo Sekine's huge sculpture as a gift on condition that the museum paid for the transport of the 12-ton work from Venice, where it was exhibited at the Biennale.

"All these acquisitions have suddenly become topical after having been discussed with the artists for years, and we at Louisiana are agreed that action should be taken now," he writes. And action was taken, but the pressure of business did not stop here. In the same year, Hugo Arne Buch argued for the principle that the older Danish collection should be sold to other museums, where the works would be more at home than in Humlebæk, and in this way the museum bid farewell to the last remnants of the old Louisiana that had opened in 1958

Alexander Calder's sculptures have stood together on the terrace since summer 1976. "Sculptures should be treated like living beings, and all living beings – including man – need their own territory in order to be able to flourish and realise themselves," said Knud W. Jensen. Only sculptures by the same artist share the same space.

as a stronghold of Danish art. The front cover of the first catalogue showed Niels Lergaard's "Landscape, Gudhjem" (1932). The same painting was now for sale. The Danish sculptor Astrid Noack's two big figures were sold to Holstebro Museum of Art, so Louisiana was more easily able to afford three sculptures by Max Ernst, "which have been offered to us at casting price provided we decide quickly," announced the always quickly working one-man committee Knud W. Jensen. Hardly had one picture been hung than his eye fell on the next work that the museum could not do without. As soon as a new sculpture had been placed in the park, he was tempted by another one. He was in permanent correspondence with the Carlsberg Foundation, which became indispensable for the young museum, but applied for funds wherever there was the least possible chance: "Shall we ask the Sonning Foundation for the grand piano and The Good of the Fatherland for chairs?" he asked when the concert hall was approaching completion, but he ended up by paying for both chairs and piano himself.

And then the Henry Moore matter. One Wednesday in April 1976 Knud W. Jensen spent the whole day together with Moore in his home at Much Hadham 40 odd miles north of London. The idea was that he should see the sculpture from 1969 that the museum had already decided on and buy one more. Preferably one of the older ones. At first it seemed that his trip had been in vain because they had all been sold. Every single one. But Knud W. Jensen was nothing if not adaptable and decided straightaway to buy a large new sculpture that had just arrived from the foundry Berlin and been placed lying in three parts in the field outside the studio. As is customary for sculptors, each sculpture was cast in three copies, and here one copy had already been sold to MIT in the USA, another to a town in northern Sweden, and the third, well the third "may also have been sold in a few months!"

Louisiana took it, and "in this way the dream of Moore's large resting women by the sea seemed to have been fulfilled!" Knud W. Jensen bargained the price for the two sculptures down from 40,000 pounds a piece to 35,000 pounds, that is 420,000 kroner each. With the sculpture back home the museum now had three works by Moore. Three was the ideal number – three by Moore, three by Calder, three by Arp, three by Kienholz and so on.

"From fairy tales we know that one means loneliness, two means infertility and three is the number of fertility, possibility. Thesis, antithesis, synthesis," he said "Flaubert once said that when you want to describe a new unknown situation, three selected details are necessary in order to create a reality for the reader, to give a sense of living three-dimensionality. Freud also says quite a lot of things about three."

When someone had given the museum a painting, he would look at it and say: "It's so lonely there hanging on the wall," after which the donor often paid for

Moore sculpture
backlighted.

a partner, but that was not enough either. "Two, that's such a boring marriage, you know," Jensen would say. "Three, then things liven up a bit." Nor could the Carlsberg Foundation resist his indomitable optimism when one day he talked his way to a grant of four-five million kroner only to continue the conversation the following day cheerfully assuming that the figure had been six-seven million.

1976 saw the influx of the sculptures that would become Louisiana's special feature. In June the two big Calder sculptures were erected in front of the cafeteria – "Almost snow-plough" and "Little Janey-Waney". Arp's "Stacked Bowls" had already arrived and been set up next to the two other sculptures. And the massively heavy Sekine sculpture – a piece of rock on a tall steel plinth – just had to be brought home from Venice in the autumn. And then there was Max Ernst, who came in when Astrid Noack went to Holstebro.

Towards the end of the good and busy year of 1976, the museum – primarily in the figure of Knud W. Jensen – felt that the time had come to round off the Giacometti collection with new acquisitions. And in addition to expand the collection of Colourfield Painting and Pop Art. Louisiana had just bought a large Andy Warhol picture of Chairman Mao at an auction in New York and negotiated for a diamond-formed painting by Kenneth Noland. And just a couple of weeks before the inauguration of the new concert hall, he also felt that it was vital to obtain a permit in principle for building a south wing while Niels Matthiasen was still minister of culture. Onwards, onwards, onwards. For a moment the museum had time to derive pleasure from the fact that its persistent critic, Chief Curator Erik Fischer from *Statens Museum for Kunst* seemed to have had to surrender. He registered a palpable lack of foreign modern art in the collections of Danish museums and wrote in the journal *Kunst og Museum* that "one has, as it were, tacitly allowed Louisiana to take over the field. One can therefore imagine that Louisiana should be given funds and endurance to become the country's main museum for international contemporary and future art."

And Louisiana tried to fill in the holes through the purchase of 1960s and 1970s art, especially American. "If we succeed, then there'll only be a gap of fifty years in the Danish museum world!" said Knud W. Jensen about the first half of the century, the main actors of which were still absent: Picasso, Chagall, Mondrian, Klee, Kandinsky, Miro, Dali, Magritte. He regretted Danish thriftiness and his own mistakes. A lot of opportunities had been missed, he thought. Also

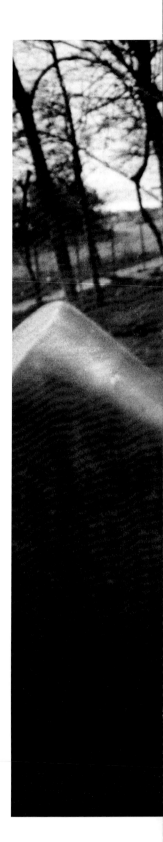

Henry Moore on a visit. Calder and Moore are placed as far
a possible from one another in the park. They were tired
of often being represented at the same museums.

"As soon as a new sculpture has been placed

One of Moore's heavy recumbent women in sun and snow.
To the far left a sculpture
by Henri Laurens.

by himself. Had the Louisiana collection been internationally oriented from the beginning, some amends could have been made, and had the Ministry of Culture supported the museum early enough and covered the operating losses in the 1960s, there would have been enough money not only to arrange exhibitions, but also to buy art at these exhibitions.

The pressure of events was never-ending: the art collection grew and grew and had suddenly become so big that the buildings were too small. The collection had to be put in store for three-quarters of the year and stood there like dead capital without providing any return in the form of experiences and inspiration. Certain new works were difficult to move when after an exhibition the collection had to be taken out of storage and put on display again, for instance the six-meter-long and three-meter-high Frank Stella painting "Ctesiphon" or Søren Georg Jensen's three-ton indoor sculpture. If only they could have permanent placings.

"If we are to function as Denmark's museum of modern art, which there is much to indicate, we must create a counterweight to the exhibitions in a number of rooms where our own collection is on display all the year round and from which it is never moved. This will require a doubling of Louisiana's exhibition space to reach the point at which we can show a main exhibition, a small special exhibition and the major part of our own collection," he informed the board in November 1977.

He thought it stupid to buy art in order to send it directly into storage, but he had no plans of stopping. The solution was typical for him and Louisiana: both things at once. "We shall have to try to carry out the extension of the buildings and the collection at the same time," he suggested. No depressing having to do without. Seen in that perspective it is understandable that he was pleased at the entry of a new person into the museum's enchanted circle: Peter Augustinus, the 33-year-old son of the founder of the Augustinus Foundation and the only member of the family who was active in the companies owned by the family. In some ways he resembled Knud W. Jensen. The lives of both were determined by their duties to the enterprises owned by their wealthy families. Augustinus would never have become the head of a business if he hadn't been forced to do so by relatives and guardians. He was to study law or economics and then take over

The South Wing and Nobuo Sekine's sculpture. The new wing doubled the area of the old Louisiana.

the tobacco company. That was that. It was irrelevant that he himself wanted to be an organist or a geologist.

The family's companies made huge profits in the 1970s and transferred a portion of the surplus to the Foundation, which could therefore afford a big gesture. The art collector Peter Augustinus was thinking of giving Copenhagen a museum of contemporary art and had the idea of discussing his plans with Knud W. Jensen, whom he did not know beforehand. Jensen invited him to tea at Louisiana and marched surprised and a little out of balance up and down the room while he listened to Augustinus. "May I call you in a week's time and tell you what I think?" he asked. He was not uneasy at the prospect of competition from a new museum with the same focus as his own. As a businessman and perfectionist he always thought that competition was a sign of health that could stimulate Louisiana to become even better. He was worried about the money.

Next time they met he spoke about Louisiana's economic difficulties and the problems that Augustinus would have in building up a museum of contemporary art at an international level. It would be beyond both men's strength to do the job properly on their own. Neither of them had the money for the unique project they were discussing. Jensen proposed a joint effort at Louisiana, and Peter Augustinus gave up his own museum plans in favour of Louisiana's. Later it turned out that they had been wrong about the extent of the task. Not even together did they have sufficient funds. Other foundations, grants, donors and the State had to be involved. A large community has contributed to the building of Louisiana.

To his board Knud W. Jensen wrote that Peter Augustinus was "very positive" towards collaboration on a large scale, so he ought to be given a seat on the museum's board, which happened. Four and a half months passed. In April 1978 the Augustinus Foundation decided to pay for Louisiana's wished for doubling its area – the South Wing. Undeniably a turning point. "Now it can become a museum in the best sense of the word," Knud W. Jensen rejoiced and perhaps believed for a moment that Louisiana had really finished growing.

The American Pop artist Roy Lichtenstein as a Viking in Tivoli with his wife Dorothy and Knud W. Jensen as Batman in 1977.

Poul Kjærholm

1950-1980

Louisiana
16. januar - 28. februar 1982

It is not in Louisiana Man's nature to let himself be dragged down into the trendy 1980s depression cultivated by the avantgarde. It's too far out. The poet Michael Strunge complains at being only maniodepressive when it's cooler to be schizophrenic. It's in to be crazy and on drugs, to knock at the door of the closed psychiatric ward and to make sure that someone sees it. Christiane F. replaces Gudrun Ensslin as the new dangerous heroine. Art worships the darkest chambers of the heart, says the musician Martin Hall.

We are speaking of ten years in the city, ten years with the unlimited focus on "I" at the centre, ten years in the dark of the night. Pathos and paranoia at the same time. Black mood, black sun, black beer. Louisiana Man's reaction is as always moderate, cautious, but he shaves off his beard and airs his carefully maintained three-day stubble on the death routes of the inner city, not drawing attention to the fact that he lives in a middle-class suburb (and loves his garden). At the uttermost, he develops an ironic style, a muted world-weariness and adheres to Louisiana's more gentle interpretation of the decade, which culminates in a resolute settlement of accounts with the 1970s. A rapid abandonment of the collective and the political. Out with the group, with the revolution. Art must be relieved of its idealistic burden.

Suddenly the forbidden is permitted and what is most important: Louisiana says one may paint again. Painting is not reactionary any longer, all the international signs point in that direction. After decades of wandering through minimalism and concept art, where it was primarily a matter of using your head and grasping the artist's idea, the Germans and Italians are painting with a broad brush. After works of mud and field stones, horsemeat and honey, the time has come for canvas and oils. This evil bourgeois genre had otherwise been declared dead as a doornail, because painting with its heavy tradition blocked the prospect to something new, but also because it could be removed from the easel and sold. Not good for an artist in the service of the revolution. But just as Paris dictates short hemlines after long ones, Louisiana is now saying painting, and that's got to be good enough.

Louisiana Man no longer needs to conceal his passion for Great Art and paintings that express feelings, for *the work*, which is the code used when interest is focused on the tangible product of the artists' efforts rather than on the more freely floating ideas about its context in society, its political consequences and inherent criticism of art as an institution. *The work* as an autonomous aesthetic experience has always interested Knud W. Jensen, Louisiana and Louisiana Man much more than the other stuff. There has to be something to look at, not just something to think about. Louisiana Man never managed to understand why the art of the 60s and 70s strove to be as anonymous, analytical and "purged" as possible, and why feelings were always mentioned as something subjective and repulsive. It was like a competition in cleaning mania and anti-individualism. Everything one wasn't allowed to do. In the 1970s he got to know the peculiar idiosyncrasies of the artist by closely studying the bulletins from Humlebæk. He knew that most of them had clearly profiled attitudes to "the values and norms of capitalism and the collapse of the Western world", and that they felt that as artists they were paid with stolen money – that is the surplus "taken from the worker", as *Louisiana Revy* put it. He knew that most of them refused to paint, and when Per Kirkeby did so anyway, he was "romantic", which was an expression of scorn. And then the unexpected message descended from the highest authority:

"Now the studios are again full of paint cans, and one rarely sees an empty easel at the art schools. Anyone who looks around in Europe or the USA will notice artists everywhere who have rediscovered the pure pleasure of painting," *Louisiana Revy* reports in 1982. An old painter like Chagall is rediscovered as *the narrator* by the new young figurative painters. But Baselitz, who had held on to the recognisable, appears in the spotlight together with Kirkeby and others who couldn't not paint either, For instance de Kooning. When he painted female figures, he was called the, figurative traitor. After an interval of decades, the key in art is once again the personal. Previously it had not been the idea that the artist himself should be at all perceptible through the work – now he is present in full force.

With increasing astonishment Louisiana Man leafs through the spring issue of *Artforum* 1982, in which "die neuen wilden" and other figurative artists are given 80 pages of mention. 80 pages! Quite extraordinarily it proves necessary to print this German journal in a second impression. There is a hunger for pictures. It as if the moralising schoolmasters of recent years are already far away, and other forces than indignation are at work in art, for instance fascination. For twenty years the avantgarde has spoken of painting with repulsion. It is not only acceptable to paint again, but also to use the entire history of art as one single big storehouse from which to quote. Everyone speaks and writes abut the leading stars in the cult – the Germans A.R. Penck, Georg Baselitz and Helmut Middendorf, the American Julian Schnabel and the Italians Sandro Chia, Enzo Cucchi and Francesco Clemente. Louisiana shows them all in the course of the 80s and buys the Germans

Health sandals and a bowl cut are no longer *truer* than patent leather shoes and a parting. The 70s' belief in the "natural" does not appear as a reality but merely as a choice. Women and men in clogs and sensible cotton underwear slowly but surely disappear from view. Louisiana Man gets rid of his flax curtains, basket chairs, corduroy trousers, coir mats and everything that is faintly reminiscent of nature. Forget it. Nature has no place in the decade in which the wise are pale. One goes around with one's well-behavedness, one's dyed hair, one's tattoos. Louisiana Man reads Rimbaud for his own sake and Fay Weldon for the women's. But just so his suburb can participate ever so little in the festivity, he lays chequered linoleum in his corridor, puts up Venetian blinds and buys four slender x-line chairs in the museum shop.

"History turns yet another notch," *Louisiana Revy* writes about the exhibition Homo Decorans in 1985. Wood is now covered with thick glossy paint; plastic and other artificial materials are displacing natural materials. Patterns and strong colours are gaining popularity; flowery textiles, pink stoneware, gilded china and glass harmonise with the punk-inspired clothing of the day. You write your own history while it is happening. You don't wait for the clarity that comes with the passing of time, but interpret yourself immediately and constantly and are quite certain that you are standing on the verge of a great liberation.

"Even though we have not definitively determined on post-modernism as a general designation for the style that in 100 years will be designated as the style of the epoch in Denmark during the sad/glad eighties, we can at least agree that something decisively new has happened. We have left functionalism behind and something has made itself powerfully felt. A new style. For we dare once more speak of a style, recognise triumphantly that we have to do with a style after having suppressed the concept for 50 years and used it only in a figurative and at times pejorative sense," writes Mirjam Gelfer-Jørgensen in *Louisiana Revy*.

Puritanical dogmas about moderation, simplicity and honesty are shot down, and at the chalk-white and extremely simple Louisiana, which was built on the basis of the self-same modernist principles, the Italian architect Alessandro Mendini is given the floor to express some heretical ideas: "Wouldn't it be beautiful if architecture also had its fashion shows, it seasonal manifestations and changed just as often as the fashion in clothes design?" he asks in the museum's magazine. "I think we live in an epoch in which the world seems to have settled down in a state of controlled chaos, where life is again regarded as fantasy.

One September day in 1985 Louisiana Man takes the train to Humlebæk to hear the lionized young poets read in the concert hall: Thomas Boberg, F.P. Jac, Bo Green Jensen, Klaus Lynggaard, Nina Malinovski, Juliane Preisler, Michael Strunge, Morti Vizki, Pia Tafdrup, Camilla Christensen and Søren Ulrik Thomsen. The programme is seriously exhausting and includes new music and three intervals. The poets have been on tour together many times previously. Like the painters who are slipping so easily into galleries and museums (and sell!), the poets are also enjoying acute success. No doors are closed to them. A large public has been missing real literature and real painting, and the artists are marketed as breakaway groups with strong messages: We want to paint, we want to write – we don't want anything to do with Leninism or hippie piss!

But rebels may feel it to be the ultimate humiliation to be found in a museum while still alive. On that very day in 1985 at Louisiana Søren Ulrik Thomsen felt that it was overdoing things a little: "There was something quite wrong about these time-honoured punk poets coming to a museum and reading their stuff while a group of classical musicians strummed away in a corner; all that was missing was that we could have been stuffed."

Art changes its status in front Louisiana Man. It has its breakthrough in the 1980s. The state of war that, according to Knud W. Jensen, prevailed between the general public and the new art had at any rate been called off. Now art spread out over everything – there is not a café, church, institution, library or shopping bag with respect for itself that does not have changing art exhibitions. *Berlingske Tidende's* critic Henrik Wivel is sick and tired of the "disturbing tolerance" with which Europeans meet art in the late 80s. They have become pacified by too much good living. Where's their anger, their indignation? In Denmark the number of art museums rises from 34 in 1970 to 51 in 1985 and instead of one million two million people now visit an art museum each year.

The avantgarde enters a state of dissolution – it is amorously embraced by its old enemies, by art museums, galleries and the middle class, which catches the young artists on the way up and pushes their prices up at auctions. Hardly are their pictures dry before they are sold or exhibited. Collectors spend manically – stuffing themselves with contemporary art, which is beginning to resemble a vulgar lifestyle product. When Louisiana opened in 1958, very few people took the newest art seriously. Either people ignored or they hated it, but now they cannot get enough.

"The silent, manic collector and the cool investor are the fascinating heroes of artistic life today," claims museum inspector Lennart Gottlieb. So much success makes it difficult for artists to maintain the classical position of rebellion, for where the hell is the opponent? And then there is the competition from all the new private bohemians who spend all their time exceeding limits. The struggle to distinguish oneself as a real artist by being *really peculiar* is becoming increasing screwed up. The avantgarde can no longer derive strength from its outsider role, for now everyone wants to be an exciting outsider. In the 1930s the surrealist Wilhelm Freddie risked going to prison for indecency "Today the most you risk is a separate exhibition," write Frederik Stjernfelt and Poul Erik Tøjner in their book "Billedstorm" [Picture Storm]. Even graffiti gains entry to the museum, and an unusually young public studies the new New York phenomenon at Louisiana.

Postmodernism breaks through in earnest in Denmark in the middle of the decade. The week after the poetry show Louisiana Man is again in Humlebæk for a round table discussion "What is postmodernism?", and a couple of months later he reads in *Politiken* a prominently placed interview with the historian Carsten Juhl, who has been in Paris and learnt from the French thinkers. The headline runs: "Marx is dead – but there is life in the postmodern". Now the unthinkable has been said. The consequence of the old man's death is that art is allowed to be itself again and is only answerable to itself and not to grand ideals and goals. Experimentation is the only thing that really matters for the artist, who does not need to subscribe stubbornly to one tradition or school, but is able to work freely in many. There is talk of unpredictability, irony, chaos, ornament and pastiche, while content, message and honesty are redolent of the old days. The later director of Louisiana Poul Erik Tøjner is in his mid-twenties and a student. Together with Frederik Stjernfelt he writes an article in *Information*, "The time has come". The essence of the article is that art and utopia no longer go hand in hand. That one can no longer judge art by the extent of its contribution to the world revolution. And art and Zeitgeist no longer belong unambiguously together. There are no *oughts*. Many years later Tøjner will bring these ideas with him to Louisiana. Postmodernism also makes its way to the Academy, where the students go amok and paint hundreds of pictures in no time. It is a huge release at last to be able to dip one's brush in paint, even though many of them had no idea whether they could. None of them had really painted before.

Louisiana twice as big

"Is it all going to be ruined now?" people ask when Knud W. Jensen reveals his grandiose plans for doubling the area of the museum. They like it that the museum is not bigger, and the press and the international art journals are enthusiastic about Louisiana exactly as it is. Even the architects become nervous at the prospect of having to alter their unqualified success from 1958. As one of the architects of the place Vilhelm Wohlert sad: "The first building is everyone's favourite."

But the buildings are beginning to tighten their grip on Louisiana. The long fragile glass corridors contain little more than formidable sections of landscape. The extension on the left immediately after the old patrician villa is in full flow as an exhibition machine, and then there are only a couple of rooms down by the cafeteria to show Louisiana's own collection of art after 1945. If even that. The museum is growing out of being a pleasant, modestly dimensioned childhood home. Knud W. Jensen's alter ego – the fictive, eccentric uncle in the country, in whose beautiful private home everybody is to feel at home – cannot keep up any longer. His rooms are too small, too low-ceilinged and too few and his own

"It's not an architectural jewel, nor is it a rationally designed building, but today we can't do without it. In fact we've never even considered getting rid of it and replacing it with something else – it's an essential part of Louisiana physiognomy," said one of Louisiana's architects Jørgen Bo of the old villa in 1985.

Old Willem Sandberg from
the Stedelijk came for
the South Wing's opening
celebrations. Far left sits
Marlou Bode, the widow after
Documenta's inventor Arnold
Bode. Far right: *Politiken*
journalist Malin Lindgren.

ambitions are too comprehensive to find room in them. Louisiana must be a *real* museum, a grown-up museum. It needs a collection.

The remark many years ago by the head of a Copenhagen museum to the effect that Louisiana is not a museum, but an exhibition gallery still hurts Knud W. Jensen. Without a collection one is nothing in that world, but Louisiana does in fact have a collection, which begins historically where others stop. Something decisive must happen now – a qualitative leap into a new category. He is aware that it looks like a reversal of policy. From outside it must look as if Louisiana is suddenly abandoning its original idea of *not* resembling a real museum, *not* becoming large and confusing, *not* burying its head in its own collection, but to keep life in the house by filling it with exhibitions, so there is always something new to come for. To focus so strongly on a permanent collection is new coming from Louisiana, and Knud W. Jensen defends himself: "I can't see that a museum should either be extravert or introvert," he says. He himself is disinclined to choose – better to have it both ways. His strategy is to create a need by continually offering new things. "After all they are just opportunities one chooses to make use of according to one's temperament," says the man who detests compulsion. And afterwards? Afterwards, of course, "one has an almost euphoric urge to relax, to eat and drink, to leaf through books and posters, and one kind of experience does not exclude the other."

He promises his sceptical public, which like most regular customers hates change, that just like the old one the new wing will end in a wonderful space where one can take a break with a view of the sea, comfortable furniture and new ways of avoiding being overwhelmed by the art. It is still not entirely common to have a museum director urgently assuring his public that they can escape from art, but he sticks to his original idea that people should not be plagued or pestered beyond what they themselves want. He knows very well that half of the visitors come for the sake of the place rather than for the art, but perhaps they manage to see a couple of pictures on the way towards the pastries, perhaps they will come again, but perhaps that's their own affair. When the journalist Lawrence Weschler visits Louisiana in 1982 to draw a portrait for the *New Yorker*, the American immediately sees the difference between this and other museums:

"From the front edge of the veranda I couldn't help noticing a special feature of Louisiana: a clear demonstration of the origin of art in human beings. People swarmed back and forth in the late afternoon sun, sat and lay on rugs, slumbered on the lawn or sought the shade: they were more like neighbours than visitors. There was a distinct atmosphere of something relaxed, something family-like – none of that stiff correctness and soreness at the back of my knees and in my back that I normally experience on museum visits."

While the two men are sitting on the stairs up to the veranda and looking out over the park, Knud W. Jensen describes the special nature of his museum in relation to others. The Tate Gallery in London or the Museum of Modern Art in New York remind him of arsenals, incredibly impressive and exhaustive in their thoroughness. Other museums resemble cemeteries with endless rows of tombstones; some are like modest mausoleums, devoted to the eternal flame of a single artist. The Guggenheim always makes him think of a temple, Centre Pompidou in Paris of a funfair. "At Louisiana," he says, "we have tried to create a place of refuge, a sanctuary, a kind of Shangri-la."

Everything he does is extravert and directed towards the public. The introvert upsets him. When he decides to register his collection – most because this is required by officialdom – he hates to see his staff spending their time on the job. It is unproductive. In the same way, if he had lived long enough, he would undoubtedly have preferred to have put up new buildings instead of renovating the entire complex, which became the lot of his successor Poul Erik Tøjner. It wasn't in Knud W. Jensen's nature to spend 218 million kroner on something that that wasn't clearly visible. Other invisible things, like the control of the indoor climate, security and research, interested him infinitely little. It was a shock for him when a fire broke out at Humlebæk shopping centre, and a ban on smoking was at last introduced at the museum, also in its cinema with its coir carpet.

The new wing is much more closed than the first one. Knud W. Jensen realises that many square meters went to glass in the old wing, and he is happy to get more walls, while the painters who didn't think that their art could stand up to the landscape outside are no longer confronted with it. Finally, the works themselves are getting bigger and bigger, so the rooms have to follow suite: "Developments in art have determined what our buildings should look like," said Vilhelm Wohlert. But there is also another insistent party involved: the spirit of the place, the villa itself and the beautiful park running down to the sea with tall rustling trees, the gently undulating lawn, the peace and quiet. These are the crown jewels.

When in 1958 Vilhelm Wohlert and Jørgen Bo discreetly placed the first wing along the edge of the park, they decided the museum's future at the same time, since a second wing would logically also have to be placed along the edge. Now the main building stands like a sphinx with two arms out in the landscape and an unhindered view over the park and the sea. "The original thing about Louisiana's architecture is and remains the museum's ground plan, which seems to have a kind of inevitability about it, and which has developed organically like a plant or rather like a system of roots," writes Knud W. Jensen in the 1990s, when the third and last wing, the subterranean extension, has also been completed.

"There was a distinct atmosphere of something relaxed, something family-like – none of that stiff correctness and soreness at the back of my knees and in my back that I normally experience on museum visits," wrote Lawrence Weschler in his full-length portrait of Louisiana in the *New Yorker.*

"A place of refuge

sanctuary, a kind of Shangri-la"

To walk from the old to the new wing is to experience a rapid review of the history of architecture over 25 years. The south wing is felt to be high-ceilinged and spacious, where the first wing is lower, more intimate, cosier. It is the 1980s against the 1950s: the smooth coolness of the 80s against the warm materials of the 50s. The 80s' neutral, closed white box against the 50s' opening towards nature. The 80s' international, more institutional style against the 50s' Danish tradition. The materials become more and more expensive for each new extension. In the new wing, there is no woodwork and no red tiles, but the underlying driving force is the same in both wings: one is on an exploration and doesn't know what is in store around the next corner.

For Knud W. Jensen an axial sequence of rooms has a disastrous effect. To be able to see down through five or more rooms all at one go makes him feel tired before setting off. The new rooms are not placed in a straight line, but transposed so the visitor has to move diagonally through each room to reach the next one and is unable to get a complete overview. Knud W. Jensen was interested in behavioural psychology, read the biologist Konrad Lorenz's works and transferred his findings about animals' territorial behaviour to the sculptures in the park: he didn't want to have so many that they got into fights for their natural territory. If others came too close, they would get angry. The same applied to the museum's visitors: they should be gently persuaded, not subjected to pressure.

The new wing is not monumental either. It hugs the ground like the first wing. It does not stretch cathedrally towards the sky like the spectacular new art museums that are shooting up at this time everywhere in Europe, USA and Japan, as if they were the architects' own brilliant works of art and which now and then overshadow everything around them, including the art they contain. For reasons of discretion the South Wing is partially dug into a mound that slopes upwards towards the coast. Trees have been spared, views have been kept open. Louisiana is still understated, still secondary to the works. In direct opposition to all international trends in museum building, the wing is intended to attract as little attention as possible and not compete with the park, the nearby town, the neighbouring landscape or anything else in the neighbourhood. The whole idea is that the museum should not draw attention to itself.

"Louisiana is the only modern museum whose architecture I have never heard criticised by anyone who has seen it," writes Harvard professor John Coolidge in his book "Patrons and Architects: Designing Art Museums in the Twentieth Century". He likes the quiet Scandinavian understatement: that the glass corridor edges around the old nine-trunk beech, that the buildings exploit their surroundings maximally and in no way harm them, and that everything from door handles to lamps is subordinated to the total visual experience.

Queen Margrethe and Knud W. Jensen at the inauguration of the South
Wing in 1982. Behind them Prince Henrik and Peter Augustinus and
sons. Now Louisiana would be a *proper* museum, an adult museum,
even though the original idea had been *not* to be like a proper museum.

The new wing ends like
the original wing in an
"interval room" with a
view of the sea, so people
can escape from the art
and get their breath back.

"The nicest person in the museum world"

When the exhausting building project is over, the Queen has been there, and the collection is in place, Knud W. Jensen still doesn't feel that Louisiana is a big museum. "Big museums scare people," he says to the *Herald Tribune* the following year. "Louisiana's harmony with nature makes people feel less threatened." At this time, he is in fact mostly thinking of how Louisiana can become even bigger. He is brooding on new plans and looking for 35 million kroner for the next extension, so that the two arms can be linked via a subterranean wing. The situation is pretty impossible and therefore wildly interesting for an activist of his type with a crammed museum, exploding prices for just those pictures all modern art museums want to have and a period of national retrenchment. There is no doubt that he will have to manage without the State's help. He develops his role as a charming beggar who will not take no for an answer and turns once again towards the foundations, the private collectors, the artists or their widows.

Honour and glory

Each time a foreign journalist or critic travels to Humlebæk, they write about what departs from the norm. The result is a focus on Louisiana in opposition to the established art world. "We have no art historians here," says Hans Erik Wallin, while showing the Canadian newspaper *The Globe and Mail* round. And thereby sets the tone. The *Readers Digest* seizes on the same approach: "In many of the world's museums the mood is cold, the furniture uncomfortable, and art bombards us from every angle. But not at Louisiana." The journalists catch sight of kids climbing about on Moore's soft bronze women as if they were being paid to do so. "Henry is very happy about that," says Knud W. Jensen to a journalist. They see that no one checks the tickets and that books have been placed at the free disposal of the public in the Interval Room. They see people lying in deckchairs or on the grass, tapping their feet to jazz. They see visitors swimming in the sea, and they are charmed by the man that the *New Yorker* portrait calls "the nicest person in the museum world", and who asserts that the books in the Interval Room don't get stolen even though they do. The *Herald Tribune* describes the museum as quiet, self-assured, and friendly.

Susan Sontag, who is now and again described as America's most intelligent woman, gives a reading in the concert hall one evening, and Knud W. Jensen shows her round the museum. A couple of days later she says in an interview

Conga line at Louisiana – far from the trendy Eighties depression cultivated by the avantgarde.

The Louisiana: A Museum Itself as Fine

COPENHAGEN — Each museum has its personality, Knud W. Jensen says: The Pompidou Center is a marvelous culture machine, the Tate is a place where people go to love the Turners and to hate the rest. The Louisiana, the museum of contemporary art outside Copenhagen that Jensen founded and directs, is a quiet, confident and friendly place: lovable may well be the word.

The center of the Louisiana is a mid-19th-century wooden country house surrounded by

MARY BLUME

magnificent trees. From either side of the house, modern wings project to form a semicircle; they can hardly be seen from the outside.

"The whole idea is that the museum should not be showing off," Jensen says. He wants a visit to be like an uncharted journey. "The idea is that you should just walk through and see for yourself, that you should have this feeling of expectation, of what's around the next

name and I like the idea that the owner and his wives are not forgotten."

Deftly diverting the town council's plans to convert the estate into a sewage plant, an old people's home and a graveyard (a combination that still makes his bright blue eyes widen), Jensen acquired the property, hung some Danish paintings on the walls and put a key under the mat so that anyone who wished to might visit.

The casual air remains today. Entrance tickets are sold but no one collects them, guards are invisible, a comfortable reading room decorated with 18 canvases given by Jim Dine has unlocked bookcases. Visitors enter through Brun's old wooden manor house, because Jensen wants them to have the impression that they are calling on an eccentric old uncle in the country.

Very much on the international arts map now, the Louisiana has a full schedule of temporary shows, lately the luridly fashionable young Italians Cucchi, Chia and Clemente. The show was not a popular success (10,000 visitors over a month compared to 10,000 on a single Sunday for a Chagall show) but Jensen [...] show current trends as well as [...] xhibitions and modern mas-

THE TIMES

[...] is dedicated to contemporary [...] sen says, no Copenhagen mu- [...] d Matisse. "When I started I [...] mistake, I started as a museum [...] he says. The mistake was not [...] f his Danish art but that he [...] to buy on the international [...] ces were still low. As a result, [...] only one American painting [...] a Sam Francis given by the [...] terrible gaps. We don't have [...] which is disgusting," Jensen

[...] the collection is gifts, often [...] ine, Francis), their widows [...] uis) or dealers (Leo Castelli, [...] rsons). The collection is more [...] mprehensive: with dealers en- [...] etition between high-flying [...] ll museum doesn't have much

[...] a receives some government [...] tenance but not toward pur- [...] ids come from entrance fees [...] ,000-member Louisiana Club; [...] erg Foundation gives money [...] of one new work a year and [...] Foundation financed the

Galleries

Spectacular Danish dream

[...] e Louisiana Museum must be a [...] culiarly Danish institution. Belying [...] name – which derives from the [...] rious fact that the builder of the [...] iginal house had three successive [...] ves, all called Louise – it is not in [...] me steamy [...] uff, looking [...] eden, in [...] openhagen. [...] e of the mo [...] ns of mode [...] ll as, since [...] tension wh [...] e Queen o [...] e of the mo [...] It is all, ess [...] c man. Kn [...] mily chees [...] 56 and put [...] o realizing [...] modern a [...] nish art, ar [...] at, though [...] n bought, [...] pressionisti [...] eir leader [...] ered pretty [...] t in 1959 [...] ocumenta e [...] d his eyes [...] Arp, Mo [...] erican A [...] inters. Bec

man, and financed the museum completely by himself, he had perforce to discover new talent, recognize neglected worth when he saw it, and forge personal relationships with his favourite artists.

right up to date with new installations just created for the site by Mario Merz and – enchanting, this – a young American called David Stoltz, whose *Utica II* sets coloured lines twisting and wriggling along and

Knud [...]

through [...] told th [...] sive, t [...] them. [...] I prefe [...] self-est [...] with na

"Here [...] trees, t

"We [...] arts, a [...] eternal

The [...] planni [...] signers [...] imagina [...] um sho [...] also a r

"A l [...] idea is [...] be used [...] wrote in

Seate [...] with a [...] one red [...] and Sw [...] thing b [...] view fo [...] museum [...] somethi

The [...] front st

Aug. 30, 1982   **THE**   Price $1.25

NEW YORKER

❋❋ P R O F I L E S ❋❋

LOUISIANA IN DENMARK

FROM its name—the Louisiana Museum—I was half expecting some bayou vista. The view from the window of the director's office, however, was of a broad green lawn girdled by a profusion of tall, dense trees; a smattering of modern sculpture; a dip about two hundred yards

estate's founder, one Alexander Brun, during the eighteen-fifties. He was a comfortable landed gentryman, with a strange fixation: over the years, he wed a succession of three wives, each of whom was named Louise. Somewhere in there he founded the estate, and named it after one or all of

Wie ein Tempel am Meer

Besuch im Louisiana-Museum in Humlebaek bei Kopenhagen mit seinen wertvollen Sammlungen zur Moderne

„Eine Symbiose von Natur und Kunst", ein Museum im Stil „Louisianas" wünschte sich Lothar-Günther Buchheim für seine Expressionisten-Sammlung. Während der Poltergeist von Feldafing im Dezember seinen „Traum zu Grabe tragen" mußte, kann sein dänischer Freund Knud W. Jensen in diesem Jahr das 30jährige Bestehen des Louisiana-Museums feiern. Und zwar in dem Bewußtsein, daß in Humlebaek, 35 Kilometer nördlich von Kopenhagen, dieses Zusammenspiel von Natur, Architektur und Kunst in einer Weise realisiert wurde, die — von der Fondation Maeght in St. Paul bei Nizza vielleicht abgesehen — in Europa einzigartig ist.

Buchheims geplatzter und Jensens verwirklichter Traum haben eins gemeinsam: Ausgangspunkt ist eine Villa am Wasser. Der Däne entdeckte „sein Gelände" bei einem Spaziergang. Das verlassene Gebäude und das verwilderte Grundstück erregten sein Interesse. Er stieg über den Zaun, besichtigte den parkähnlichen Obstgarten und wußte: Hier und nirgendwo anders wollte er seine „Freistätte für Menschen schaffen, die sich für die Kunst der Gegenwart engagieren". Es gelang ihm, die Villa samt Grundstück zu erwerben. Den Namen „Louisiana" behielt er bei. Er geht auf den Hofjägermeister Alexander Brun zurück, der das Haus deshalb so benannt hat, weil seine drei Frauen alle den Vornamen Louise getragen hatten.

Jensen, der in der Schweiz promovierte („Die Einflüsse der primitiven Kunst auf die Moderne" — ein Thema, dem er vor zwei Jahre eine bedeutende Ausstellung widmete), schwebte zunächst vor, nur einheimische Künstler zu präsentieren. Es zeigte sich jedoch bald, daß dieses Konzept unrealistisch war. Kunst läßt sich heute nicht mehr geographisch isoliert betrachten; mehr denn je lebt sie vom gegenseitigen Austausch, von der geistigen Auseinandersetzung mit der entstehenden Weltzivilisation. Provinzielle Enge, Abkapselung — das wollte der dänische Kosmopolit Jensen nicht.

Seine Sammlung erhebt nicht den Anspruch, alle Kunstströmungen des 20. Jahrhunderts zu dokumentieren. Bei der Fülle der Objekte wäre das eine Aufgabe, die den Rahmen jedes Museums sprengen müßte. Ausgangspunkt für Louisiana waren die Jahre nach dem Zweiten Welt-

Blick in das Louisiana-Museum für Mo

treten der jeweiligen Richtung zu prä
Eine besondere Rolle in Louisiana s
Skulpturen. Als Schwerpunkt sieht Jen
Arbeiten Giacomettis, darunter die „F
Venice" und die vom Künstler als E
trachteten Werke „Femme débout", „E
marche" und „Grande tête". Der G
Raum im Nordflügel mit Blick auf ein
hört zu den schönsten der gesamten

ARTE

I grandi musei

UN PORTO DELL'ARTE NASCOSTO NELLA NATURA

Una raccolta modernissima
immersa nel paesaggio danese:
il "Louisiana" congiunge
al passato la più viva attualità.
Entriamo a visitarlo insieme.

TESTO E FOTO
DI ANDREA BATTAGLINI

NEUE ZÜRCHER ZEITUNG

25 Jahre Museum Louisiana

Hs. Mit einem Alter von 25 Jahren ist — | nem ganz einmaligen, spezifisch dänischen
selbst heutzutage — ein Museum so jung, daß | Frühimpressionismus hingeführt, der Gefühl

Un grande avvenire dietro la porta

Louisiana

di KAREN DISSING

I N EUROPA il futuro si chiama Louisiana, si trova appena fuori Copenaghen e ha già compiuto 25 anni. Per il suo anniversario, rinnovato e allargato, il piccolo museo-gioiello dell'arte moderna ha pensato ad una grande mostra dedicata a Gauguin, che si apre il 16. Ma dell'esposizione diremo in fine. Adesso raccontiamone la storia.

Quando nel 1957 il ricco industriale Knud Jensen decise di fondare un museo di arte moderna in concorrenza con quello del centro storico di Copenaghen, c'erano due considerazioni, uno

uno stile leggero, misto tra architettura scandinava e giapponese: hanno lunghi corridoi di vetro che fanno entrare alberi e mare nelle visioni delle sale. Sia la parte originaria che la nuova sono state costruite dagli architetti Jorgen Bo e Vilhelm Wohlert. Nel parco, le grandi sculture di Henny Moore, Jean Arp e Alexander Calder.

E Moore e Arp sono anche i grandi giocattoli dei bambini che si arrampicano e si nascondono nelle braccia e nei grembi materni delle donne sdraiate di Moore. Le sculture di Calder, composte

E intanto Firenze sogna un museo per domani

IN DANIMARCA si costruisce scommettendo sul futuro delle strutture espositive, in Italia si discute del problema. La città degli Uffizi: i musei del futuro è infatti il titolo della mostra inaugurata sabato scorso a Firenze, nelle sale a pianterreno di Palazzo Medici-Riccardi. Si tratta dell'ultima esposizione del ciclo dedicato al quattrocentesimo anniversario della fondazione degli Uffizi.

Sono progetti, disegni, prospettive e bozzetti che illustrano le soluzioni che si sono venute stratificando in anni di pro-

nei dintorni fino a Prato, i musei che mancano alla città. La parte del leone la fa naturalmente il Museo d'Arte Contemporanea, sia perché è veramente paradossale che una città d'arte come Firenze non possega una struttura espositiva dedicata al moderno e al contemporaneo, sia perché è questo

campeggiare nella prima sezione della mostra il progetto firmato da Gregotti, Battisti, Dezzi Bardeschi e Mattei (che cura anche la sezione stessa); se mai si farà, il Museo d'Arte Contemporanea di Firenze avrà questa faccia. A meno che non si torni all'idea iniziale di costruirne

gettare un museo tutto per loro, in risposta a quello tutto fiorentino: ed ecco la seconda sezione della mostra di Palazzo Medici-Riccardi. Firma il progetto un architetto meno noto, Italo Gamberini.

Le altre sezioni (dieci in tutto), si snodano poi attraverso una serie di temi che vanno dal Museo del Tessuto (da realizzare a Prato) a quello di Arti Applicate (per Firenze), dal progetto di ristrutturazione per la casa di Galileo a quello di utilizzo dei giardini abbandonati [...]na. Un gioco di sogni [...]etto che sarà visitabile [...] 6 gennaio ogni giorno [...]alle 13 e dalle 16 alle 19 [...]ra tutti i mercoledì). Il [...]d'entrata è di tremila li-

[...]ufi».

[...]futuro» a Louisiana si chia-[...]auguin, dal 16 ottobre fino a [...]gennaio, oltre alla ricca col-[...]e danese, ci saranno i qua-[...]el Metropolitan Museum, [...]uvre e dei musei di Mosca e [...]grado. Quest'inverno, poi [...]re e retrospettive del foto-[...]. Robert Cartier-Bresson e

---

PROGRESSIVE ARCHITECTURE

Additions to Louisiana Museum, Humlebæk, Denmark

Art inhabiting Nature

Evolution of Denmark's renowned garden museum, opened in 1958, continues in new additions by the original architects, Jørgen Bo and Vilhelm Wohlert.

The museum wraps irregularly around a sculpture-studded lawn. Even the 1982 wing (below) is subordinated to the original villa (bottom).

For decades, architects have been [...] grimages to a little seacoast tow[n ...] penhagen to see a building that is [...] in form, yet vividly memorable a[...] ence. Since 1958, the Louisiana [...] offered a rare integration of art-[...] enjoyment of the landscape, i[...] tectural setting that mingles with [...] ery and frames vistas in the grac[...] of Zen temple pavilions.

The Louisiana owes its existenc[e ...] of its special character to its found[er ...] Knud Jensen, who foresaw a nee[d ...] less institutional kind of museum [...] art. In 1956, Jensen sold the f[...] business, then devoted much of t[...] and all of his time to the projec[t ...] and the museum's are well tol[d ...] *Yorker* profile by Lawrence Wesch[...] 30, 1982, issue.)

EPOCA

VIENI C'E' UN TESORO NEL BOSCO

In Danimarca, a pochi chilometri da Copenaghen, sorge il Louisiana, il più bel museo d'arte moderna del mondo. Raccontiamo la sua affascinante storia e quella dell'uomo geniale che lo ha creato.

Copenaghen, novembre

I ragazzini adorano quelle superfici lisce e scure da accarezzare, da scalare, dalle quali scivolare sull'erba. Le prendono d'assalto ridendo d'entusiasmo, s'intrufolano nei grandi buchi, giocano a nascondersi. Le sculture di Henry Moore, nere «figure reclinanti», appaiono come mamme protettive per gli scatenati bimbi danesi che i genitori hanno

Dal nostro inviato Alberto Salani

During the 1960s and 1970s, the Louisiana

nmark's fine m

contemporary

det finns i Danmark

ned på en sportlovsresa till kulturellt.
Louisiana. Från Kalmar tidigt
i morgonen och tillbaks igen
samma kvällen. Men det var
en väl använd dag!

□ Strålande vårväder
med tiograd kyla på morgonen möttes vi av strålande väder i Louisiana. Knappast
ett snökorn fanns. Folk satt
och åt sin lunch ute i det fria,
njutande av solen.

Ligstadieläraren **Birgitta**
Svensson från Lindsdal hade
tagit med sig dottern **Jeanette**
och åt verkade njuta intensivt
av både resa och utställning.

— Vi är båda konstintresserade och hade väl tänkt åka till
Stockholm och se Chagall-utställningen. Det blev så i alla
fall. När vi såg att den skulle komma till Louisiana ville vi inte

□ Marc Chagall
Han har sin egen stil, Marc
Chagall. Han har inte blandat
dit sig i massa intet som
fiertalet andra konstnärer.
Med sin fantasi upphäver han

har jag mycket att berätta för
eleverna. Jag målar dessutom
en hel del själv och det var oer-
hört intressant att studera den
store mästarens teknik.

□ Givande bussresa
Att åka med på bussresa till
ett sådant evenemang är givande. Man kommer i kontakt
med olika resenärer och har
frågor.

lånade från museer och pri-
vatpersoner från hela världen.

De ryssarna har släppt
ifrån sig många tavlor, de blev
knalle vara restriktiva i sådana
frågor.

ra sig om någonting. Den guide som följde med vår buss het-
ter **Britta Johansson** från KB-
resor. Hon har bott en stor del
av sitt liv i utlandet, varit re-
sekribent i olika vecko-
tidningar och är väl insatt i det

Men när hon skulle beskriva
Ven — som ligger inom syn-
håll från Louisiana — gick hon
på några verkliga minor. Det

ouisiana gjør Norden stø

ÆK: I 1954 sprang en mann
und over hagegjerdet til den
en forfalne eiendommen
i Humlebæk, nord for
n. Mannen var Knud W.
unnlegger av det nå så ver-
nte museum for moderne
uisiana.

Landlig idyll
Den nye sydday, som har gjort
det mulig å vise museets egen
samling permanent, er Knud
W. Jensens hjertebarn. Da pla-
nen om utvidelsen ble kjent,
vakte den en storm av protes-
ter. Men arkitektene Jørgen Bo
og Vilhelm Wohlert har på et
mirakuløs måte forstått å kom-
binere den opprinnelige 1800-
tails elegante villa med moderne funksjonell arkitektur. Byg-
ninger som føyer seg i harmoni
med landskapet.

Louisiana ligger på et platå
ved Øresundkysten. Den hvite
villa fra 1855 virker som en inne-
tekommende og fortrolig repre-
sentant fra en svunnen tid. Den
landlige idyll, understreket av
den åtre hundre år gamle kron
på toppen av bakken, blir hur-
tig brutt så snart man er inne
bak hoveddøren. De moderne
føyene er bygd i enkle materia-
ler i hvitt murverk, ubehandlet
furu og massw glass, og fremstår
som et skulpturelt mesterverk.

— Kunstformidling betyr for
oss at verkene får optimale ut-
foldelsesmuligheter. Vi søker å
plassere samlingen slik at den
oppleves under de beste for-
hold. Også for besøkende som
ikke er fortrolig med moderne
kunst. Vi tror verkene vil tale
for seg selv, sier Knud W.
Jensen.

Det høytidelige og pompøse
som ofte forbindes med begre-
pet museum, er unngått. Man
befinner seg i behagelige og av-
slappede omgivelser hvor det
annes som et livstegn at barna
leker med skulpturene. Og når
været tillater det, spiser man
matpakke under de skyggefulle
trærne på gresset. — Hvem vet,
sier museumsdirektøren, kan-
skje husker en eller annen at
han eller hun som barn engang
har kravlet på et mesterverk.

Moderne verdenskunst
Louisiana er ikke et museum
som bare viser egne samlinger.
Det «åvheles» ikke til å gjøre, internasjonalt
aldri tapt seg i løpet av de

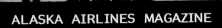

ALASKA AIRLINES MAGAZINE

INTERNATIONAL TRAVEL

Danish modern: *The Louisiana was named by a man who married three different Louisas.*

The Northern Ligl

A Danish museum that breaks all the rules. By Roger

The approach to Denmark's Louisiana Museum is as ...   come to the Louisiana, the white-washed two-story building behind   lands
the e

SCANDINAVIAN DIARY
Anthony Clarke

contemporary art, so the decision
was made to concentrate on certain highlights — hence their fine
representation of works by Arp,
Moore and Giacometti.

Private sponsorship is crucial to
Louisiana's acquisition and expansion programme
tobacco — thr
berg Foundati
tine Foundati
patrons.

The New C
finances one
year, a recent
asso's 1961 pa
sur l'herbe'. T
dation provide
lion for the la
Louisiana.

In complete
den setting of
den's Culture
building set ri
Stockholm, al
banks and dep
in its own way
zest.

The Culture
maintain its o
but fills its seve
elling art and a
resource area
reference libr

eries I visited
e above all
of its kind —
urne would do

a, Denmark's
of contempo-
its collection
ust be one of
of art gallery
in the way it
and exterior
iting whole.
as a gallery in
rief of provid-
est in contem-
This aim was
y the goal of
tative collec-
contemporary
ding a venue
ry exhibitions
owing when I
Tahiti', with
m collections
and America.

on spacious,
ground. Its
nce is an 1855
ceilinged and

e been sculpt-
pe and seem
nost a natural
e land. In the
d Louisiana's
including fig-
Henry Moore,
alder and Arp

MODERNA MUSEE

TA

LOUISIANA

Danmarks
levande museum

Av Maurice Shadbolt

le vid Öresund ligger
ropas förnämsta konst-
En gång avfärdade man
n excentrisk osthand-
rier. Idag har det blivit
me för andra museer

Jensen är ö
vanligt. Ka
hit och delt

Lite sena
lerstensgård
stora 1800-
växtbevuxna
nerande sku
och hamna

READERS DIGEST

MUSEUM OF THE
UNEXPECTED
BY MAURICE SHADBOLT

KWJ: Våra besökssiffror svänger starkt beroende
på vilka utställningar vi har, och eftersom vi främst
visat avantgarde det senaste året har vi bara haft lite
mer än 200.000 besökare sedan förra hösten.

MB.: Men det innebär att ni inte behöver basera er

rje år ca 3 miljoner
iljon kr kommer
ett lokalt stöd från
gefär lika mycket
så ganska bra på
tställningen såldes
och den och andra
det, ungefär 3 mil-

tt underskott på ca
ck Louisiana Fon-

MB.: Hur fungerar samarbetet
senterar ni konkreta förslag på
att bygga upp museet och dess

KWJ: Nja, det är olika; jag sk
att det sker via en löpande dial
Carlsbergsfondet presenterar v
inköp, och i fråga om Augusti
det om en stor engångsinsats;
fem år sedan och när vi två oc
äntligen fått alla instanser att
visade det sig, naturligtvis, at
att bygga kvalitet i dag. Kost
mare 10.000 danska kr, men
framtiden kunna förbinda de
man kan vandra genom hela
ning.

Thomas Mann har skrivit
mänskliga själen finns en star

that in Louisiana she has found a paradise on earth that is just as delightful as the new Musée d'Orsay in Paris is vulgar:

"I loved Louisiana. The atmosphere is so special, democratic in a good way, friendly and radiant with love of art and nature. A kind of model for what a good society could be – both very open and welcoming and in addition of very high standard. As a rule a high level shuts people out, and openness has a tendency to lower the standard. But you have something that does not make compromises but is at the same time for all. The world should be full of Louisianas – and I don't just mean museums!"

During the 1980s Danish and foreign journalists come in throngs – because of the opening of the South Wing in 1982, the 25th anniversary the following year and the choice of Louisiana as Museum of the Year at the City Hall in Paris in 1984. While the 1970s were a decade of consolidation for Louisiana, this decade forms itself as a decade of celebration, in which honour and glory pour down on the parvenu. The Danish Academy for the Fine Arts manages to make Knud W. Jensen an honorary member in 1979 before the others come rushing along. The Finnish newspaper *Hufvudstadsbladet* places him in the Top Ten of international museum directors together with the Swede Pontus Hultén as the only representatives of the Nordic countries. And the new director of *Statens Museum for Kunst* since 1985 Villads Villadsen puts a lid on the big museum's former irritation:

"Louisiana, which with a broad international horizon, with an excellent collection of international painting chiefly from the time after 1960, and with highly appreciated exhibition activities, both approximates most closely to the foreign models and has quite irrefutably had a colossal importance for the dissemination of international modern art," he says to *Berlingske Tidende*.

One spring day in 1984, Knud W. Jensen is made an honorary doctor of the university in Lund and crowned with a laurel wreath in the cathedral. In white tie and tails he processes through the Swedish city with the other newly created doctors and he is particularly glad to have received this honour because it has come from the heart of academia to one who wavered between a business career and family obligations on the one hand and art history and passion on the other. Like a good boy he chose duty, but the conflict ended with his getting everything: the cheese firm in the first twenty years of his adult life, from 20 to 40, and Louisiana for the next 40 years (it would turn out), but he never became formally qualified as an art historian. In its citation Lund University motivates the award by referring to the fact that without actually having received a formal education in the field Knud W. Jensen has become an internationally recognised connoisseur of art, and that in collaboration with architects he has made Louisiana a model for other museums.

Surrounded by jubilant staff, who have travelled to Lund, where
the university's motivation for the doctorate it confers on Knud W.
Jensen is that he has made Louisiana a model for other museums.

German TV during a visit in 1983.

And two years later, at a private audience, Queen Margrethe awards him the rare gold medal *Ingenio et arti*. Certain members of the aging avantgarde still call him Cheese Jensen, for instance Jørgen Nash, who complains that "the emperor of the coastal commuters, Louisiana's mighty creator" has never had the courage to break with middle-class values and the environment he was tied to by birth.

The Swedes are regulars at Louisiana, which they consider to be Southern Sweden's most important and best museum. Every third or fourth visitor is Swedish, which makes the museum something of a border station and a naturally bilingual area. "The Danes understand Swedish with the greatest ease, at any rate the kind of Danes who turn up at these arrangements," said academic and critic Torben Brostrøm about the Nordic writers' meetings at Louisiana. 140,000 Swedes crossed the Sound to visit the Pompeii exhibition alone. "Louisiana is perhaps the only institution that has realised the idea of a joint Øresund Region," says Wallin to *Ystads Allehanda*. This irritates part of the Danish public on big days. During Matisse in the summer of 1985 convoys of buses roll ashore filled with Swedes who queue well-manneredly in front of the entrance and hear a sibilant: "The Swedes shouldn't be allowed in on such a day". Later they stand in line well-manneredly in front of the cafeteria and hear a muttered: "With all the Swedes having to change money, no wonder it takes such a long time." And so on. When the queue grows, the Danes are always quicker to notice the Swedish ladies' profoundly provocative fur coats. Scandinavian solidarity is under pressure during modern myths like Dali, Picasso, Chagall, Gauguin, van Gogh and Toulouse-Lautrec. Oluf Palme writes a little letter to Knud W. Jensen and thanks him for his invaluable efforts to "raise the cultural level in both southwest Sweden and the rest of the world."

"The strangest thing is that people queue up for this museum," writes *Göteborg Posten* and thinks it knows why: "Louisiana isn't like a museum at all; it is full of life and contains things to wonder at, even for a three-year-old, even for someone who does not know so much about art." It sounds like the time when, Louisiana opened, and what pleased journalists and critics most was how little it resembled a museum. The same opposition between a visually and a theoretically based art museum reoccurs in most reactions 25 years late: "Where ordinary museums are severe houses of learning for earnest studies, Louisiana is as light as a feather, an intoxicating, enchanting stimulant for the mind and the imagination. No desiccated museum technocrats can create a museum like Louisiana," writes *Dagens Nyheter*.

Knud W. Jensen asks his secretary to copy the best foreign articles and enclose them in letters to new and old sponsors. He turns 70 in 1986, but is by no means finished yet. In the course of the decade, he writes to two of the men who have been spoken of as his replacements to tell them that he cannot after all imagine himself sitting in his home in Sletten and reading novels or going for walks in the district, while Louisiana proceeds with its life only a few minutes away. "I quite simply feel like continuing for the time being," he writes to Øystein Hjort at the beginning of the 80s. "I want to fortify and further develop Louisiana, whose possibilities I think I know better than anyone, and to which I am attached by so many tied that it would hurt to tear them." He places himself in the group of "self-appointed fogies" – politicians, choreographers, conductors, stage directors who have created their own worlds and remained in them as long as they had something they could achieve.

When the museum's administrative director Børge Hansen suddenly died in 1987, Louisiana was cast into a crisis. The board pressed for a replacement, in case Knud W. Jensen should also die. And Knud W. Jensen asked the director of Silkeborg Art Museum, the highly gifted and very solemn Troels Andersen to be his lifebelt. Two years later he got cold feet and wrote to Andersen that his own departure was not immediately in the cards after all and he found it difficult to believe in a winding down of his activity: "I cannot imagine a life without this tension between current and long-term concerns – a motivation that sets its mark on one's way of living," he explained and stayed for another six years.

Nude-nude

In Finger B of Copenhagen Airport there hung for a short time a nude male figure. The British sculptor Anthony Gormley had made a plaster cast of his own twenty-something body and clothed it in lead. The genitals play a prominent role in the sculpture because they form its geometric centre and are in addition fairly voluminous. From the penis a thin white line is drawn to the man's brain. *Got it?*

It was the airport's own fault. It had asked Louisiana to exhibit a work, and now the passengers were complaining about the aggressive figure. Knud W. Jensen cared about what other people thought. He didn't want to offend them, and at bottom he didn't like this demonstrative nudity (or any other kind of demonstrative nudity) either. He made haste to bring the work home again.

The founder of Louisiana was quite simply a modest man, almost Victorian. He loved art, but not all art and kept away from what a museum inspector at Louisiana calls *nude-nude*: the flesh and sexually insistent. The over-nude. When he acquired his exquisite collection of Giacometti, he always went after the older artist, not the young, violent and sensual Giacometti. Knud W. Jensen did not care for Edward Kienholz' macabre sculpture of two chained old and naked persons with spread legs and bloody groins ("The Middle Islands", 1972), and thought that Hugo Arne Buch had persuaded him to buy it. Louisiana showed the sculpture very

"The strangest thing is tha

"Where ordinary museums are severe houses of learning for earnest studies, Louisiana is as light as a feather," writes the Swedish daily *Dagens Nyheter* about the favourite museum of Southern Swedes.

eople queue up for this museum"

rarely, and the easily moved Knud W. Jensen did not want to have it on display when the Queen or distinguished visitors from the Augustinus Foundation were expected. On such occasions Kienholz was removed. The Queen had once during a guided tour expressed distaste for the sculpture. That was enough.

Knud W. Jensen was not a red-blooded person. Despite his ground-breaking. museum as a proof of the opposite, he often found it difficult to break with the conventions. It required an effort for him to do so, and he was slow to surrender to the modern. There were many of the artists that he dared to exhibit, but not to buy for the collection. Louisiana had an exhibition of the Ukrainian-American sculptor Louise Nevelson as early as in 1968, but the museum didn't buy her until 1987, when she was a venerable old lady, and "Royal Tide III" from 1960 cost 800,000 kroner. The museum virtually never bought "before breakthrough" and was rarely sufficiently self-confident to buy artists who were only up and coming. The museum invested in the established successes, and Knud W. Jensen paid dearly for his waiting policy, as he was the first to admit.

In 1982 when the American artist Jim Dine was in Copenhagen and visited Louisiana with Herbert Pundik, he sat silent on the back seat of the car on the way home. The visit had made an impression on him, partly the meeting with Knud W. Jensen, who did not hide his enthusiasm, partly the place itself. "Then give them a picture!" Pundik exclaimed. But when he phoned Humlebæk with the news, Knud W. Jensen's first reaction was hesitant. "He was afraid of confrontation, you know, and worried about what would happen if he didn't like the result and all the trouble there would be," says Pundik, who was surprised at the response since Dine was already represented in the collection and his pop art was often hung.

The matter developed as Knud W. Jensen had feared it might. Jim Dine rode every day on a racing bike from Copenhagen to Humlebæk and disappeared into a room that he had made his studio at the museum. One day he came out of it with a series of 18 pictures! They extended across the entire library room in the South Wing, which definitively became Dine's room. When Poul Erik Tøjner arrived on the scene in 2000, he took them down because the room was to be used for many things. One day Dine took his new wife up to show her his room, but now the pictures had been put in store. He offered to give the museum one picture if he got the 18 back. Tøjner asked the Ministry of Culture for permission for the exchange, which was refused for the reason that the works had been created for the place and were therefore intended to remain there. At any rate close by. Now they are in a cellar, and Dine is "somewhat bitter," as Pundik puts it.

To receive gifts without becoming dependent on the donor is always difficult, a great gamble, but in the 1980s a number of major foreign collectors

"Th

Dance in the concert hall on the museum's 25th anniversary.
As a private museum Louisiana was from the start entirely
dependent on how many people felt like dropping in.

orld should be full of Louisianas"

discovered Louisiana in earnest and made the situation less acute. Louisiana was suffering twofold under the entry of Wall Street millionaires into the international art market and the building of the South Wing. Ninety percent of all American art collectors were exclusively interested in modern art. "Who still collects ivory works from the Middle Ages?" complained the director of the Metropolitan. Museums were thriving everywhere, except Denmark. Thirty new or much expanded museums in the USA in only five years. Lots of new museums in Germany, in Switzerland, in Japan, and they all wanted to be filled with big names. The market was boiling. Even business magazines began to mention the phenomenon and the incredible auction prices. If Louisiana bought just one single picture by one of the internationally popular modernists, this would exhaust its cash reserves for decades. Knud W. Jensen himself no longer had enough money to keep up with the game. He had spent every single penny, and his capital – including the house in Sletten – was tied up in two foundations, which were quietly bleeding to death in order to cover the museum's deficit. There was no question of buying art.

Something had to happen, and it did. Other people's money and other people's art works began to play a significant role in the 80s: Mr. Riklis, an American businessman, who had become rich from supermarkets, donated a fine collection of 200 constructivist paintings, drawings, sculptures to Louisiana, the so-called McCrory collection:

"Here it is truly a matter of an international enlargement that shows Knud W. Jensen's unique ability to procure gifts for Humlebæk, yes procure, for gifts rarely come on their own. Not only the background, but also the museum must be of the highest class. One has to have a net out all the time in order to bring home the big catches. At this point, he is working with a skill that the heads of Danish museums can learn from," Alex Steen wrote in *Kunstavisen*. According to Steen, however, there was a reverse side of the coin since Knud W. Jensen' success meant that he had become a good excuse for the politicians, who failed to make a serious effort at creating a museum of modern art. The politicians could relax – Louisiana was doing well enough.

There also came three works by Mark Rothko from the Rothko Foundation and some works from the American art patron Celia Ascher. The Carlsberg Foundation bought not just one but two Picassos, and "in these difficult times" the public put 800,000 kroner in the glass chest for a third. Sam Francis donated pictures, the Belgian-American collector Stephane Janssen likewise. And finally, Wall Street crashed in October 1987, the art market collapsed, and "soon we could again begin to bring the collection up to date," Knud W. Jensen wrote happily in his memoirs.

He threw a rop

Louisiana was almost crushed in the 1980s'
competition among modern museums for the
same expensive artists. Here two times Calder.

p into the air and began to climb

'Krig og menneske' [War and Man] 1981.
Billedstofsteatret's wordless performance looked like a collective suicide.

The museum was looking for new centres of gravity, younger artists to be cultivated in the same way as Giacometti, Calder, Arp and Moore. The choice fell on Per Kirkeby. As the only Danish artist of his generation to do so he made an international breakthrough and in that way returned to Louisiana, where he was elevated to a monument, a process that culminated in the big retrospective exhibition in 1990 and once more in 2008, the year of the museum's 50th anniversary. There had previously been only one Dane of real stature at the place, Asger Jorn, an artist that Kirkeby had always been mythologically interested in. They went well together. With Per Kirkeby came other artists from the big 80s wave of German painters, for example Baselitz and Kiefer. They were all in Michael Werner's stable in Cologne, and a myth arose that at the beginning of his museum Knud W. Jensen bought young and audaciously, but later lost his nerve and was swallowed up by the German gallery owner. But it is also part of the story that the art market's enormous volume in the 1980s was matched by correspondingly influential art dealers. That Michael Werner had some of the best *eyes* after the Second World War. That his artists were incontestably good. And that Knud W. Jensen had never wandered around in the studios of the youngest artists and made daring purchases. That is wishful thinking. In a actual fact, the average age of the purchased artists was lowered when Nittve and Tøjner arrived, something that is happening all over the world. Young, young, young.

In buying the German painters Knud W. Jensen chose a special path for Louisiana. The Germans knew where they came from. Their pictures were grief work. They were struggling with the national, with history, with the psychological, and they were figurative rather than abstract. He *could* have chosen differently and bought the ironical and kitschy art of the era's other dominant flock: people like Jeff Koons who adhered to the conceptual tradition with a focus on the idea rather than on feeling. Knud W. Jensen always chose something in which he found something for himself and believed that there was something for others: the existential, the humanist view of the surrounding world. It was vital for him that people should not be made to feel smaller and go home from the museum with a dunce's cap pulled down over their ears. He was above all an eye-person. Things should have a visual dimension, be visually charged, and that does not apply to a dot on a wall, or to a box with letters that you can play with yourself or to a round-table discussion. The eye is the key.

One must *see* and *see* and *see*, said Knud W. Jensen, who considered the collection to be "a kind of spiritual power field, an accumulated artistic capital" that one can return to at any time in order to elicit meaning and insight. "The re-encounter is immeasurably important, because only little by little does one

In the 80s political commitment returned
to Louisiana after 10 years' absence.
A picture of chaos from the arrangement Peace and Man, 1983.

realise what the artist has wanted to express. There are works that bowl one over at first sight, but the great majority open up for one only gradually."

The first half of the 80s were tough for the country and an inappropriate period in which to fish for state subsidies. Even for Louisiana. "If it wasn't against one's nature, one could become a misanthrope," Knud W. Jensen wrote in the Louisiana Club's magazine, and Prime Minister Poul Schlüter said on his accession to power in 1982: "I feel it to be one of my tasks to create optimism. In the final analysis, maybe I'll succeed in convincing myself." After the crisis atmosphere of the 1970s, their pessimism, stagnation, bankrupt businesses and inflation, came the cuts, economies, the reduced sickness compensation and social problems of the 1980s. But in the middle of the decade it was possible to glimpse the replacement for all the closed down farms, industries and shipyards – the personal computer combined with a quick brain. The mid-1980s exhibited the most vigorous economic progress and optimism since the 1960s, and Knud W. Jensen prepared his offensive. He wanted to have that subterranean wing, and he wanted the State to cover more of his deficit, so he could buy art for the museum's own money. He threw a rope up into the air and began to climb.

Peace

In the 1980s Louisiana refound its political commitment after an interval of ten years. Now it was world peace that was at stake. Where the museum's questionnaires and seminars in the 1960s were about near things such as the general public's hopeless taste, the blessings of modernism and the need for art subsidies, the focus had now moved further way – to international politics, the Cold War, refugees, human rights, freedom of expression. Three times in the course of the decade Louisiana held peace days, "Krig og menneske" [War and Man] in 1981, "Fred og menneske [Peace and Man]" in 1983 and the big peace camp in 1987, a colourful three-day bazaar run by Camilla Plum's peace foundation.

"A lot of our sponsors don't like the peace movement," Knud W. Jensen said to the *Herald Tribune*. "I'm not a member of the peace movement myself but I love these people because they are brave and energetic and our only hope. What's the use of hanging paintings at the right level if it all goes up in an explosion in a few years? "

▸ Samba in the concert hall, 1983.
This was the decade when the
street carnival came to Denmark
driven by samba rhythms.

It took place in the special Louisiana way, in which one invites "all the usu-als" and reckons that no one has been left out. But of course these were all the people with the right opinions, NATO-critical journalists and politicians, Nina Hagen and Kim Larsen and "The Permanent Council of Globally Wise Women", socialist economists and feminists from all parts of the world, who *as women* assumed full responsibility for the survival of the globe and demanded that the superpowers should immediately agree to remove all short and medium distance rockets. "History's severe verdict on Reagan is being drawn in the dust," reported *Weekendavisen's* correspondent, who of course couldn't know that in his obituaries many years later the president would be given a large part of the honour for the fall of the Berlin Wall and the defeat of the East European dictatorships by doing all those things that the peace people didn't want him to.

"What are we going to talk about?" asked Nina Hagen, looking as if she was about to die of boredom as she took a seat between an American peace activist and a Soviet critic. "We should learn from beings from space," she suggested among other screwball and not particularly specific proposals.

"All the usuals should be more or less be understood as the part of the population that is against or strongly in doubt about the defence alliance that has now secured peace for a longer period than has ever previously been experienced in Europe" wrote *Frederiksborg Amtsavis* coolly, while the Soviet Union's faithful mouthpiece *Land og Folk* rejoiced at "the peace and imagination" at Louisiana, which in the course of one single sunny day attracted 10,000 people, a record for one day.

Shortly afterwards, the American Secretary of State George Shultz looked in at Louisiana in connection with a 26-hour visit to the country, during which he asked Denmark to contribute more strongly to NATO. He was photographed together with Knud W. Jensen in front of a Jorn painting and revealed no faith in a Nordic nuclear-free zone. Not pulling his punches he said: "It is not a question of where nuclear weapons are launched from, but where they strike."

The Russian meeting the following year was characterised by seriousness and depth and left other traces than a trampled lawn and a sea of clichés. In 1988 for the first time Russian exile writers met Soviet writers and literary critics. For both camps the encounter seemed surreal because no one had believed that the Soviet Union would allow its writers to travel to the West in order to meet the "enemy" – defectors and traitors like, for instance, Andrei Sinyavskii, who in 1966 had been sentenced to seven years in a strict-regime labour camp for having tried to get his books out to the West.

"It sounds all the more improbable that a single man, and be it noted not a statesman or a politician, should make a breach in the wall that had been erected

Billedstofteatret's gloomy prediction during Peace and Man in 1983. 'Corpse' in the Giacometti room.

▶ The German punk queen Nina Hagen discusses war and peace with the American Quaker and peace activist Kenneth Boulding (left) and the Russian peace researcher Georgi Andjaparidze.

seventy years earlier and divided Russia into two suffering halves," writes the literary scholar Galina Belaya some years later about Knud W. Jensen, "who was the first to begin the healing of our bloody wounds."

When she was rung up in Moscow by the originator of the idea Märta-Lisa Magnusson, she couldn't help laughing at how crazy it was. A meeting with the émigrés? In Denmark? What is this nonsense? she thought. "Oh, these foreigners! They have no understanding at all of the prison we live in here." When permission from the Union of Soviet Writers actually came, she still could not grasp it. "The whole story was still like a kind of game, something we Soviet citizens were playing at – presenting ourselves as free people, and the foreigners played along and pretended to believe us."

But she came to Denmark together with the other writers, trembling with nerves at this forbidden meeting. How would it go in front of the KGB people from the embassy? How could they get to talk with the émigré writers? In Copenhagen the Soviet ambassador said that properly speaking they ought not to take part in the conference. Why sit there and listen to anti-Soviet statements? They should act as if they were only attending a friendship meeting with Danish writers.

"Afterwards we drove through the clean, white city and up along the coast to Knud W. Jensen's museum, Louisiana, where there was an en exhibition of

Defector Lev Kopelev with professor of literature Galina Belaya. The Russian Meeting was unique in that it was the first time émigré Russians met writers and litterateurs from their former country, Galina Belaya returned a number of times after the fall of the Soviet system.

Edvard Munch's pictures at that time," Galina Belaya remembers. "We walked in a tightly knit cluster through the museum, like prisoners from the same prison who were to be moved as a group to a new and unknown place, but only for a couple of days, absolutely temporarily, predetermined soon to be sent back to our old prison. I looked right and left out of the corner of my eyes and saw nothing but pictures and signs with "Munch, Munch, Munch". Then there was a blinding light in front of us, and we could hear voices. "What is it?" I asked. "It's journalists from all over Europe who have come to be present at this historic first meeting between Soviet writers and émigré writers." We continued into the cafeteria. "There you are then, my dearest," I heard Mariya Rozanova exclaim. Something heavy tore itself loose inside me and got stuck in my throat. It was fear. "Why are you just standing there, Sinyavskii", Mariya said to her husband. "I don't know really", Sinyavskii said embarrassedly to me, "but perhaps you haven't been allowed..."

"No, honestly!" I protested as if I were a free person. "Hello!" and we embraced."

Six months later Märta-Lisa Magnusson writes that the émigré theme is no longer taboo in the Soviet Union. Newspapers and journals have devoted full-page articles to the Louisiana meeting, articles in which writers previously condemned

The U.S. Secretary of State George Schultz looked in on Denmark, Louisiana and Knud W. Jensen and said in opposition to the peace people that the West gains most vis-à-vis the Soviet Union when it negotiates from strength.

255

and ignored are not merely mentioned but also quoted. There is just one year to the fall of the Berlin Wall.

The public

Salvador Dali landed in New York for the first time equipped with a two and a half meter long baguette. At a surrealist exhibition, he lectured in a diving suit, but fainted due to lack of oxygen and had to be taken to hospital. On one occasion, he arrived at the Sorbonne in a Rolls Royce full of cauliflowers to give his lecture on "phenomenological aspects of the paranoid-critical method" to a delighted audience. Liqueur glasses had been sewn onto his dinner jacket, and at the bottom of each of them one could discern a fly. As a young man, he underwent a nervous crisis suffered in consequence of delusions and lengthy laughing cramps. And so on, and so on. In other words: Dali was a real artist.

A museum should not underestimate that kind of story, but immediately tell it to its public as Louisiana did in 1989 with the Dali anecdotes. The man attracted people and in that way paid for other artists who had not succeeded in creating a myth around themselves. Other such myths attached to Monet, who painted best when half-blind and the indomitable Picasso, who said that he would paint with his tongue in the dust if he was put in prison. Louisiana was quick to realise that great artists with the proper stuff of myth in them (madness, virility, eccentricity, brutality, early death or a combination) sell better than artists who are merely great.

In *Louisiana Revy* normal people read about peculiar artists' disturbingly different lives. Of the German painter Arnulf Rainer, who exhibited at the museum in 1982, we know that without getting out of bed he drew for days in a shabby rented room emitting atonal sounds while his drawings became blacker and blacker. We know that Antonin Artaud worked in an extreme fury, breaking one pencil after the other and suffering intense inner torment. And we know that that Gauguin on Tahiti found a lovely 13-year-old girl, whom he made pregnant.

A glance at the museum's Top Ten reveals two ways to a blockbuster, for which queues extend down the road, coffee cups pile up in the cafeteria, and two people are employed fulltime to roll up posters: you can either exhibit a great artist alone or a unique collection:

Claude Monet in 1993 . . . . 448,166 visitors

Pompeii 79 AD in 1977 . . . . 416,820 visitors

Picasso in 1981 . . . . 320,716 visitors

China's Treasures in 1980 . . . . 282,329 visitors

Arne Jacobsen in 2002 . . . . 275,249 visitors

Picasso and the Mediterranean in 1996 . . . . 259,145 visitors

Matisse in 2005 . . . . 244,920 visitors

Marc Chagall in 1983 . . . . 239,901 visitors

René Magritte in 1999 . . . . 236,548 visitors

Pierre Bonnard in 1992 . . . . 219,048 visitors

The world's first blockbuster might be Rembrandt – the exhibition at the Stedelijk in Amsterdam in 1898, through which 43,000 people passed in two months. The old successes are surprisingly similar to those arranged at Louisiana and other Danish museums from the 1970s and onwards. They cultivate the male artistic genius and focus on the major works. Monet, Picasso, Dali & Co. are repeated at intervals of 10, 15 or 20 years. It is as sure as eggs that these Master exhibitions will bring the visitors in. To see new art 10,000 people will turn up in the course of an entire month, which corresponds to a weekend for Chagall. "It is as if via sensitive signalling system a part of our public consistently avoids certain exhibitions," sighs Knud W. Jensen.

With Picasso in 1981 and Chagall in 1983 Louisiana was the most visited museum in Denmark in those two years. The Eighties were a fantastic decade for the museum. First the opening of the South Wing, which the Augustinus Foundation ended up paying 37 million kroner towards. Then Louisiana applied to a number of foundations for money for the subterranean graphics wing and got it, and finally Knud W. Jensen pressured the government into giving an increased grant and got precisely what he asked for. 5,5 million kroner a year, and nobody, *nobody* complained. Twenty years after the popular Rindal revolt against elite culture Louisiana, whose founder had recklessly asserted on inauguration day that the museum would never cost the State a penny, received an adequate grant, and only one single little reader's letter of the classical type:

"What is the message in the huge picture at Louisiana that consists solely of black? It should probably be called "The World Wants to be Deceived". So do the Minister of Culture and his committees, but it was the taxpayers who once again had to shell out when five million kroner worth of their money was transferred to Louisiana the other day."

But among the public there are also always people who have a kind of revelation that is difficult to describe, and such people do not write readers' letters.

The later Academy professor, Erik Steffensen, had one of his first art experiences at the beginning of the 1980s. After having viewed the special Chagall exhibition he went into one of Louisiana's permanent exhibition rooms and looked at some aluminium boxes and coloured neon tubes:

"They too were art. Purity and simplicity. There was no distinction between new and old. Everything was madly thrilling. It was elevating. My Louisiana life began. There were white walls, high ceilings, even though the rooms were intimate. One felt the art as a human touch that had access to the soul. Spiritual plenitude. It had what I lacked or needed in my life. The experiences filled out a vacuum."

The same thing happened for Christian Gether, the later director of the Arken Museum of Modern Art: "As a student of art history in the 1970s there was no way one could afford to visit the European metropolises, not to speak of New York. One saw the great works in reproduction in art history books and as slides at the Institute for Art History. So it was fantastic to be able to buy a ticket for the coast railway and set off for Louisiana. And then to stand face to face with the 20th century: Picasso, Matisse, Chagall, Kandinsky, Henry Moore, Giacometti and many more. All that the international art public could experience in Paris, London, New York, Tokyo, etc. we could experience at Louisiana."

Hans Erik Wallin from Louisiana in China to borrow works for 'China's Treasures' in 1980. He came home with a horse, an officer, an archer and a soldier, which had been excavated together with 7,000 other life-size ceramic figures.

258

From 1981 to 1985 Louisiana averaged 394,000 visitors a year, *Statens Museum for Kunst* had 186,000 and Glyptoteket 170,000. When *Berlingske Tidende* asked seven well-known Danes what was their favourite museum, five answered Louisiana, one chose Hirschsprung and one Ordrupgaard. The newspaper asked again fifteen years later, and the writer Knud Romer answered: "Louisiana is my favourite museum, even though it's banal." Not the museum, but choosing it. The outsider from 1958 had become a matter of course.

From the very day of its opening the public was constantly at the back of the minds of all members of Louisiana's staff. It was very early for that kind of preoccupation in Denmark. An art historian at Louisiana had to and has to be able to endure the public. He or she has to be able to speak of visitor figures without blushing and to generate money, which many people in that profession still found difficult in the 1980s. One had to be able to have four exhibitions in one's head at the same time, to produce and to move on quickly. Every opening is also a conclusion: a glass of wine, dinner with artists, patrons, collectors, lenders, the museum's friends, press conference. On, on, on. The little group of museums inspectors are constantly on the go. They are not specialised, not divided into specific fields, but they interact with one another and a comprehensive team of cooks, the shop,

Prime Minister Anker Jørgensen with his wife Ingrid (left), Minister of Culture Lise Østergaard (right) and the Chinese ambassador (middle) with accompanying personages at the exhibition "The Treasures of China" in 1980. In 2007 with 'Made in China' the museum showed Chinese contemporary art – paintings, installations, videos, performances – for the first time.

The shop is a thorn in the eye of the classical puritan critic, who had also disliked the cafeteria at the opening in 1958, because of the mixture of things that do not belong together. Just as Knud W. Jensen wanted it.

the music chief, the Children's House, the Club. In the 1980s you don't just show Mario Metz, but sell the Italian with fettuccine and Parma ham, artichokes and a glass of red wine. Bonnard goes well with coq au vin, Chagall with pâté and Russian wine, etc. If some art historians don't seek employment there, it is because they want to do research, immerse themselves in archives, in collections, in an individual artist. They cannot stand the exhibition race at Humlebæk, and some cannot accept what they regard as a conservative view of art. Louisiana also has a reputation for being demanding. You give *The Firm* a large bite of your life.

When Knud W. Jensen lived, one also had to be able to put up with the fact that it was a man with no formal qualifications in art history who made the ultimate decisions. Everybody kept a sharp eye on costs. It surprised one of the inspectors that according to rumours the exhibition "Claude and Poussin" at *Statens Museum for Kunst* had taken one man 8-10 years to set up. Everything was correct and of high quality, including a comprehensive catalogue, but all the same: "There's got to be public funding involved – it can't be private money, can it?" As a private museum, Louisiana was from the beginning entirely dependent on how many people wanted to drop in.

Kjeld Kjeldsen from Louisiana was on the board for Danish art museums and heard the other members complain that their municipal boards were always criticising them for not doing enough to attract the public as Louisiana did. The museum representatives defended themselves by saying that Louisiana was based on three things: Danish pastries, sales of posters and exhibitions. Not a compliment. They still had an ambivalent attitude to the link between money and attendance. Now everyone can accept it. Briefly put, what has happened since the 1980s is that Louisiana became the model the others copied. The new art museum Trapholt is called in the press "Kolding's mini-Louisiana" or "the East Jutes' natural answer to Louisiana", and the Social Democrats in the western suburbs of Copenhagen planned their own "Louisiana" in Ishøj.

Nor is it unusual for the public to be unable to stand the public. Some people get the creeps from looking at the other visitors and can't help giving them reviews. With great relish they describe their hopeless clothes and behaviour, and the story always follows the same pattern. First, the reviewer drives up the coast road, passing the villas of the wealthy with their privileged views and expensive

◄ The launch of *Fredag*, the now deceased journal for literature, culture and politics, drew full houses. From 1981 to 1985 Louisiana had an average of 394,000 per year. *Statens Museum for Kunst* less than half as many.

Isnel da Silveira appeared at the museum in the 1980s together with other of the decade's prominent women – children's upbringing guru Anna Wahlgren from Sweden and the writers Germaine Greer, Fay Weldon and Isabel Allende.

yachts. Then he enters Louisiana and encounters a public dressed in the latest Lene Sand collection with designer shoes and project children. Then comes an ironic account of how people run into their acquaintants, "Heavens, are you here too!", of the cafeteria's carrot rolls that accompany the pumpkin soup and thinly sliced fillet of veal, and this is followed up by an equally ironic account of the art merchandise in the shop. The point each time is that it is impossible to see the works behind all that mainstream and designer taste.

Suddenly, it becomes problematic that people go on Sunday excursions and have a good time. There is an echo of the old criticism from the 1950s to the effect that open shrimp sandwiches and a view take the seriousness out of the art. Behind it lies the wish that the museum was still a virginal institution forming a sheltering roof over the works and protecting them from the filth outside the white walls. This is a typical domestic criticism of Louisiana, which in the foreign press is always lauded for being wide open to *all*. *Politiken's* Bjørn Bredal now and again represents the local public-critical school. He operates with an expression like "the Louisiana feeling", a feeling of inferiority at finding oneself amongst one's betters from the stockbroker belt. Knud W. Jensen always rejected the claim that Louisiana was a museum for the upper class. In the first place, the Danish upper class was not all that numerous, and then the North Zealand contractors and directors were too busy to visit the museum. He was well aware that it did not attract everybody, but found its public in the large well educated middle class, which had been growing larger and larger since the 1960s.

Other segments of the public cannot stand that there are many people and that they buy postcards. These critics entertain a longing for the dusty, exclusive museum, for quiet empty rooms where one can be in peace with the works without bumping into plebs who are probably here merely because they think it's the right thing to do. A classical prejudice is that *the others* always look at art for the wrong reasons. That they don't quite experience the essence of art as one does oneself. That they are not wholehearted. That they have other reasons for being here than the right ones. That they are just killing time. And finally that high quality cannot be reconciled with huge crowds of visitors.

As Knud W. Jensen said about the criticism of the crowds visiting the Monet exhibition in 1993: "The new intellectual gimmick is to designate everything that obtains a response and attracts many people as *event culture*. In this way, we who are glad to get into contact with many people (also the dream of many artists) are reduced to smart, populist impresarios delightedly rubbing their hands together when there is a queue at the entrance. Does not the concept of "event culture" underestimate both us and our public a good deal?"

The fact is that art is no longer the preserve of a single class, but of all who are interested. It has become a mass phenomenon, show business, an element in international tourism, but there are still some people who think that others should not have access to it because they do not live up to their obligations as the public. Barriers should therefore be set up so that they can't get in. At heart these people are struggling to dominate Louisiana and to be the most correct Louisiana visitors, but the great majority of the public is sublimely indifferent to these subtle distinctions. From bus trip with a provincial arts society to Nolde at Louisiana in 1987 Jane Aamund reports: "The museum's visitors have done their homework, since you don't want to make a fool of yourself when talking to others on the bus. Before leaving for home again, you buy souvenirs for your notice board, posters for the kitchen and books and art journals. This is a new Danish way of having a cosy time. There is a good atmosphere – you talk about the pictures, meet new people, feel elevated after such a good evening."

The visitors behave exemplarily. Lars Fenger, Louisiana's music chief, cautiously suggests that they are "perhaps the world's best audience for chamber music". What good is it if musicians and composer are sublime but the audience is not on

Jesper Klein and the Chamber Orchestra and "perhaps the world's best audience for chamber music," according to the museum's music chief.

a level with them? The public and the intimacy of the concert hall are Louisiana's special strength in relation to other concert halls in the world, says Fenger. "A highly cultivated audience who know how to listen; listeners who know what they are looking for and are able to appreciate the experiences they receive. The musicians notice this." As long as the museum has existed, the papers have published photos from the museum showing intensely listening people who exhibit an almost demonstrative good will towards the reading, debating or music-making centre. When the generation 68 visited the art museum twenty years later for Louisiana's international symposium in 1988, there was only one single rebellious Lenin T-shirt among the 225 participants. Everyone seemed to have passed the age of 40, and according to *Aktuelt* these were "serious and extremely thoughtful people engaged in reverent listening."

The Danes have grown accustomed to going to art museums, largely thanks to Louisiana. The worst anxiety and mistrust are over. About 16 % of the year's visitors are members of the Louisiana Club, a kind of superloyal society of friends run by the museum itself.

Weekendavisen describes the visitors as discreet people from the progressive upper-middle class. "The public? Well, they belong to the cultural segment – they can't escape from that. Other features are: middle-aged, grey hair, bifocals, black

overcoats, sensible shoes. And among them: the young couple with the infant in the Chicco stroller, the other young couple with the infant in the Chicco stroller, and then the inevitable kindergarten class sitting in a group in front of a Richter picture and gently chattering as they copy it. At last a little sound. But otherwise it is especially shuffling soles and quiet, knowledgeable conversation one hears – people discussing what they see, analysing, comparing. Some visitors have hung their overcoats in the cloakroom – they must be the serious ones."

The beautiful park over-looking the Øresund, tall soughing trees, peace and calm. These are the crown jewels. "At Louisiana," the founder said to the *New Yorker*, "we have tried to create a place of refuge, a sanctu-ary, a kind of Shangri-la."

19
90^s

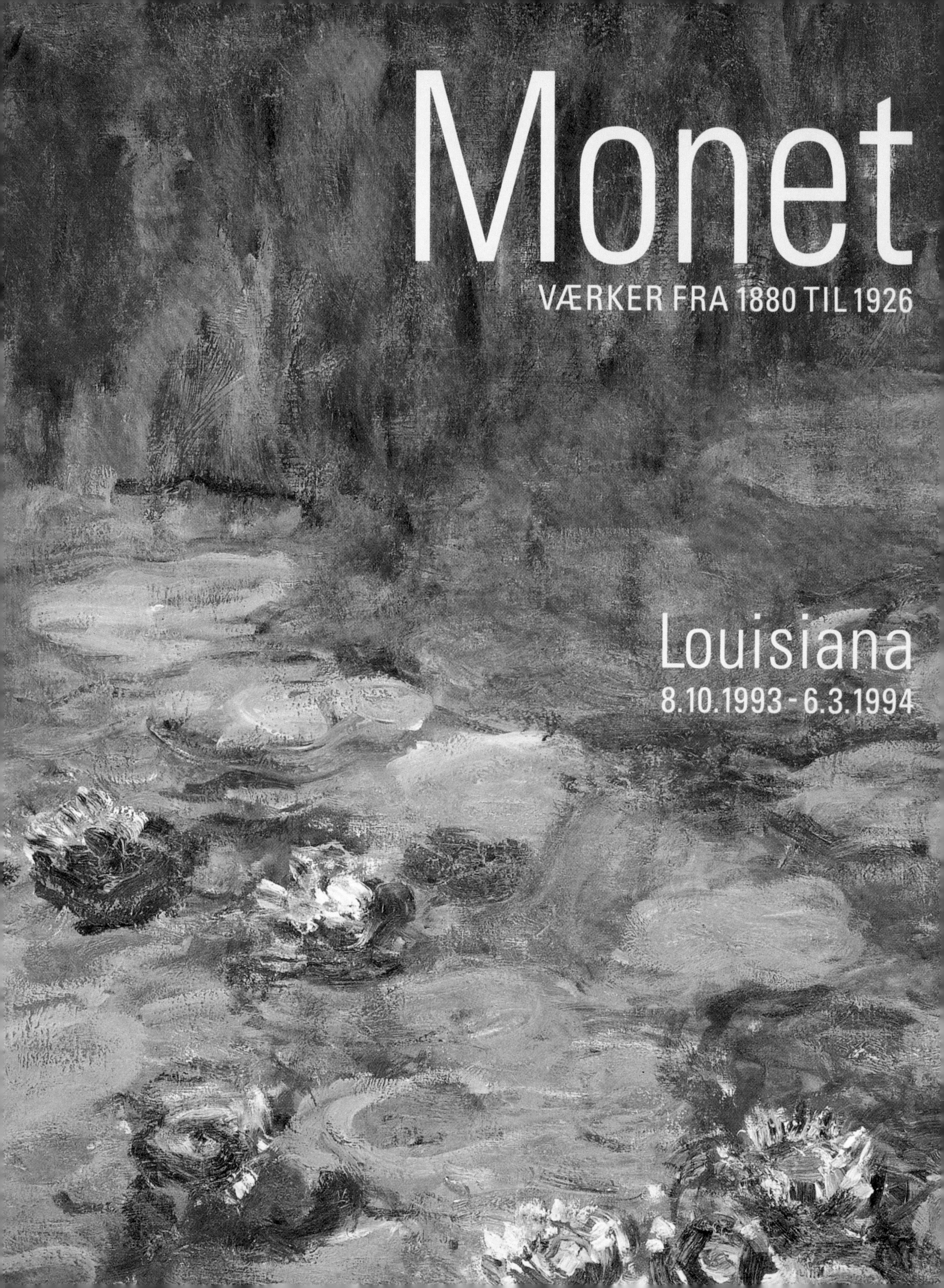

Monet

VÆRKER FRA 1880 TIL 1926

Louisiana

8.10.1993 - 6.3.1994

In the 1990s Louisiana Man sees his secure system crumble. For so many years the museum in Humlebæk has told him what is going on in art and given it names. And he has swotted up on constructivism and Russian avantgarde, De Stijl and Bauhaus, futurism and expressionism, land art and concept art, minimalism and pop art, new realism and happenings, action painting, informal painting, colour-field, monochromy, figuration, hard-edge, body art, arte povera, deconstructivism, video art, installation art and performance. Plus all the extras. He has really worked hard to keep things straight, has preserved every single issue of *Louisiana Revy* just in case he has nevertheless misunderstood something. And then it all disintegrates. No one will any longer assume the task of collecting art in a convenient ism or two. No one dares divide it up into handy trends and place the artists in groupings. Even Louisiana gives up and refuses to exert any authority. The isms have disappeared, so one must learn to swim oneself, even though it looks ungainly. There isn't one right way of doing things any longer

"The current art world is one big chaos," says art historian Jan Hoet from Documenta in Kassel in the Club's newsletter. The only small hints from Humlebæk are that "the clear trend towards pictures" from the 80s is continuing. That "the socio-critical" resembles a tendency in the midst of all the absence of tendency. That figuration has come to stay ("even though abstract, non-figurative art rejected all recognisable elements in the picture"). That the narrative is returning to art ("even though the story was for a long time excluded as reactionary, out of date and exhausted").

Knud W. Jensen sums up: "Today we are more open – it is no longer a matter of the hegemony of the various trends in abstract art!" Just look at Edward Hopper's success at Louisiana. He is a painter, he tells a story and he is figurative. There is no doubt that Louisiana loves just that combination, although there are other things at stake in the 90s. Installation art and video dominate. There are very few who paint compared with the 80s.

Knud W. Jensen is now called the grey eminence of the art world, Louisiana's grand old man. And even though Louisiana goes over board and acquires four videos from the young international art scene, in the year book for Danish art 97 he admits his scepticism towards the new genre and says that it is simply stupid having to zap one's way through 40-50 hours of video at an exhibition. He finds the new genre difficult to show and thinks in general that art is moving in a more elitist direction than in the preceding decades. He arranges "Picasso and the Mediterranean" for his own 80th birthday. A real painter!

At an exhibition of young Danish art in honour of Knud W. Jensen and Louisiana, arranged by René Block in Kassel in 1998, video, installations, photography and sound almost fill the whole exhibition. The artist group Superflex show their biogas equipment, which can transform the waste (shit) of an African family into energy. Many of the young artists could have come straight from the 70s. They don't display objects but make exhibitions that consist of sitting down and talking. They want to go out into society, participate, change, give aid to the developing world, get people to address one another and call it art. As in the 70s, there is suddenly something intangible called "social sculptures", formed by the public's reactions and participation. Social criticism is art. Debate is art. It is not always equally enjoyable to look at. Louisiana Man is close to confusing certain young Danish artists with a subsection of Doctors Without Borders.

It is a long way to Louisiana's painter heroes here, a long way to the visual, a long way to *seeing* the work. Uncompromising concept art has never been a source of strength or pleasure for Louisiana, and its broad public gives it a wide berth. At the end of the decade, Louisiana's new director Poul Erik Tøjner is quoted as saying that the problem with a lot of modern art is that it resembles all too much what we know: "The artists deliberately make social constructions, which, by being moved into an institution, are supposed to turn into art. This doesn't make it more difficult, but less challenging, and when the focus is on the institutional, it becomes tedious and formalistic for me."

But Per Kirkeby is still Per Kirkeby. He becomes more and more painter and more and more Louisiana's Danish world celebrity. In 1990 Louisiana Man sees his big retrospective exhibition at the museum, stands in front of the pictures and feels *the Kirkeby effect*, as described in *Louisiana Revy* by Peter Schjeldahl: "I connect it with the smell of newly dug earth, with the clamminess in damp woods, with a metallic taste in your mouth after too brief a sleep, with losing your way in a somehow familiar landscape, with the feeling of having forgotten something important (so important that it is unbearable at that moment to remember what it is). The effect is gloomy, indeed even threatening. But if you are patient, you experience a movement in its depths, the beginnings of a grateful joy."

At Humlebæk Station, Kirkeby constructs a monument for Louisiana, a structure in red, but there is no shelter, no protection in it. It merely stands there as a forewarning of the museum. On the platform, signboards it says "Louisiana" in slightly smaller letters than "Humlebæk."

It is as if eating was not discovered until the 1990s. Before that there were just meals – now what you eat reflects your identity. Louisiana Man eats salmon lasagne with spinach. He eats wild rice, he eats pasta. In the catalogue for the big Japan exhibition he regards with interest a photograph of "the Japanese national dish sushi". Humlebæk is strongly affected by this phenomenon, which is instrumentalised by the TV cook Claus Meyer. Gone are the bright red salami and the soft white bread of the old days, gone are the flat cheese sandwiches, the meat balls and the big plastic containers of potato salad. Even the Louisiana pretzel-formed cake is threatened. Suddenly, we are eating fricassee of Bornholm chicken with green asparagus from south Funen. Oxtails braised in Wibroe 1993 with root vegetables. Leg of Gascony duck with thyme and garlic.

The centre of the art world moves again – this time from New York to London and Berlin. Almost a half century earlier it moved from Paris to New York. That was just when Louisiana opened. People begin to use the word "global" in every other sentence. The world becomes one, and the artist's nationality means less and less. So long as he is at international level. Louisiana Man goes even further and like the rest of the population engages himself in data landscapes, fractals and chaos theories. Goes to Humlebæk and sees "On the Edge of Chaos" in 1993, which is about the new trends in the natural sciences, architecture and painting. Or to put it more cerebrally: about "disintegrated cultural systems and disintegrated ideas about art". The exhibition is one of the most ambitious projects in the Danish art world in the first half of the 90s. Oddly enough the museum isn't on the Internet yet, and when you book tickets, you are asked to enclose a stamped and addressed envelope with the check.

Other things on the edge of chaos: parking conditions at Louisiana, the queue for the cafeteria.

Monet and the money

The idea for Louisiana's biggest success ever, the Monet exhibition in 1993, came to the museum from outside, from an otherwise unthinkable source, and to start with this French golden egg rolled into a slightly sceptical Knud W. Jensen. He didn't think that Monet was anything for Louisiana. A painter born in 1840 was too old for a museum of modern art with a focus on the postwar period. But the unthinkable source insisted and continued to work on and soften up the museum. For its own sake. The source was McKinsey & Company, the international consultancy firm, which in addition to drawing up and presenting a strategic plan for the museum also gave some advice far from its customary field of activity: "Show Monet!" McKinsey was at the museum to write a report that could basically have been entitled: "The problem of generational change at Louisiana" and "How to make more money and survive in a tough business." But anyway: "Show Monet!"

If Louisiana was to retain and reinforce its position in the 1990s as a prominent Scandinavian art museum, its organisation, management and earnings had to be strengthened. Monet was about earnings. And the semi-blind bearded painter

Monet painting being installed. He became the museum's greatest success ever. "We had to close the main entrance and tell
people that they could only come in when others went out," said
one member of the staff. Some visitors asked for their money
back as they couldn't see the pictures. And they got it.

eople hated this new art museum

from Giverny proved to be good at that. "Claude Monet. Works from 1880 to 1926" was stormed by the public – almost half a million people in five months. From early morning, they formed a queue stretching from the main entrance out onto the side road, round the corner and spilling out onto the main road. At the station one saw huge crowds of people getting off the train and on again later, each with a carrier bag with the water lily poster. Many had never set foot in Louisiana before. In no time, the varnish was worn off the parquet floor in the old villa, and every day the beautiful place bore the ravages after thousands of visitors. Knud W. Jensen took a Sunday bike ride in the neighbourhood and counted 11 tourist buses, and the ladies from the ticket sales ran down to the main office with cardboard boxes filled with bank notes. The museum feared that the windows in the glass corridor could not take the pressure and began to limit the numbers that were let in. The Italian president Scalfaro was given a five-minute start ahead of the 4,000 other visitors, and shortly after his arrival they were cheerfully mingling with the distinguished party from Southern Europe while the Italian security men looked on in concern.

The museum's "excuse" for Monet was that he inspired so many modern painters, for example Knud W. Jensen's favourite artist Sam Francis, whose enormous colouristic paintings hung in the concert hall and elsewhere at Louisiana:

"Today, there is no doubt that with his ground-breaking paintings from the Giverny period Monet has contributed to creating the very foundation for modern art. The water lily paintings in particular play a significant role here, but also the colouristic, very dramatic, almost abstract pictures from the garden painted at the same time as the panels for the Orangerie anticipated aspects of painting after 1950," Louisiana wrote in the catalogue. "Thus, the exhibition finds a natural place in the sequence of Louisiana's presentations of the great masters of modern art."

When the staff arrived in the morning, Louisiana smelled of duck, and when they went home, it smelled of duck. Grilled French legs of duck, *Monet-style*. The café sold 3.2 tons of them. "I don't think I have ever eaten them since," says one guide. Two people did nothing but roll up posters all day long. They crossed the counter more quickly than hot loaves. The shop manager had suggested printing three posters, but the new growth-oriented master of business studies 28-year-old Bo Bjerggaard was quite fearless: "No bloody way – we'll have nine!" He had 10,000 of each printed, some of which had to be reprinted, and filled the house with Monet merchandise to an extent never before seen in Denmark. At Louisiana, too, Monet set off tremors throughout the organisation. "We had to get used to the idea of being popular," says one member of staff. The nausea and the

indignation were particularly linked with the Monet red wine (Lussac Saint-Émilion 1990) and the Monet cookery book, but the Monet playing cards and the Monet apron evoked similar reactions. Young Bjerggaard occupied a newly established McKinsey-inspired post as information and activities chief. At that time, not even Louisiana dared to call things by their right name: the man was director of marketing, but that sounded a bit ugly in connection with art. His job was to get more visitors, more money. Each single one of the 38 oil paintings exhibited had come from France, the USA and Japan to Louisiana in a specially built temperature-regulated wooden crate, each accompanied by its own courier who had travelled with it from start to finish. A lot of water had passed under the bridge since the director of the art museum in Basel, Otto Fischer, had in the 1930s called the water-lily pictures in the Orangerie in Paris "a completely intolerable aquarium". The insurance premium was a nightmare. Some of the pictures were valued at 40 million dollars and cost Louisiana several hundred thousand kroner to borrow. Then there were the attendants, who had to be placed everywhere. That sort of thing costs money. Two years of intense preparations costs. Travel in Europe, the USA and Japan costs. Doubling the number of employees from 120 to 240 costs. Staying open 61 hours a week costs. Not being allowed to speak about money in connection with art could therefore very easily seem unnatural.

During the Monet exhibition the house was filled with artist merchandise, and nobody had ever seen anything like it in Denmark.

"If you knew the sort of junk one can obtain for a Monet exhibition," Bjerg-gaard said to a critical journalist. "But there we're very rigorous, I think, in reject-ing stuff." He presented a selection of the big museums' Monet horrors that Louisiana had not procured. The museum had *nothing* in comparison with the profusion of authorised Monet accessories on the market. But all the same. On notice boards round about in the museum hung an article with the headline "Monet and the money", in which *Weekendavisen* wrote satirically about Louisi-ana's water-lily souvenirs. No one at the museum forgot it. They still mention it with a giggle, because, intriguingly, it had been written Poul Erik Tøjner, who later became director of the museum and soon adopted a quite different and more positive attitude to the indispensable income from the café and shop.

Seen in an international perspective Humlebæk conducted itself with tact and discretion, but it nevertheless made a sensation in Denmark. Monet broke all bounds, heavily underlining the revolution that was under way at Danish muse-ums. Any museum with respect for itself and its customers now had a café, sold books and postcards, ran an association of friends or a club, and rented out localities to business enterprises. Gone was the image of the museum as a sanctuary that maintains the opposition between art and money; the image of the museum as an experiential forum of an exclusive nature," as Tøjner wrote.

Some people hated this new art museum, this "supermarket for elite cul-ture", as Mai Misfeldt called Louisiana in *Information*. She complained of not being able to catch sight of Monet himself among the perfume and fur and "a confused public" constantly checking their watches in order to make it to the cartoon film, the cafeteria and the Turkish bazaar. Art historian Morten Lerhard poked fun at the biscuit tin art and "the idiot culture" of the mid-90s, when some art museums had to be reassessed on the premises of the entertainment industry: "No one is called to answer for the populism that with visitor figures as the most important motive prevails at the art museums," he thought and like all other critics in this field felt that he was able to see through the big, stupid public that streams in when conformist museums show expensive masterpieces, but without going into any depth with them. Without really understanding.

This sort of thing always made Knud W. Jensen angry. Since 1958 he had lent his ear to the complaints of the elite about *the others'* wrong and "isolated" art experiences. He was accustomed to the wrinkled noses of the art historical republic every time the museums suddenly had too many visitors:

"All this talk reminds me of the complaints of the bourgeoisie and "the individual traveller" when the travel agencies began to send every Tom, Dick and Harry to the South. I just think that it's a really good thing that everyone has a chance of a holiday in the sun with cheap booze!"

Children

When Louisiana opened in 1958, people noticed a little room to the left of the main entrance. It was a drawing and painting room called "The Children's Museum" At that time, it was not just a good idea – it was impressive, different and the first in the country:

"If you want to get rid of your not always terribly art-hungry offspring for a time, a laboratory has been set up for the next generation, who with classical models on the walls can occupy themselves directly with the elements in the form of water colours and coloured pencils. The rest of us may be allowed to admire the lovely model study by Karl Isaksen, which shows the way into the collection," wrote Erik Clemmesen from *Kristeligt Dagblad* on the opening day, and *Berlingske Aftenavis* also praised "the new and entertaining form of museum at which visiting children can freely work with paints and hobby materials and cover the walls with their products."

But in the course of the years, Knud W. Jensen became less and less satisfied with the Children's Museum as he gradually realised how it could be done with a real investment of interest and effort. The painting room functioned respectably as parking and to mitigate the worst boredom for the smaller children, but it was not on a level with anything that he dreamed of: "We give the children a piece of paper and some oil crayons – an easy way out. Art basically bores children even though they can often be brought to say something nice about it or indeed something brilliant. After all they so much want to please us. In reality they probably don't get much out of going to an art museum before their teens."

There was something of a child about him. His niece Hanne Engberg relates that already as a young man he liked to talk with children. With him you could cross the railway tracks and go into people's gardens, and if you met anyone, he talked with them and charmed them. Out on a walk, he found the twins Leif and Lydia for his sister's children, who had just moved to a town in the provinces and had no playmates. They were friends for years. A typical and early feature of Knud W. Jensen's character was that he always hit upon something. If things were becoming a bit sluggish at the big family get-togethers, he would dissipate the boredom in some way. His restlessness released a constant attention directed towards what one could now think of doing. New experiences, new adventures, new people. Having ideas before anyone else was also embedded in his business instinct.

When the old drawing and painting room began to look a bit tired in his eyes at the end of the 1970s, he began to to read Danish and foreign books about playgrounds and to study what had been done elsewhere – from Disneyland in Los Angeles (unpoetic) via Legoland (OK) to Brændesgårdshaven on Bornholm (wonderful) – so when the UN's Year of the Child was approaching Louisiana

The first children's museum, inaugurated with coloured pencils and watercolours in 1958. Children are the most difficult task a museum has, Knud W. Jensen wrote later.

This mysterious "other people"

pulled out all the stops and opened "Children are a People" in 1978. The museum learned what children think is fun and not fun. There was a grass-clad Volvo, a huge womb one could go into, and a big flying apparatus with wings. The lake garden's aerial ropeways, climbing trees, rope bridges and ferry across the lake taught the museum that children prefer to have physical challenges, to use their strength, and have many choices.

Once the wish for a special place for the 60,000 children who visit the museum every year had been registered in Knud W. Jensen's idea bank, he set about realising it. In the first place, there was only one good place left on which to build – a 55-degree slope down towards Humlebæk Lake next to the Giacometti room. Secondly, it would cost a bomb. Claus Wohlert, son of the Louisiana architect Vilhelm Wohlert, solved the first problem by placing an organically swung building in three storeys outside on the existing buildings, so the children could go directly from the museum into the top floor of the Children's House and out to the lake from the ground floor. Two generous foundations solved the second problem with large donations.

The Children's House opened on 16th September 1994 and was so delectable that it immediately evoked criticism from child culture bigwigs and researchers in a direct broadcast on the radio. What did children need such luxurious surroundings for? With architect-designed furniture? With heating under the Asian wooden floors? With that modernistic style that didn't seem all that child-friendly? The critics feared that there wasn't room for the children, and that they would just be window dressing among all that exquisite taste. In their view the Children's House was nothing but play and storage, that the Lego blocks proved that Louisiana was not serious. The new departure was pursued by criticism in the beginning – and by the chaos that ensues from success. Once again, Knud W. Jensen had hit the bull's eye, revealing an enormous need, for Louisiana was swamped. The House had mainly been intended for Club members; no one had thought of schools, kindergartens and youth clubs. And they arrived in awe-inspiring numbers, ten to twenty institutions a day. Adults also wanted to see the new Children's House in such numbers that the staff had to position themselves at the top and bottom doors and refuse them admission. There were days with 500 children and the House was only manned between 10 a.m. and 2 p.m. The staff began to seem bad-tempered and desperate. There were

▶ Vilhelm Wohlert's son Claus designed the new children's house as a chrysalis clinging to the mother museum, here seen from the woodland lake.

▶ Too beautifully finished for children? The critics were in doubt.

half-eaten sandwiches and sandwich paper everywhere, and it had not been foreseen that the exciting blackboard landscape with its projecting corners would be used to slide down instead of to draw on, and the staff said secret prayers when the children landed with an eye just next to a dangerous point. Something quite essential was missing: calm and a door to close, but neither were present. After only one month the institutions had to book in advance, and the staff discovered that they had to conduct activities with the children. This was in conflict with the founder's innermost convictions.

He was persuaded that children can manage everything themselves and he did *not* want the Children's House to become a kind of school and yet another authority in the endless sequence that children have to encounter. Therefore, he would not accept any teaching either. The children could meet living artists and learn their techniques, and in the breaks they could draw and paint. But it developed into a drawing and painting room along the previous lines: Here you deposit your umbrella, here your overcoat and here your child. Knud W. Jensen was enormously interested in the Children's House, but his view of children – and perhaps also of artists – was romantic. Not all the artists who passed by

The interior changes with the changing exhibitions.

284

were equally good at communicating, and too few came. And not all children
could sit down without being encouraged to do so and create sparkling original
works.

Knud W. Jensen's view on children can in a way briefly be described as reminiscent of Enid Blyton's "The Five": campfires and twistbread and autonomous
children that are best off in their own world without any corrupting interference
from grown-ups. He believed in this mysterious "other people" and their ability
to produce art intuitively. When he came round to look at their pottery, he was
delighted, for he and Jean Arp had spoken about casting the children's clay figures in bronze. Together with many others from their generation they believed
that children have an artistic ur-idiom that grown-ups spoil with their control of
everything. Knud W. Jensen was afraid that the children would be infected, and
he vehemently opposed the staff's proposal that the children should do sketches
while being shown round the museum. "Imitation," he said dismissively. But he
became wiser. When the House held its fifth birthday, he was as always present in his blue Mao shirt. He confessed that he himself had once enjoyed doing
sketches in Rome. That was a start.

Ideologically, the Children's House has changed substantially since its open-ing. Whereas Knud W. Jensen thought that the children spend their time as they wished, they are today out in the museum with drawing-board and pencil first and only then inside the Children's House working with the materials themselves. "The other people" have been integrated. They learn something, but the word school is still banned at Louisiana. Children don't *have* to do anything when they come. If they want to doodle on a piece of paper, that's OK, but the Children's House would like to inspire them to produce something with a point of departure in the art, for instance in Louise Bourgeois' spiders, Giacometti's figures or Norman Foster' skyscrapers, and there must be a possibility of obtaining help. In accordance with Knud W. Jensen's generous spirit, his wish to give children the best of everything, there is no rationing of paper or clay. If a child takes 30 pieces of paper, so be it.

A teenage class can be difficult to open, and the Children's House loses the children when they turn 12 or 13. They become afraid of the materials, of the assignments and that they can't make proper pictures. They become afraid because their awareness that there are right and wrong pictures grows. Perhaps Louisiana will not see the children again until 20 years later when they stand with crossed arms during a guided tour for fear of 1) making fools of themselves and/ or 2) of being fooled. But if they have once sat on silk cushions on Arne Jacob-sen's little black Ant Chairs and heard Humlebæk grandparents tell stories or produced American pop art themselves, there may possibly still be a way in and the art may not appear so frightening.

Everyone wants to be Louisiana

In the decade in which Knud W. Jensen turns 80 and Louisiana 40, there is no doubt about who is wearing the trousers in the Danish museum world: Louisiana has won – catastrophically, some people think. There are simply far too many imitators who in their eagerness to copy Humlebæk's success stuff their muse-ums with "experiences". Certain artists and critics miss the nerdy museum, and in an editorial *Politiken* writes that Louisiana was a much needed and outstanding counter-reaction to the museal traditions, but:

"Today, almost 40 years after the first tentative start, everyone wants to be Louisiana. No one wants to be – oh, horror – an "institution". And then Louisi-ana's triumphal progress begins to be destructive. For the truth is, of course that Louisiana's success has very little to do with the museum's permanent collec-tion – and everything to do with the spectacular succession of exhibitions from Chagall to Monet, from Mexico to Pompeii. The picture as an event, a destination for an excursion, total experience with drive along the sea, queues, coffee and cakes – this is the essence of Louisiana culture – and there is no cause to think

Women picnick-ing in company with Henri Laurens' 'Large Standing Woman With Cloth' (1928).

Birthday party. When the rebel Louisiana turned 40, the other Danish museums had long since begun to copy it, and new museums like Arken and Trapholt placed themselves in its slipstream. Since 1960 all museum construction and activity have had to relate to Louisiana's practice.

Louisiana 40 years of age. None of the confused struggles that took place behind the walls leaked out to the public.

badly of it. But when this culture becomes universal, also at the museums that have other obligations and tasks, then it begins to do damage."

Here the newspaper is thinking of a desperate *Statens Museum for Kunst* clad in fashion-designer Erik Mortensen's dresses to attract people to the house. (Bubber's Picture Bingo, the sales exhibition for Georg Jensen silver and the religious services with well-known public figures are still to come). But already in 1996 *Politiken* thinks Louisiana is making itself felt in places where it has no business to be. When museums across the country lose their interest in the thorough long-term work on research and the collections in favour of media stunts, Humlebæk has conquered too much territory. *Politiken's* congratulations to Knud W. Jensen on his 80th birthday are therefore spiced with an invitation to everyone else to stick to their last and not try to follow Louisiana. "Anyway no one can come close to imitating Jensen."

To use a later director's phrase, Louisiana has a *disgustingly* good press. When Louisiana's monopoly was finally broken, and competitors appeared in the shape of Arken (1996) and a strongly expanded *Statens Museum for Kunst* (1998), both were inevitable compared with Louisiana, but nowhere were they declared to be winners, neither for architecture nor for content. Not even though they opened with a fully evolved Louisiana concept: café, bookstore, children's museum, special fares, membership club and multi-purpose room. Also called culture comfort.

At the beginning of the 90s, *Statens Museum for Kunst* is still seen as "The Sleeping Museum", also when it isn't. The two previous museum directors Leo Swane and Jørn Rubow, who together headed the museum for almost 50 years, gave it a dusty/exclusive image: the museum was for those who were already interested. The public was not to be enticed with special exhibitions and sensations. But even though Rubow left the museum at the end of the 1970s, the museum was met with an ingrown scepticism and automatic yawns. That develops a sense of martyrdom.

"I am quite convinced that the selfsame Edward Hopper exhibition, which had such a great success at Louisiana, would not have attracted nearly as many visitors if we had held it. Hopper was previously fairly unknown in Denmark, but the mere fact that it was Louisiana that showed him was a guarantee of quality," protested museum inspector Kasper Monrad in 1992. And although Allis Helleland as director set a quite different and innovative course from any of her predecessors, she also felt that she was a victim: "After all it's an old tradition. *Statens Museum* is just there to be criticised, and Louisiana is there to be praised."

But perhaps the historical explanation was not the only one. As long as Knud W. Jensen was in doubt, one heard nothing from him. The museum closed itself hermetically around bad stories, internal conflict, fiascos. Only when everything was all right, would he bounce out of the museum and tell the press about the latest visitors' record, an impressive acquisition, an important donation, gifts from American millionaires, a new indispensable extension of the museum, or how Louisiana had miraculously bagged yet another Picasso exhibition. There was always something *first* and *biggest* about Humlebæk.

When *Statens Museum for Kunst* did something, it was criticised. When Bjørn Nørgaard's sculpture "The Human Wall" in front of the entrance was removed, it was a problem. When the Parisian dresses were shown, it was a problem. The way in which the collection hung was a problem. The management was always a problem. Internal conflicts leaked to the press every time. The house was so accustomed to being given a pasting that in 1998 it promoted itself after the huge extension building via a bizarre campaign in which the museum tried to give the media's malevolent art and architecture reviewers the blame for the unceasing criticism: "HM the Queen will open the museum on 5th November. Henrik Sten Møller/Torben Weirup/Poul Erik Tøjner will close the museum on 6th November. *Statens Museum for Kunst* ... we shall see." Also this attempt at museal state irony fell to the ground, as the media criticised the campaign for being defensive, libellous, provincial, elitist, populist and unserious.

Helleland also lost in the Matisse Affair in 2005, when her museum put a little exhibition with nine paintings by the French master on its programme at exactly the same time as Louisiana launched a huge exhibition based on solid research and 150 late works borrowed from all over the world. *Statens Museum for Kunst* was taking a free ride on the back of Louisiana's big initiative, wrote *Politiken*, and found a name for Helleland's new invention – a parasite exhibition – and went on to intensify the humiliation: "And it must be frustrating to be Allis Helleland. Up north in Humlebæk there stands a museum that succeeds in all that it touches. The architecture is masterly, the press is usually enthusiastic, and the public pour in to nearly all the exhibitions. It's quite different at *Statens Museum for Kunst*."

▶ Niels Barfoed guides the fatwa-threatened Salman Rushdie down the corridor to a secret meeting in the boat house in 1992.

▶ The Swedish actor Ernst-Hugo Järegård presents his personal view of Picasso in the concert hall.

▶ Swedish writer Per Olov Enquist, Danish poet Søren Ulrik Thomsen and Norwegian writer Erik Fosnes Hansen at an arrangement. Partly via its ownership of Denmark's largest publishing firm Gyldendal Louisiana had a strong connection with literature.

▶ In 1990 and 1993 the pianist David Helfgott played for ecstatic audiences.

Politiken's art critic Peter Michael Hornung once explained the difference between the two museums with reference to Knud W. Jensen:

"Since Louisiana opened in 1958, it has had the same top leader, who was also the person who built up the museum from scratch. This provides the background for a quite different kind of administrative continuity and effective management. The institution has been able to gather experience for more than 35 years, experience in being Louisiana in optimal fashion," he wrote. In the same period *Statens Museum for Kunst* had been on varying courses with four very different directors, who all wanted to change everything. "From the ringside we have seen that every time a new leader was to be found for the museum, it had to be one who was as different as possible from his or her predecessor. Now the patience of the cultural-political circles was exhausted. Now something radically new had to happen in Sølvgade."

This sort of thing creates confusion. What was unthinkable under one director, is absolutely thinkable under the next. What one will in no circumstance have under his roof is welcomed by the next. This weakens confidence in the museum and scares off generous collectors. "As the situation is today, Louisiana appears to be despite its much shorter history Denmark's most self-assured and professional institution," Hornung concluded. Louisiana acted as a unified organism, a total organism.

That none of the confused wars contested at Louisiana in the 1990s seeped out to the public was partly because everyone in the museum remained loyally silent, partly because the media didn't think of looking for scandals there, and partly because Knud W. Jensen was good at controlling his and his museum's public image.

No one else had the right to make decisions. If some people nevertheless worked in considerable freedom, this was because they moved within the limits of the spirit of the place. People who were not themselves able to sense or accept the founder's limits got along badly. When Niels Birger Wamberg refused to remove Knud W. Jensen's characteristic swear words from their joint conversation book, "Mens kunsten er ung" [While Art is Young] (1992), silence descended between them. And McKinsey found it a problem that Knud W. Jensen always did precisely what he wanted to. That he didn't respect rules, that he changed decisions that had already been made and put people to work on projects when it suited him, and that he was at the centre of the organisation, a point to which every one else had to refer. "We all already knew that. We didn't need McKinsey to know that," says a member of the staff for 30 years. "But Knud couldn't change himself – that's how he was. We put up with it because the good result always came in the end."

Knud W. Jensen was a kind and friendly boss, always present where things were happening. Whether it was Blixen or Rifbjerg, he'd be on the spot.

The daily round

"This is Knud!" he said on the phone early one summer morning. "What does one do about dandelions in the lawn?" It was 6 a.m. and he had called the home of one of his employees, who had been woken up by his little child four times during the night. That was not the sort of thing that Knud W. Jensen recognised. He found it strangely half-hearted when one of the new art historians asked not to be disturbed during his holiday. So did the more long-serving members of staff. That was not how one worked at Louisiana.

"Hello. This is Knud! I hope I'm not disturbing you in the middle of your supper?" he asked another.

"We've just sat down," was the answer.

"I'll keep it short," he replied and did not ring off until long after the food had got cold. Conversation was his way of purging his ideas. Often he would ring from his own office to the office next door. "This is Knud! Come in a moment and see something amazingly exciting," he would say to a person heading for home with his overcoat on. This was also the fashion in which he approached the foundations, which couldn't get themselves to reject him either. Under everything that he said and did lay the conviction that this particular thing would be fantastic. People liked the place and they liked him. They were ready to work for him.

One of Louisiana's sponsors, the natural gas company DONG, wished to present the museum with an expensive specially designed gas lamp for the park, but Knud W. Jensen had calculated that there was room for 18, and if DONG laid pipes down everywhere in the park, the lamps could be switched on at the same time from the same switch. The gas pipes were laid.

He was a curious man, who lived off his curiosity all his life. A strange combination of a man of the moment and a man with strong connecting links to the future. He thought in possibilities, not in problems. The method consisted of not being able to see uncomfortably far ahead. He "forgot" that after each extension came larger operating costs, but built "and we'll see what happens". To his board he often reported a smaller figure that would be more readily accepted. The building projects *always* ended up by exceeding their budgets. The cost of the subterranean graphics wing was set at 37 million but soared to more than 50 million. A hole of that size put board members in a cold sweat, but Knud W. Jensen covered the excess expenditure via the foundations. "We owe the board of the Augustinus Foundation many thanks because they have now (again) rescued the old museum and myself," he wrote to his own board in 1990, when the Foundation gave 10 million on top of the already granted 10 million.

Many people around him felt the urge to restrain such wildness, but Louisiana's importance and position today are due to the very fact that he did not sit

View from the museum.

down in his white villa with his collection of Danish paintings and say that that had to be enough. Things went well, but they could have gone wrong. Denmark profited from the fact that he was unrealistic. "Danish artistic life would be *nothing* without Louisiana. The museum moves at a high international level," says artist Erik Steffensen. And the director of Arken Christian Gether has said that Knud W. Jensen simply taught the Danes to go to museums. As a child Mikkel Bogh, now rector of the Royal Academy of Fine Arts, obtained his first experience of 20th century art at Louisiana, where his parents were members and frequent visitors. He remembers the bombardment of big, beautiful colour pictures in *Louisiana Revy* at a time when the country otherwise seemed strangely pictureless. At Louisiana, he had the feeling of a larger, more generous space, where what mattered was art and nothing else.

In his last decade, Knud W. Jensen built the Graphics Wing with Vilhelm Wohlert as architect, and as soon as the comprehensive and complicated work was completed in 1991 and Wohlert totally exhausted, the indefatigable founder presented his idea for a children's house in three storeys clinging to the main building like an organic chrysalis. At this time, only five months had passed since Wilhelm Wohlert concluded his opening lecture on the Graphics Wing with a polemic "and what now?" He didn't have the energy to gets to grips straight-away with a new project, so the task passed on to his son, Claus Wohlert, whose Children's House opened in 1994. The expansion of the shop plus the broad white marble stairs down to a new, airy basement floor were ready for the museum's 40th anniversary four years later. And that same year, Knud W. Jensen also found time to get the Høst Museum in Gudhjem up and running. He was now 81 years. Afterwards he concentrated the remainder of his energy on erecting a building for architecture on the beach – it would have been his ninth extension in 40 years.

At heart he was at least just as interested in architecture as in art, perhaps more so. Loved special places, views, atmosphere, light. He consistently went in for the idea of building the architecture of our day, also in the most lovely parts of the landscape that the conservationists always wanted to protect. "I am against uncreative conservation orders – let's rather build something beautiful and useable and thus connect nature with the works of man," he wrote to an acquaintance and would like to have seen the Lake Pavilion in Copenhagen torn down and replaced by public swimming baths designed by Utzon. Down with the New Stage of the Royal Theatre "it's not even *good* art deco" and up with some-thing new. He paid profound attention to detail – for the sake of the whole. The details had to be *right*, for everything can be sensed, noted.

At a job interview for a manager of the shop, he lifted his spoon and said: "You will have to be able to see whether a teaspoon like this one is worth having

Now Louisiana can't get any bigger. In the middle stands the old villa with the main entrance. The old wing from 1958 is on the right and the South Wing from 1982 is on the left. The subterranean Graphics Wing can in the nature of things not be seen.

at Louisiana." And when the big grey granite stairway down to the sea was completed at the beginning of the 90s, he was not satisfied until he had had the edges rounded – for a small fortune. Otherwise, the steps wouldn't be comfortable to sit on – they would cut into the backs of one's knees.

At the opening of "Workshops of Architecture: Frank Gehry" in November 1998 a guest at the reception put his foot in it. Inspired by the relaxed atmosphere the man knocked on his glass to obtain silence for a few improvised words. It felt good to be in the high-ceilinged, rebuilt boathouse and he praised Louisiana for showing Gehry. At last some elite culture. The phrase triggered an outburst of rage from Knud W. Jensen, who weighed into him in front of all the guests. Enormously embarrassing. Later the unfortunate man tried to explain, but Knud W. Jensen wouldn't listen to him. Without suspecting it the man had run head-on into Knud W. Jensen's hatred of that particular term. That was not what he thought he was showing at his museum. What he was showing was just quality, the best. And he detested the discrimination that the concept operated with. When he received the Adam Elsheimer Prize at the opening of Art Frankfurt in 1993, the speech in his honour emphasised this very reluctance to impose anything at all on anyone:

"In his museum no one is to be instructed with a raised forefinger; no one is to be subjected to pressure or made to feel like an ignorant philistine, but on the contrary the visitor is given the opportunity through play to experience the multiplicity and beauty of art," the German collector Rolf Hoffmann had said. And then someone came and told Knud W. Jensen to his face and at his own museum that he showed elite culture. His credo was that art should not be allowed to disappear into a ghetto, but now and again it nevertheless slipped between his legs and into the ghetto. *Louisiana Revy* can be a ghetto of incomprehensibility, a wilderness of jabberwocky, an elite cultural trap. From the first issue in 1961 to the most recent, one can find small pockets of elitist writing that are clearly not accessible to or intended for all. Unfortunate texts remind one of malicious but funny parodies of art criticism with their opaque references to "Goya's slumbering rationality" "Braque's prismatic cubism".

Difficulties often occur when an individual painting is to be interpreted, for instance Sigmar Polke's "Apparizione", whose forms are "as it were being worked

The public relax by the entrance to the Graphics Wing. "I can't remember ever being without plans for the future," said one of the museum's architects Jørgen Bo in the mid-80s.

"No one is mac

o feel like an ignorant philistine"

Sigmar Polke's 'Apparizione' releases "almost religious feelings, sensations of being close to something sublime, of seeing the world come into being, of being exposed to the radiation field of the numinous," the museum suggests in an interpretation of the work. Not for beginners.

out, emerge and disappear, assume new shapes, allow us to dwell in depths, wander through portals, be met by fabulous beings, by enigmatic glances; they let us float around in blue infinitude, whirl around in a pounding red dynamic or be met by the alien, the burlesque other that laughs its mocking, secretive, challenging and slightly scary laughter." But that is not all. More is expected, for the picture also releases "almost religious feelings, sensations of being close to something sublime, of seeing the world come into being, of being exposed to the radiation field of the numinous."

This sort of thing creates high expectations among the public who three days later stand staring at "Apparizione" – and see and feel nothing of all this. Not only is there museum fatigue, but there is also museum anxiety because a reaction has to be produced in front of the works. Enigmas must be solved, an understanding arrived at. That's what people believe anyway.

In its introduction to "New Art from Denmark and Scania" the museum tried to explain what the world looked like in the year of grace 1997:

"The world does not appear to the same extent as formerly as a linear relation between delimited temporalities and spatialities, but on the contrary as a network with simultaneously existing, rapidly changing nodal points formed by the relations and contacts one establishes mentally, socially and physically. Whether one lives in Cologne, Copenhagen or Katrineholm is increasingly unimportant. The decisive factor is how one makes use of the possibilities of navigating freely between the global and the local. That many people for a time bind themselves locally in a nodal point does not therefore mean that they cut themselves off from the rest of the world, but on the contrary that a temporary concentration of meaning is established in the network's horizontal structure – a concentration of meaning that on an equal footing with other local nodal points now necessarily attracts far greater interest than the formerly hierarchically fixed centres can do. For the same reason there is very great international attention directed at what is taking place at the new regional nodal points. It is probably here that art – like so much else – is occurring."

It requires a determined reader – and probably at least a higher education – to work one's way through *Louisiana Revy* on one of its bad days. And this at a museum that is often accused of being popular. Also under Poul Erik Tøjner Louisiana's writers are now again punked for being incomprehensible and for other sins that beset academics. His defence is that painting is a special experience that cannot simply and exhaustively be translated into another medium: "To pretend that one can write simply about art is just dishonest," he writes in the members' magazine. "Art has to do – no matter how we put it – with frontier-seeking formulations. Art seeks new country, a new language, a new idiom, and

it is probably rather naïve to imagine that the interpreter – of all people – should stand at the end of the rainbow with his language already clarified."

It is for this reason that the reader continues to encounter fantastic descriptions of a work. It may be "radically hesitant and heroically thoughtful", or it may cohere "like a novelistic prism", or it may "throw off sad associations with painless duplications, imitativeness and other soulless activity".

In the 1990s Louisiana entered, for the first time, into a phase in which new blood was called for. People who did not belong to the self-elective Louisiana. People who were not old business contacts, schoolmates, friends, friends of friends, children of friends or other enthusiasts who had slowly risen through the hierarchy and received their training there. There was a need for specialists, even art historians. The McKinsey year, 1991,was a new beginning for Louisiana, a kind of normalisation process in which the museum signalled to the Ministry of Culture and the other museums that it was professional. That it was like the others. One of the art historians did not feel convinced that in reality the museum felt respect for the art-historical museal world, since already in the 1970s Louisiana was at a level that the other museums had not yet reached in the 1990s. The others were dependent on grants while Louisiana was almost self-supporting. This underpinned a strong sense of self-esteem in Humlebæk.

The first team of art historians lasted little more than a year. The next not much longer. On the one hand, they felt like henchmen in a centrally controlled organisation and got into conflict with Steingrim Laursen, who in the opinion of many exercised an old-fashioned authoritative form of leadership at the level just below Knud W. Jensen. The leadership structure crumbled because the founder was trying to delegate and withdraw although the right replacement had not yet been found. On the other hand, there was the usual gap between "unschooled" Louisiana and the academically trained art historians, whose ideas were now and then too highbrow in relation to the museum's culture and they themselves too namby-pamby for its commercial and practical activities. Suddenly accreditations and titles began to be important because the new staff wanted to have their academic degrees on their business cards, which upset those who had for decades been arranging exhibitions without. Louisiana exhibited a brilliant facade and concealed a less brilliant rear in the 1990s: while the public rooms presented exhibitions of outstanding international artists, behind the scenes savage battles were taking place for power over the place.

Generation change I

Knud W. Jensen had long since passed the age limit of 70 that applied to everyone else in the institution and its board, but not to the founder, the solo dancer, the top figure in Louisiana's friendly, but solidly established hierarchy. Every one had to refer to him – it wasn't particularly modern. Already in 1991, McKinsey pointed out the acute need to have a replacement ready. So one spring day in 1994 40-year-old Swedish Lars Nittve received an approach from Louisiana. Would he be prepared to enter the museum's leadership. He would head the beloved Danish destination of his childhood excursions together with the experienced exhibition curator Steingrim Laursen, who for decades had learnt the names of the major collectors' children and dogs by heart in order to be able to procure the great modern classics for Humlebæk. It was said that if he couldn't sweet talk a work of two out of a hard tried, much pursued collector, no one could. And Knud W. Jensen, whom Nittve had always observed and admired from a distance, would also have a small role. To be realistic the two elderly gentlemen would have only a few years left at the head of Denmark's most visited art museum.

But Lars Nittve ended by declining. The mandate was not acceptable. If he was to be director, he wanted to be alone in the post and have the final responsibility himself. As Øystein Hjort had put it many years previously, he wanted to have his artistic freedom. Like Hjort, Nittve didn't fancy having someone looking over his shoulder, especially not in a one-man show like Louisiana, which had not only seen the light of day as Knud W. Jensen's private museum, but simply *was* Knud W. Jensen. The two of them had long ago merged into a single organism. Where one began and the other ended could not be discerned with the naked eye.

So Nittve remained as director of Rooseum in Malmø, where his task was to establishing an internationally hot exhibition institution, an uncompromising and exclusive Mecca for art in a provincial corner of Sweden. He was good at it. He succeeded in creating a Scandinavian forum for young or at least youngish art and "in creating waves abroad", which in translation means that international journals feel impelled to write about one's exhibitions. Visitor figures were very low, but Nittve did not allow that to worry him. High ticket sales were irreconcilable with the task he had been set, which was to produce spearpoint exhibitions and introduce new artists. Most important was not how many but who came. And the right people did come. Artists, critics and open-minded persons who were not so likely to be thrown off balance by complicated, concept-based exhibitions. In comparison with Rooseum's narrowness Louisiana resembled a broadly embracing cultural machine, but the idea was that Nittve's different viewpoint and international contacts should be merged into Louisiana's program and Steingrim Laursen's network of contacts, which was a generation older.

Exactly a year later Louisiana rang again, this time in the shape of the chairman of the board, Allan Philip. The scenario had changed, according to Philip at any rate. The board was looking for a definitive replacement for Knud W. Jensen, who was to retire fully and completely, only have a place on the board and otherwise live in his house in north Jutland or that in Spain and write books. He had promised to step aside. Nittve wouldn't compromise on this particular point and was assured that he had understood correctly: Louisiana was his. Agreement was reached all the way down to a company car ("we drive Volvos here"), and when Nittve began in the summer of 1995, Knud W. Jensen tried to handle his board's decision. He behaved with impressive self-discipline – for the first three months. Later less and less so.

"It should be no secret that I regard it as a great honour to take over as Knud W. Jensen' successor at Louisiana in Humlebæk. I think it's fantastic!" Lars Nittve said to the Danish press. "Of course I represent a change of generation. Some will call it "fresh blood"! But I have always considered Louisiana to be one of the best-run museums in Europe. On the one hand, I shall maintain the big, classical exhibitions that generate the long queues, but I will also develop the interaction between them and a number of smaller, more contemporary exhibitions just as Louisiana did 15-20 years ago, when the museum's leaders were younger. But let me stress: I feel that it is my main task to preserve Louisiana's soul!"

A sensitive transfer process was under way. One man was handing over his life's work to another, who had made his independence a condition from the very start, but nevertheless would be functioning completely enveloped by the former's work. The problems arose when the new man began to make serious changes to the family enterprise. Without asking for permission.

In the concert hall Lars Nittve made a fiery speech to the staff, and the great majority fell for him immediately. The art historians gave a sigh of relief: for the first time, there was a specialist in charge of the museum! That's how they saw him, even though Nittve was had in fact studied economics just like his predecessor. Nittve gave the impression of being a young man with fresh antennae, whereas Knud W. Jensen had in fact become an elderly gentleman no matter how fond one was of him. He was no longer at the cutting edge. The new director was stringent and well-formulated. He promised to bring the museum back to its international position in the 1960s and 70s. Nittve did not refrain from openly criticising the national jewel that he had taken over and thought that Louisiana had lost ground in the course of the 1980s and 90s. That this had been noticed in the professional international art world and in the final resort might make it more difficult for Louisiana to borrow works and collaborate with the best museums in the future, since they do not lend their things in order to help a museum to make

Steingrim Laursen and Knud W. Jensen in 1998, when they were again alone on the stage after an unsuccessful attempt at generation change.

money, but to show new aspects of art and expand the frontiers of knowledge via an original and in their view crucially necessary idea for an exhibition.

The problem, according to the new director, was that Louisiana had too much of a safety first policy and took over too many exhibitions from others. The museum had, so to speak, put the cart before the horse and arranged exhibitions to fill an ever bigger house and keep it alive. As if it had forgotten the real reason for its existence. As if the programme was drawn up with a view to earning money, to put it crudely. A crisis was in progress, and Louisiana also lacked contact with young Danish artists, who could not be bothered to come to the museum, neither for exhibitions nor for openings. They ought to do so. Nittve wanted to get hold of the right public – the arts establishment of (preferably young) artists, certain galleries, certain critics – this marginal group of people who virtually never have the same taste as the general public, but whom no museum seriously dares to neglect. Louisiana's own voice had to be heard more clearly and sharply. More *cutting edge* to use Nittve's favourite expression. It was there, on this sharp edge, a museum of modern art should be. He would place Louisiana on the same level as the avantgarde, so that it was there the very latest was exhibited. This too was a breach with Louisiana's practice of adopting a slightly cautious attitude to the teeming scene of contemporary art.

Where Knud W. Jensen's Louisiana always placed the raw crisis moods of modern art in a warm and optimistic setting, Nittve was cooler. He did not care all that much for the first museum wing from 1958 with its reddish violet tiles and homely 50s atmosphere, but preferred the chalk-white rooms in the South Wing from 1982. Nor incidentally did he care for fruit, landscapes or animals. But Louisiana has never been cool. Rather the museum is fairly cosy with the old villa, domesticity and nature always at hand. The collection is not cool either. It has to do with human beings and inter-personal relations rather than abstract ideas. It is not particularly interested in concept art or installations, but seeks the visually attractive. That is why Knud W. Jensen never felt any enthusiasm for Nittve's purchase of Andrea Zittel's caravan "A to Z trailer unit customized by Kristin and Todd". The idea was that it would stand in the park among the other sculptures, but it never emerged onto the lawn of honour devoted to Henry Moore and Henri Laurens, because Knud W. Jensen thought it looked far too much like – a caravan.

On the way out of the door to America Nittve sent the staff a detailed letter about his plans and doings and signed off with a *I love you madly*. Knud W. Jensen was not pleased. Down by the beach he sat in his beautiful high-ceilinged office – a cathedral for Danish design – and through intermediaries followed what was going on up at the museum. He didn't take part in the meetings, was not involved, not asked, but he would have liked to. Naively he imagined that as the founder and financier he could keep his huge office, take part in meetings, participate in the planning of exhibitions and nonetheless have an autonomous man at the head of it all. And that this other man would be able to feel free. Knud W. Jensen was Mr. Louisiana and could never be a visitor who was just passing by. It was a surprise for him that Nittve wanted something different from what he wanted, because he had grown accustomed to getting what he wanted with the others. Knud W. Jensen gave himself assignments. To start with he focused on the extension of the shop and the new subterranean section, and after that he moved on towards the beach below the museum, where he acquired an old red-brick villa and made expensive plans for an Utzon project. This was not Nittve's priority, far from it,

The slender glass corridor in the old wing from 1958. The famous Danish art historian Christian Elling said at the time that the museum with its self-effacing subjection to the land-scape was "the beginning of the end for architecture".

but "one cannot say no to Knud," he says. "It was almost a standard phrase. One couldn't refuse to allow Knud to go on with his life's dream."

Although he had an enormous desire to spend the money, Knud W. Jensen had restrained himself and reserved ten million kroner for Nittve to buy art for. And Nittve bought works; they arrived at Humlebæk and were unpacked. Knud W. Jensen was not invited to participate in any of this, which both disappointed him and made him angry. He had not imagined that anyone would do this without asking him. After the meetings up at the museum his intermediary reported back to the boathouse, and Knud W. Jensen began increasingly to communicate with Nittve via others: "Knud says so and so. Knud is mad about this and that." The two men did not quarrel directly; there were no open aggressions between them, but in time the whole thing became more and more wearisome and irritating. Nittve hung the collection up in radically different constellations that broke with the old chronological ism-based hanging scheme: Yves Klein together with video works, for instance, and Knud W. Jensen came home from holiday and took many things down again. Still without either of the two men speaking directly about it. The staff suffered and were deeply frustrated by the distribution of power and territory.

Before Lars Nittve began at Louisiana, he saw a vacuum he could fill. Something unfinished that he could complete. "The interesting thing about the place is that it is a free institution, independent of society, the state and politics.," he said. "Its exhibition tradition has been characterised by openness and by Knud W. Jensen's unlimited curiosity about what is going on in art and culture. Louisiana has no ideology. That means that it has a development potential that can make the place one of the most interesting museums in Europe."

Knud W. Jensen always emphasised that Louisiana "presented a material", so people could form their own opinions. They could hate it, they could love it, they could ignore it. And here came his successor and said: "Louisiana has no ideology". That is to say, no wish to influence the public in a given direction. No underlying agenda. That approach was not what Nittwe wanted. He favoured a breach with the past, as the public would soon see. Alongside the broad exhibitions with a classical Louisiana profile – Calder, Picasso, Francis Bacon, Design and Identity – he showed new and difficult art. Very big and very expensive. In the

Conflict potential: Lars Nittve's caravan, which Knud W. Jensen couldn't endure seeing parked among Moore and Calders classical works.

"Louisiana has no ideology"

final resort this led to his having to leave. He showed the voluminous experiment 'Nowhere', which was by far the costliest exhibition in the museum's history.

"'Nowhere' constituted a dramatic change of generation," wrote *Art in America* in 1996. "Where Knud W. Jensen regarded modernism (in all its mixed forms) as the true way for the art of the 20th century, Nittve made his debut with an exhibition expressly based on the conviction that, as he declares in the catalogue, "we can no longer rely on the idea of dominant tendencies or 'isms', however new and up-to-date, to help us to structure what we see happening in art".

Where Knud W. Jensen was a modernist, Nittve has become postmodernist. Where the modernists sought the whole, the postmodernists see an infinite pluralism and wealth of interpretations and possibilities. In the middle of the 1980s Lars Nittve could not catch sight of any alternative to the idea of a unified vision and a chronological basic structure for art. Ten years later he gives up the idea. It is quite hopeless and moreover authoritarian to look for a common denominator for the big exhibitions, a common concept under which one can forcibly slot the

The South Wing was more closed and traditional. Nature was kept outside.

314

works. He does not want to assume the task of showing a single way forward into the mysterious, confused landscape that constitutes the era's cultural environment. "I believe that it is clear to most people that art today resists all attempts at definition except – and even here there are grounds for a certain caution – that which defines art as what "the art system" *perceives* to be art."

Because postmodernism does not think linearly, an avantgarde can no longer exist. There is no forwards and no backwards. Everything is possible, including going back in time, against the current, and absorbing older art in one's own. And because everything is possible, Nittve cannot abide by a monolithic curator ego who like an absolute monarch chooses the Right Art. He must have a number of views on the matter. For 'Nowhere' Louisiana invited four foreign curators, plus two from the museum's own staff to arrange five mini-exhibitions, which filled the whole house. In this way the power to select was divided (even though it was still of course a question of power).

The five rebellious sections had one thing in common: they all kept modernism at arm's length and thereby also Louisiana itself, which descends directly from Alfred H. Barr, the founder of the world's first museum of modern art, the Museum of Modern Art in New York. As one of the critical guest-curators Iwona Blazwick said: "Louisiana's beauty can also be seen as a form of stagnation. As a storage place for a special type and period of art work it expresses power, authority and conclusion."

In the catalogue Nittve asked himself: "What should a modern museum do if not continually question its own premises?" The sceptical critic from *Art in America* could easily think of alternatives: "A museum might resist the general slide from high culture to pop, might distinguish the intellectually significant from the trivial and separate the aesthetically good from the bad. But of course that would require a criterion of quality, which although it seems self-evident in other areas of endeavour – e.g., sports, dentistry, opera – today somehow eludes (or frightens) us in art."

The year after came the next major breach. For the first time since 'Tabernakel' in 1970, when Bjørn Nørgaard, Per Kirkeby, Poul Gernes and Peter Louis-Jensen walked out in protest against Louisiana's reactionary policy and Knud W. Jensen's resistance to the killing of the horse, the museum invited quite young Danish artists into the house. Virtually all and sundry. Up to this point, the museum of international modern art had in the nature of things shown only Danish artists of international standard. To be purchased by Louisiana was the ultimate endorsement, but now Nørrebro, the artists' quarter in Copenhagen, was hoovered empty for the big arrangement 'New Art from Denmark and Scania'.

True, Rooseum-Nittve had said in an interview that the nationality of the artist no longer played any role – it was as dead as mutton. Somewhat respectlessly, he had asserted that taking its size into consideration Denmark would at the most be able to display one major artist. Now he found it odd that Louisiana's public were shown young and for them unknown Japanese, English and Swiss artists, but never their Danish counterparts, who were in fact beginning to gain a footing in the international arts scene of the 1990s. There was no logic in this, he thought, and the museum was also contributing to a kind of suspiciousness of the Danes in the international art world: if they weren't at Louisiana, they couldn't be any good. So he invited 50 from Denmark and Scania. "That corresponds to arranging an exhibition at Moderna Museet in Stockholm, entitled 'New Art from Sweden and Funen', a critic sneered.

Protests were heard: "Louisiana has long since qualified itself as an international whetting stone on which Danish art can be sharpened. But with the upcoming parade of Danish art, the museum will squander that position. And that's a pity for Denmark," argued the sculptress Elisabeth Toubro. "It is impossible to find 50 artists of international standard in Denmark and *the whole of* Sweden together. The exhibition will pull yet another Danish cultural institution down into the normalcy of society's equality ideology." Louisiana's sudden reluctance to select and exert authority distressed her as it had distressed the critic from *Art in America* in connection with 'Nowhere'.

This was the first time that Denmark experienced curator rule. And the concept could be experienced in full figure in connection with Denmark/Scania, where these curators were photographed visiting artists in their studios and appeared in *Politiken's* special issue. Suddenly the people behind the scenes appeared on the front page. The invisible became visible and received attention – for a period. The idea was that Denmark-Scania should be repeated every fourth year as a recurrent event, but there was only one. After Nittve the museum stopped placing the curator on a level with the artist. "It's not us, dammit, that people come to see," one of them says.

"It feels good!" answered Knud W. Jensen, when he was asked in 1997 how it felt to have another man in charge of his lifework. "I could have gone on a little longer with Louisiana's good staff, but my biological age means that compared to the forty years I have worked at the museum I don't have many years left. In other places I would have succumbed to the age limit long ago. I have great confidence in Lars Nittve. He is professionally on a level with the best museum directors in the world. It's true that Louisiana was on the world map before him,

Lars Nittve with curators. It was in his days that they first received prominence.

but he keeps us at the cutting edge of developments while not deviating from Louisiana's main course."

At the same time a certain discontent at the museum's changes begins to be heard round about. After 'Nowhere' and New Art from Denmark and Scania' there is a fear that that some part of Louisiana's popular appeal is disappearing to be replaced by an incomprehensible, elitist avantgardism. Or, as *Ekstra Bladet* put it after Nittve's departure: "Under Lars Nittve's leadership Louisiana became a place for the small, sexless collection of youngish, intolerably pretentious and academic art historians who unfortunately decide, also internationally, what is in at present. One could almost hear the problems piling up when one saw their plans, which aimed to make Louisiana a meeting-place for contemporary art."

A reader's letter in *Politiken* called the place's new trend "bin-liner art", while certain sections of the young public were jubilant. They danced till sunrise at Nittve's techno raves and looked forward to a more progressive, less conservative Louisiana. In this way Louisiana resembled its old self: the public divided up into the two usual camps: a small trendsetting camp and a large camp that paid the bills. In the power struggle that later unfolded between the founder and the new director, the latter camp won Louisiana back to their side.

A viewpoint between the two opposing sides is that Nittve brought fresh air, only too much of it all at once As an artist represented at Louisiana puts it, he laid the whole house waste, wrought havoc in the main flower bed and changed a lot of things in one hell of a rush. But afterwards when he looked around for his public, they were dead. The exhibitions were very total, both in their physical extent and in their ideas. Quite exceptionally the museum closed for a month in order to set up 'Nowhere'. The guides withdrew to the wind and cold of the park, and one day the only visitor was a young man from northwest Jutland with red cheeks. In his urgency Nittve forgot the importance of traditional Louisiana logic: there must always be more than one single exhibition. And cold exhibitions should alternate with warm.

The visitor figures for 1997 proved depressingly low. The public did a u-turn at the sight of video screens, installations, prosaic everyday objects. They did not care for what a curator calls *contemporary contemporary*. The newest of the new. Things had gone downhill ever since Nittve's arrival in summer 1995. From a record high in 1994 with 640,000 visitors to a record low in 1997 with 410,000. If things continued that way, the museum would go bankrupt. Not only did people not come in sufficient numbers, but the exhibitions themselves were very expensive to arrange. The economic situation was slipping rapidly. He was unlucky as well. A classical Miro exhibition that might have straightened things out was postponed, but in the board there was neither the good will or faith to be patient. Already in 1997 the chairman Allan Philip wrote a number of times to Lars Nittve asking him to adopt a more public-friendly line in accord with Louisiana's policy hitherto. Philip was ready to enter into negotiations concerning his departure.

Knud W. Jensen convened the board for a secret meeting at Allan Philip's home. With him he brought a list of complaints, at the top of which figured the fall in visitors. Between the lines could be read his own disappointment at being kept out, even though the director's contract fully entitled him to do so. In January 1998 Nittve sensed that there was a risk that Knud W. Jensen would test his power in the board and get it to choose between him and Lars Nittve. He realised that this contest would be hard to win. The following month Knud W. Jensen tried to persuade *Weekendavisen's* cultural editor Poul Erik Tøjner to join the board to provide a kind of specialist counterweight to Nittve, which Tøjner declined.

What in the house would later be called the *Nittve experience* was drawing to a close. It was quite simply a relief for both parties when London miraculously rang up, and Tate Modern came into the picture as a brilliant new workplace for Lars Nittve. A direct dismissal was thus skilfully transformed into a typically Louisiana happy ending. Now the conclusion of an unfortunate three-year attempt at generation change looked like something quite different: an irresistible career leap (which it was in fact) to the largest and hottest museum of modern art since Pompidou in Paris and an honour for Louisiana that its director had been headhunted to build up the new supermuseum, while the truth was that Lars Nittve would have had to quit Louisiana no matter what. Professionally, he had not succeeded in preserving the spirit of the place in the form of its broad appeal and large number of club members. From a human point of view it was untenable to keep Knud W. Jensen away from all influence. Nittve had to leave Humlebæk and accept that his artistic and political line had failed to carry the day. "He was an excellent museum director, but just employed at the wrong place," says a long-serving member of Louisiana's board. The daily newspapers except *Information* were content that the challenger had now disappeared from the scene. They preferred the old Louisiana in the founder's spirit.

Years of confusion

Throughout his life Knud W. Jensen would make promises to people that he couldn't keep. The sequence of crown princes that never became king is just one example. No sooner was Lars Nittve out of the door than Knud W. Jensen started negotiations with art critic, writer and literateur Poul Erik Tøjner, born 1959 into a middle-class home with culture and art. Jensen saw a humanist in him, a man from the world of literature as he himself had once been. They had got to know each other at press showings at the museum and at Gyldendal's annual receptions, where they always ended up talking together. Knud W. Jensen was a close friend of Kurt Fromberg, the director of Gyldendal, with whom, as was his wont, he often spoke on the phone for hours. Fromberg knew Poul Erik Tøjner as the editor of Gyldendal's literary journal *Kritik* and had once asked the young man with the cigar what he wanted to be when he grew up: either director of Gyldendal or of Louisiana was the answer, which was primarily designed to shock. Nor did Fromberg forget it.

Knud W. Jensen admired Tøjner for many things, big and small. First and foremost for his intelligence, and because he could write, but also because he could listen to Bach's 'Wohltemperierte Klavier' and at the same time do the

carpentry for installing a kitchen sink. For being able to cook supper for his wife and three children. For suddenly being able to marshal his energy and make things happen. For being an omnivorous reader and for being able to translate his reading into articles and books. For being direct, but not stubborn. For having a sense of humour. Such a man could take care of the link between culture and art at Louisiana.

Steingrim Laursen had recommended Nittve. So incidentally had Poul Erik Tøjner when Knud W. Jensen asked him for advice. Now it was the founder's own turn. He made the astonished Tøjner an offer that the latter would not even in his most ambitious dreams have been able to anticipate. It created a state of highly wrought mental turbulence, and slowly he began to think himself out of his post as cultural editor on *Weekendavisen*. In the beginning reluctantly, later with greater conviction. He couldn't say no to becoming director of Louisiana. It was that simple. Agreement was reached almost all the way down to the dotted line. Poul Erik Tøjner drove expectantly to Humlebæk to fix the last details and knocked on the door of Knud W. Jensen's office.

The meeting was excruciatingly embarrassing. "It can't be done all the same," said Knud W. Jensen, and Tøjner didn't hear the rest. He wanted to get

Poul Erik Tøjner.
Dress code: T-shirt,
sweater, crumpled
shirt. Never a tie.
Knud W. Jensen didn't
dare make him direc-
tor – first time round.

away. "I must be able to give you something," said a flustered Jensen and looked around his office. His eye fell on a fine, leather-bound edition of Achton Friis' "De danskes land" [The Country of the Danes], inherited from his father. He insisted and the two of them began to fuss around with plastic shopping bags and carry the volumes out to Tøjner's car.

Steingrim Laursen had intervened and proposed himself as director for the next three and a half years up to his 70th birthday. Knud W. Jensen abandoned his promise to Tøjner. This was cynically done, especially by a man who himself punished faithlessness in an almost medieval fashion and got really angry with people who were disloyal to Louisiana. The museum had even written a draft press release, in which it looked forward to working together with Tøjner. The founder excused himself saying that no harm would ensue from a young man becoming three years older. What was the hurry? The boyish Knud W. Jensen did not understand that he would have to make up his mind if he wanted to nominate his successor. Instead, he promised Steingrim Laursen that after long and faithful service he should have his last years without being encumbered with "a new Nittve" – that is a person who took his job seriously and didn't necessarily do what the old guard said. The confusion was comprehensive – Louisiana acted in a labile and unprofessional fashion. Tøjner was invited to join the board, which he declined once more with reference to his objectivity as a critic and editor of *Weekendavisen*. Nor did he want to have further dealings with them.

Knud W. Jensen told the media that Louisiana did not wish to nominate a new director after Lars Nittve before Steingrim Laursen retired. Until then, he would head the museum together with economy director Christina Lage. The change of generation and the revolution had been cancelled, the museum's capital had been drained by low visitor figures and, and Steingrim Laursen who, had been behind most of the big money-spinners' seemed a convincing choice. With him one could be certain that Louisiana remained as Knud W. Jensen wanted it to be. The museum quickly returned to business as usual, and disappointment spread. Two museum inspectors immediately resigned because they saw the new management as a reversal for experiments and contemporary art. Other members of the permanent staff considered doing the same. This was clearly an interim solution, the opposite of a generation change, and not a fresh and optimistic signal from the museum of modern art. Such things can be postponed, but not indefinitely.

"From here we express our congratulations to Nittve, but cross our fingers that Louisiana does not solely focus on visitor statistics, but is willing to take a risk now and then," *Information* commented. "Under Laursen's management of Louisiana the museum is in safe hands – perhaps too safe." And Louisiana's 40th anniversary was accompanied by headlines like "Tumult in the cultural playground",

"Operation save Louisiana", "Dark clouds over Louisiana" and "Louisiana asks minister for help". On top of this, there was quite new competition from Arken, the extended *Statens Museum for Kunst*, Kunstforeningen Gammel Strand, Brandts Klædefabrik in Odense and, on the other side of the narrow Sound, Rooseum and Malmø Kunsthal. The ever optimistically minded Knud W. Jensen adhered to the principle of only speaking of his successes, not about sad failures and defeats, but he admitted to the national media that the museum was in a state of "limited turbulence".

Behind the abrupt annulment of Tøjner as the new director there were a number of other factors in addition to pressure from Steingrim Laursen, who despite his position as Knud W. Jensen's long-serving right-hand man and roving ambassador, could only have a short period of time left. As always, Knud W. Jensen rang a number of advisers and close friends, this time to hear what they thought of, Tøjner, and some of the heavyweights were uncertain. The new chairman of Louisiana's board, Kurt Fromberg, and the chairman of the Carlsberg Foundation, Hans Edvard Nørregård-Nielsen for instance. They were slightly hesitant. It was one thing that the man lacked museum experience, and Louisiana's economy looked bad, but didn't he also seem slightly arrogant as he sat there smoking his cigar? Hadn't he always had things his own way? Wouldn't it be good for him to encounter a little adversity, so one could see how he took it?

"He's a bigmouth"," said Hans Edvard Nørregård-Nielsen to Knud W. Jensen, who was afraid of what would happen if Poul Erik Tøjner did not get money from the foundation that had been the museum's biggest supporter ever since its start. The new director preferably needed to be someone Hans Edvard Nørregård-Nielsen could go in for. When his advice was asked, he said in his laid back fashion that it was basically a good idea "but start by beating him up for three hours".

Eighteen months passed. During this period a number of prominent persons engaged in lobbying for Poul Erik Tøjner. The painter Per Kirkeby did his best for him. As did gallery owner Bo Bjerggaard. *Berlingske Tidende's* cultural editor Henrik Wivel had a three-hour persuasion meeting with Kurt Fromberg. Also the rector of the Royal Academy of Fine Arts and board member of the Carlsberg Foundation Else Marie Bukdahl advocated the bigmouth. Kurt Fromberg allowed himself to be persuaded. Finally, he became afraid that Tøjner would fly away. They needed to hurry. And then once again the telephone rang miraculously at Louisiana: economy director Christina Lage accepted a job in TV, so the way was suddenly open for Tøjner to head the museum alone, as he had stipulated all the time. Fromberg said to Knud W. Jensen that they had to act now and see that they disentangled themselves from their commitment to Steingrim Laursen. And they did so.

Midsummer on the beach.

Tøjner can be a man of
letters in the morning and
a picture specialist in the
afternoon. Or something
else. Fairly omnivorous.

"But start by beating him up fo

Generation change II

"A rumour that has been buzzing in the air for the last two years was confirmed yesterday when *Weekendavisen's* highly competent cultural editor, 40-year-old Poul Erik Tøjner, was appointed director of Louisiana in Humlebæk," wrote *Information* on 18 November 1999 of the next gifted young man to occupy one of the most important posts in the Danish art world.

Tøjner was welcomed with the closest to unadulterated enthusiasm possible for the Danish press, which noted his unpretentious openness and well developed awareness of the importance of communication. They mentioned his intelligence, his respected, indeed admired name in art circles, his knowledge of the needs of the broad Danish public and his unsurpassed ability to think with art. Here was a rare combination of an intellectual top reviewer for an elitist weekly, who could write both a highly specialised work on Søren Kierkegaard's aesthetic and also a broad bestseller on the museums' best pictures. A boyish man with an unusual disposition for abstract thinking but at the same time with practical abilities. When he opened his front door for *Politiken* and showed his "childishly chubby face with the brown eyes", the photographer was on the verge of asking: "Is your dad at home?"

When Tøjner called for a taxi, the switchboard operator congratulated him. He was on morning TV, local TV, national TV – everyone agreed that he was a brilliant choice even though he didn't have the remotest experience of arranging exhibitions, running a workplace with 250 employees or managing a budget of 80 million kroner. His point of departure was that he thought Louisiana was a fantastic place, and that he was fond of Knud W. Jensen. At his first press conference he exhibited a rare restraint in his ambitions. He wouldn't change anything right away, but get to know the house from inside. The only certain goal for Tøjner the aesthete was that he would stick to the visual in art, *see* the work as the most important thing rather than all that surrounds it, such as the work's concern with its own relation to the institution and so on. Unlike Nittve he had always found the contextual boring, and all this very modern discussion could not excite him. The work itself could. As a critic he sought to describe his immediate experience and to theorise a little afterwards. "One should not hide one's own set of values – for me art criticism means that one writes personal criticism. I hate disinterested criticism," he said.

The key point was to put oneself in the place of the observer. He hoped to be able to do the same at Louisiana and said to the press: "Experience has become such an ugly and deprecated word, but after all that's what Louisiana must give its public in the sense that something enters into connections with people's worlds. It is there the discussion of our lives and existences begins."

ree hours"

Among the art critics there were few objections. "There are those in the art world who think that you have a reactionary view on art, that you don't like contemporary art," a journalist said at a press conference. Others had touched on more or less the same subject in their "reviews" of the new director. "On the face of it his preference for classical art with emphasis on names like Goya, Titian, Velazquez, Rembrandt, Vermeer makes the choice of him as head of a museum of modern art seem a little unmotivated," wrote *Information*. And "Poul Erik Tøjner has not concealed his love for the art of the world of yesteryear," wrote *Berlingske Tidende*.

"Contemporary art?" answered Tøjner. "What I find uninteresting about the preoccupation with "contemporary art" is the professional correctness it reflects. The mantra that "someone produces art at an international level", which is just another way of saying that they produce something that everyone else produces. It is such an automatic view of what counts. It is just as if one has to buy the right make of car to become a member of the right golf club."

20
00 ˢ

LOUISIANA

GEORG

BASELITZ

10. FEBRUAR – 5. JUNI 2006

The typical Louisiana Man has in reality long been a woman of over 40. Without her evening schools would close, female authors would go hungry and the country's museums would echo emptily. Louisiana carried out its first survey of its visitors at the beginning of the 1960s and was surprised to find that the great majority were men, until someone at the museum discovered that the wives handed the forms to their husbands, who filled them in their own names and were therefore disproportionately represented. That doesn't happen any more.

Louisiana Woman belongs to the social group of what is still called "nice" people in Denmark: interested, cultivated, open-minded and sensible. She does not allow herself to be intimidated by the growing queue behind her, but takes her time getting to know all the dishes in the café. She eats her sandwich with knife and fork and praises the kitchen for the quality of the bread and the spinach. That spinach really tastes of something! She is fond of continuity: Calder on the lawn, a fire in the fireplace, lit candles on the tables. As a member of many years' standing she feels she has a share in the place. That it won't be long before they recognise her. Jazz, classical, organic, gastronomic, slim. Doesn't look down at *Politiken's* cultural programmes for its readers. Would never touch a theme park, pre-packed marinated meat, commercial TV or Risi Frutti. In this way, she resembles Louisiana Man, and as a rule they form a couple. She has become one with the museum shop, its girlish aesthetic and pang colours, its slender Ditte Fischer ceramics and ethereal Rigetta Klint scarves. She would like to live like that. No other train ride brings you closer to healing.

It's hard for her to put it into words, but there's something about Louisiana, that makes you feel clean. As if your hangovers disappear to be replaced by clear-eyed Nordic coolness when one goes through the door. In the shop a salad bowl is not just a salad bowl, but also a piece of sculpture. A football is made of attractive, strong, naturally coloured leather, a vase is legendary, a flower broach unique, a briefcase is minimalist, a sofa cushion handmade. If she has erred too far in the direction of ghastly good taste, she buys a *crazy* raincoat for 2,500 kroner. There is a feeling of OK luxury about it all, acceptable overconsumption for thinking people, far from the brown mink and unconcealed materialism of the stockbroker belt. Design is different although you don't quite know why.

She belongs to the *Cosmopolitan* segment, the largest individual group of people in the Louisiana Club (16 per cent), but as a self-confident individualist she would hate to be put into a category. Especially with other people. The Cosmopolitans are unmistakably the wealthiest Danes. They have lengthy academic educations, two cars, top jobs in their own or other people's enterprises and live in spacious houses close to the sea and the woods, typically along the coast road north of Copenhagen, typically in Rungsted Kyst, the country's most expensive

postal code and the beautiful place where Knud W. Jensen spent his summers as a child and young man.

As the most natural thing in the world, her mother brought up her daughter to appreciate art and culture and life membership and has herself moved up into the group of *Hedonistic older people* (eight per cent), who travel south to go to the opera, shop at local special stores and attentively follow the trends in shares and bonds while their grandchildren attend the highly popular summer school at the museum. Louisiana is often inherited, chiefly on the maternal side. Like all other art museums in Denmark and in the world Louisiana finds it difficult to get young people interested in earnest, but the same also applies for groups liked *Stressed Families with Children* and *House Owners in Provincial Towns* and *Tradition-bound Farmers.* Well-educated families with children and high positions in public service, called *Redbrick Houses* after their typical type of home, are the next largest group with fifteen per cent of the members in the Louisiana Club. They go in for the welfare state (their employer), skiing holidays, the less popular radio programmes and, if need be, TV. They take the train to work in town, but have two cars standing in the garage and compensate by buying organic, environment-friendly articles. It is very indicative that a large proportion of Louisiana's younger club members are gathered in the consultant category *Career Starters* (ten per cent), the members of which resemble older groups in having academic educations and money along with a fondness for newspapers, fashion, interior decoration and specialist shops. They are just younger.

Louisiana Woman knows that much is as it always has been. Many young artists still prefer to be pariahs and feel excluded because it makes them more authentic and artistic. They want to be outsiders, but have to learn to do their VAT accounts, apply for grants and talk on the phone. They still hate the idea of an "art work" (that the things can be sold) and try to protect their works against "the institution" (that the things can be exhibited), but on the other hand a number of young Danish artists are enjoying international careers and selling their works for millions in London, New York and Berlin.

Some people find this opposition artificial, for instance Søren Ulrik Thomsen and Frederik Stjernfelt in their strongly provocative debate book "Kritik af den negative opbyggelighed" [Critique of Negative Edification] (2005) take issue with the dominant trend in art – to define oneself negatively and work negatively. As a writer, artist and debater. Everyone considers it necessary to adopt the role of the outsider. Already in the 80s, Thomsen and Stjernfelt noticed that one could be a member of good society only if one sneered at it. When Jytte Hilden

was minister of culture she said cheerfully that art should be "like a bacteria in society". Nonsense, they answer. Provocation is not the only criterion for art.

Modern art still expends much energy on reflecting on itself as art. Drawing has suddenly become hot, as painting was *not* for a lengthy period. Video art has long been so. Louisiana Woman reads in the club magazine that post-colonial art with a political agenda fills the whole of Documenta 11 in Kassel, while other artists are not political at all. There is still no route to total understanding, but nevertheless a striking common feature in art: "Irony is as natural a part of the new painting as sugar in candy," writes *Politiken's* art critic Peter Michael Hornung. Fervour, passion and naked feeling are out or reserved for amateurs. The modern painter challenges and teases his or her public, speaks in tongues, hides the message and employs juicy, private clichés. Hornung sees irony as a shield behind which the artist hides his or her innermost core and as an appeal to an over-stimulated and over-fed public that has moved around among intensified expressivity for so long that it has become blasé.

Louisiana's finances looked gloomy at the turn of the century. Not even with 450,000 visitors a year was it possible to run the museum.

Desperado

In Poul Erik Tøjner's office hangs a typewritten sheet of paper framed and under glass. This is a certificate of exemption from the Ministry of Culture that permits him to be the director of Louisiana without having academic qualifications as an art historian.

At Denmark's easily most visited art museum, founded by a cheese wholesaler for his own money and run for decades without an art historian for miles around, the authorities now demand one of that ilk in the director's chair. At the place where an entirely new and habit-forming museal concept saw the light of day, perhaps because it was free of art historians, there is now a requirement for one. But if it cannot be helped, then it is acceptable, as in Tøjner's case, merely to have reviewed art for sixteen years, merely to have written eleven books about art, merely to have studied Danish literature and philosophy, merely to have a post-graduate degree for a treatise on Søren Kierkegaard's aesthetic and have received the N.L. Høyen Medal, which is awarded for work of a particularly high quality in relation to research into the interpretation of or the mediation of art. But, in fact, that was not quite good enough. The National Museum Board required evidence, and Tøjner had to send a packing case with the books, catalogue texts, articles and reviews he had written over the years so that they could see whether he had against all the odds mastered the curriculum.

The new director came in through the door on the first day of the new millennium and proved to have a number of characteristics in common with Knud W. Jensen. Also, Tøjner was profoundly restless. He too was able to talk with people in an unimpressed and natural way, perhaps even charm them, which is vital for a semi-private museum that constantly has to raise money. The director soon proved to be the perfect fundraiser. In that he resembled Knud W. Jensen more than the board had dared hope, but as it happened he had no choice. The first thing he saw was a financial hole that was quite automatically growing deeper and deeper. It would not be possible to run Louisiana with the money there was. Not even with 450,000 visitors a year. Poul Erik Tøjner would without delay have to try to replace whatever personal modesty and inherent Danish reluctance to ask people for money he possessed with the down-to-earthness that flourishes so naturally in American museum circles. He became a desperado. Didn't know how one did that sort of thing, just knew that he had to have the money.

He went to the Ministry of Culture and presented his problem to Undersecretary Erik Jacobsen: the museum was balancing on the edge of bankruptcy and couldn't possibly be run without a larger grant from the State. The civil servant answered that there was a problem with Knud W. Jensen's plans for a new and expensive building on the beach, because it is difficult to ask for money and spend it at the same time. Tøjner was obliged to drive home with the depressing task of explaining to Knud W. Jensen that they would never ever get more money if he continued to run around on the beach plot with his measuring tape and markers. To the Ministry Tøjner reported back with aplomb that he had things under control, but during a conference at Louisiana attended by Minister of Culture Elsebeth Gerner Nielsen Knud W. Jensen nevertheless buttonholed her and showed her the plans, while Tøjner tried to avert the danger with his repeated: "Of course we are *not* going to build it!" Knud W. Jensen behaved like an indomitable developer to the very last. Tøjner had to promise him on his deathbed that he would some day build on the plot.

After his meeting with the undersecretary, Tøjner wrote a letter to the minister, who directly told him that she didn't have any money. "You must talk with Mogens about it," she said. "The annual budget negotiations were approaching, and a nervous Tøjner wrote to Minister of Finance Mogens Lykketoft, but without having a clue as to whether he had received the letter. He called the minister's

The beach below Louisiana. Classically Danish.

personal secretary, who at first refused to inform him about the letter's fate, but was pressured by Tøjner to go into the minister's office and return to the receiver and say: "He's sitting at his desk with the letter. He *has* read it and says it has made an impression on him. And that's all I think I can say."

During the budget negotiations Tøjner could barely stand the tension. He felt that the museum's entire life and future lay in the events of the next few hours, and in the middle of his evening meal he rang one of the crucial left-wing representatives in the Cultural Committee, who said that it had gone through. Louisiana was granted an additional six million kroner a year by the State, a decisive sum and the first major portion of money for fifteen years. Rejoicing in Humlebæk. For a moment the desperado imagined that the worst was behind him.

From the very first day, Tøjner knew that he was serving two masters. The key was to find a balance between regard for Louisiana and regard for its founder.

Some of the new initiatives could make Knud W. Jensen indignant – until he learnt that they came from Tøjner.

In his view the two did not always coincide. He had a headset installed in his car so he could talk to Knud W. Jensen all the way up to Louisiana in the morning and all the way home again – 70 kilometres in all. Otherwise, Knud W. Jensen would telephone in the evening. The task was to communicate. To say where the museum was going, argue for it and win the founder over onto his side. Not to make him unhappy. This required great endurance, a lot of strength, a lot of time. In the nature of things, Knud W. Jensen held many views on Louisiana. On art they should show, on art they should buy, on the place's identity, on the root of the problems. He looked back into his own era and dated the museum's golden age to the 1960s, and they had daily discussions as to whether one could save Louisiana by returning to the past. Tøjner didn't think so. Nor did he think that a man of 83 should head the museum.

Knud W. Jensen did not leave Louisiana, but sat in his office by the beach with two secretaries and worked. Calmly and quietly. It was a stroke of luck for him to have found Poul Erik Tøjner, who did not challenge his authority and therefore acquired it. Three months before his death, Knud W. Jensen wrote to his acquaintance Petra Kipphoff from *Die Zeit*: "Louisiana and I can only be satis-fied with our young, new director Poul Erik Tøjner. From the very start he rolled his sleeves up and got down to work. For him it was undoubtedly a big change to move from a post as an art critic to being Louisiana's director, but despite the many demands on him he seems to feel like a fish in the water. For me there is no doubt that he *is* the man, that he will be able to *handle* the job."

Their relationship developed from mutual respect and sympathy to some-thing personal, almost familiar. It was therefore acceptable that the younger man could both be fond of the older man and from time to time unable to stand him. Tøjner teased him disarmingly when he got excited about *yet another* thing that was to be changed in his house. That is to say his life and identity. Some of the new initiatives could make Knud W. Jensen indignant – until he received an intimation that they had come from Tøjner. Then he would discreetly withdraw his protests and let things happen, but he no longer had the same strength as in Lars Nittve's day; he didn't have the same energy to interfere even though he now and again gatecrashed an exhibition meeting. After repeated attempts and detours the change of generation at Louisiana ended successfully in a father-son relationship that extended all the way to Knud W. Jensen's deathbed. It turned out to be quite simply a question of individuals and the relations between them.

To the relief of neighbours, the board and the Ministry of Culture, Tøjner succeeded in having the building project by the beach placed on a diplomatic standby. Throughout his forty-year-long museum life, Knud W. Jensen loved and respected the spirit of the place and adapted his simple architecture to the spirit

of the landscape, but at the very end his faith weakened and he wanted to have something grandiosely conceived, unified and monumental. A millennium project. And he wanted to round things off: when he bought Louisiana, he asked young Utzon to draw a museum, but the architect was absorbed by the Sydney Opera House. Since then, the world-famous architect had not really built in Denmark, and now amends could be made with a tower down on the beach. On the phone Knud W. Jensen said to an employee: "My directors don't understand me. They always think that when a new extension has been carried out, then we'll just continue with it, and that has to be good enough. But it's I who have the visions, and in the long term I know I'm right. The public must be brought down to the sea and feel the closeness of nature."

Furious public meetings were held. After one of them Jensen found his car with all four tyres slashed. On another evening, he met a dog with a gentleman who hissed "If only you were dead" after him. To his friends and acquaintances, on the other hand, Knud W. Jensen said that the people who protested most in the idyllic old fishing village of Humlebæk were architects who had grown fat from covering the country with ugly one-family homes in the 1960s and 1970s.

Knud Wadum Jensen 1916-2000

In the middle of November, Knud W. Jensen fell ill and was admitted to hospital, first to Hillerød Hospital, later to Rigshospitalet. When Vilhelm Wohlert visited

Tough public meeting about the building by the beach.

him, he was still talking about the museum by the beach, from which Utzon had withdrawn, but which Jensen still wanted to build despite local opposition. Once again. "I know I'm right," he said. He told Tøjner that he had dreamed how the first issue of the new, Louisiana Magazine should look and had edited it in his thoughts. He never let go of his museum for a moment.

On 12 December 2000 Knud W. Jensen died in hospital shortly after his 84th birthday. He was born in the middle of the First World War, experienced the Second World War as a young man (and got into trouble because of it), lived through the Cold War as an adult and witnessed its surprising conclusion as an elderly man. His life spanned almost an entire century, in which Denmark changed radically, a process he followed as he gradually freed himself from his duty to his dominating father, who couldn't stand bohemians, and from the expectations that friends and acquaintances entertained of him. At halfway point he changed and became another person. Art too had become unrecognisable. At Sankt Thomas Plads he grew up in a pompous apartment with five reception rooms and Golden Age paintings on all vertical surfaces. As a child he was scared by P.C. Skovgaard's engraving of the big bear killing a hunter under a huge oak tree. As an adult he loved the Californian Sam Francis' happy abstract colour orgies, but "I have also grown used to minimalist white". He bought his first picture while at high school – a painting by the Dane Jens Søndergaard. The last was a portrait of a woman for Louisiana by British Frank Auerbach – for Louisiana.

As a child, he lived in a now vanished world, where one changed for dinner, used the old-fashioned spelling and addressed one's mother formally as in "Dear Mother, Would you be so kind as to put out a hymn book for me tomorrow morning, so I can read a verse that is not to be found in the school's song book. Furthermore 30 øre for "The Coal Collection for the Society for the Protection of Lonely Old People?" Your Knud."

His museum set a high standard at a time when others went in for gas concrete, eternit and vinyl, women wore dralon and perlon and washing powder ads "whispered about her tea towels...!" One ate breaded meatloaf and switched eggs, and Afro-Americans were called negroes in the papers. He lived to see fourteen ministers of culture and at least twenty palpable isms, witnessed how the art scene moved from Paris to New York and later on to London and Berlin. He experienced painting's death and resurrection and the birth of video art.

When he opened his museum, art was to save the world and the souls of the population. In the end, the goal was more modest. Art could make do with being an event for the people who wanted it as "the momentary possibility for sensed, reflecting secession from the network of other everyday projects," as Poul Erik Tøjner had already written at the end of the 1980s. As a young man interested in art in Denmark of the 1930s, Knud W. Jensen had very little to choose between – as an old man far too much. Minister of Culture Julius Bomholt's fervent wish of covering the country with a dense pattern of cultural institutions has definitely been fulfilled.

As a young and ambitious business man, Knud W. Jensen had moved among farmers, shopkeepers and dairy managers and was sent by the Ministry of Agriculture to America in 1946 to sound out the market for cheese. As an adult, he associated with legendary artists, museum directors, patrons of the arts and other big shots from a very different sphere. As a young man, he flirted with Nazism, as an adult, he was considered by the social democrats as a possibly minister of culture, and as an old man, he was canonised while still alive. His life work was transformed from a provincial museum into the leading museum in Denmark, to which ten per cent of the population bought a ticket each year. From 7 to 250 employees. From glad amateurism to comprehensive professionalisation.

When he opened Louisiana, he read in *Dagens Nyheder* how under the headline of "Circusiana" art historian Svend Eriksen charged what he called "the world's most beautiful art motel" with lack of respect and care in its handling of the works. He and most of the other art historians feared that the new museum's success with the public could seriously harm "quiet institutions", if they were to be compared with Louisiana. But Knud W. Jensen would have plenty of opportunity to observe how from the 1970s Danish museums consistently followed Louisiana's lead.

He would see how painting and other classical art forms that still reigned unchallenged on the elite-cultural scene in the 1950s became a special case. How pop, cartoon strips, bungee jumps and graffiti were not merely tolerated, but were called art and culture. And he lived long enough to see the appearance of an opposition to museums of modern art like his, namely the even newer museums of contemporary art. All over the world small MoCAs (Museums of Contemporary Art) emerged out of the big MoMAs (Museums of Modern Art). He registered how modern art changed its status from being suspect in the 1950s to being embraced in the 1970s and virtually exploding in popularity in the 1980s. Everything changed in those years, but Louisiana, which had in the course of time grown almost by a factor of ten, resembled itself most of the time because he was keeping hold of it.

When as a young man he was told by his doctor that he couldn't have children, he was deeply upset. His friend Thorkild Bjørnvig comforted him in a letter and assured him that his life would nevertheless form itself beautifully. "You will be a perfecter, not biologically but spiritually, he wrote. "You have the spontaneously happy within you."

Knud W. Jensen, loved and pampered, with his mother. He was the only child in the family whose socks were ironed.

"I have never been able to draw, play the piano or write poems. I also knew that I would only have become an average art historian. It is the environment around art that has interested me," said Knud W. Jensen. Here speaking with the composer Herman D. Koppel, who performed at the museum from as early as 1958.

Daily life

Already during Tøjner's first exhibition in 2001 – the German painter Sigmar Polke – the representative of a German art museum inhaled deeply through his nose, noticed an unpleasant odour of damp and announced that this was the last time that Louisiana would borrow works from him. He was not the only one to pronounce this verdict. During a tour of the exhibition the major German collector Ingvild Goetz from Munich asked her assistant to write Louisiana's name on the list of museums she did *not* lend to. The house seemed tatty and smelt strange. If you looked carefully, you could clearly see the damp stains on the walls of the only 20-year-old South Wing, where Polke's pictures hung. It became necessary to bring plastic buckets in at night. The roof leaked more and more. Not only did it rain *into* the South Wing – it also rained *inside* the South Wing. Louisiana could not live up to international standards everywhere, neither with respect to indoor climate nor to security. And in the South Wing it was not possible to obtain National Indemnity, the state insurance. This in a world where lenders want to see humidity print-outs and graphs before they would even begin to consider lending their works.

The museum's works manager was asked for a rough estimate. He thought that 12-15 million might do the job. This was a mind-boggling figure for the board and Tøjner. How could so much money be procured? The six million from the government the previous year had been hard enough. When Tøjner spoke with Aino Kann Rasmussen from the Velux Foundation at a lunch with three kinds of marinated herring at Louisiana, he couldn't even get the monstrous figure to pass his lips. He had not yet learnt to pronounce eight-figure sums, but he would do so. The usual supporters were warned. The Augustinus Foundation called for an in-depth examination of the whole museum's condition, not just the South Wing. And then the shocking revelation burst out of the mists: the museum had to be totally renovated throughout. It would cost not 12-15 million but 218 million kroner! And who would give money to something as unsexy, invisible and boring as repairs?

Tøjner began to argue his case even though as a new director he could find other and more obvious things to focus on than consolidating the firm. Art, for instance. He admitted to foundations and sponsors that these were unexciting investments, but they were necessary. His only argument was that if all that Louisiana had been and meant was not to end on the scrapheap, something had to happen now. The Augustinus Foundation gave 40 million in a first payout, the Velux Foundation 15 and later more. The Realdania Foundation 40, the Ludvig and Sara Elsass Fond 25, I. F. Lemvigh Müller's Foundation 1 og C.L. David's Foundation and Collection 10 million. Then, the train shuddered to a halt. There was no one

else to approach in the Danish foundation landscape, big or small, for all sums were welcome. All! Tøjner began to ask people if they knew anyone who was rich. He came in mind of one person he had borrowed a couple of pictures from for the Roy Lichtenstein exhibition in 2003. A collector that he had not initially known to be particularly wealthy, but who later appeared in the media as an American/ Hungarian billionaire with a liking for Denmark. Tøjner phoned Charles Simonyi, who at the age of 17 left Hungary for Denmark in order to work at the data company Regnecentralen in Valby. From there he moved on to computer studies in the USA. From there on to a friendship with Bill Gates and a job in his firm Microsoft, at that time with only 25 employees. There Charles Simonyi developed the Word and Excel programmes, and from there he later started on his own. Now he sat on his yacht in the Caribbean and listened to Tøjner's story about the vital renovation. "I can write a check for a million dollars now," he said, but the Dane answered that he needed nine million dollars, not one. "I'll have to think about that," said Simonyi. A week later he called and offered a typical American match challenge: for every dollar Tøjner could obtain himself, he would give one. Up to the missing nine million. Louisiana obtained the other half in the Ministry

Poul Erik Tøjner and multi-millionaire Charles Simonyi, who presented him with an irresistible and typically American challenge.

of Culture, where Brian Mikkelsen extraordinarily found 100 million kroner for three Danish museums with building projects in progress. Louisiana got 30 of them, thus meeting the American's challenge. Charles Simonyi ended up by paying 4.3 million dollars, so Tøjner had got 3.3 million dollars by his boldness. Louisiana was reinaugurated on 31 October 2006 almost as itself and without having been closed for one single day during the three years that the renovation work lasted.

Where Knud W. Jensen was constantly extending and expanding, Tøjner concentrated instead on looking after what there was. He improved the museum in depth, cleared up, not having taken up his post with promises of radical renewal – on the contrary. He stressed that he absolutely went in for the policy of popular backing that Knud W. Jensen based his museum on. Nor did Tøjner have anything against the homely atmosphere or that it was a destination for family excursions – the sort of things that are not particularly exclusive.

"I'm fundamentally opposed to the belief that there is a crucial distinction between art and the way in which it is represented. I dislike the churchly aura that some people want to surround art with. It is out of step with the way in which art comes into being. Artists listen to music, drive cars and eat and I would be sorry if the public at Louisiana couldn't get a bite to eat afterwards. I go in for people coming to the museum and it's all right to have a Turkish bazaar atmosphere with the Children's House and areas where people crowd together. Louisiana is alive and must combat the clerical attitude to art, but this doesn't mean that there shouldn't be pockets of quiet where it is possible to immerse oneself," he said prior to his arrival.

The unspoken criticism he was answering here was exactly the same as 40 years earlier, when the museum opened the door to the white villa and in Lars Nittve's words "for the first time in the world put the customer first". Not art, not research, but the visitor. Throughout all the years the same trickle of criticism has run through the pleasure of the broad public at the coffee and food, the post cards and the tumult, the beauty and the sure taste.

Tøjner aligned himself to Louisiana's classical tradition: "We are not running a museum for the inner circle – that's not the idea of Louisiana. It would correspond to running the Zoo for zoologists only and not for people who want to see wild animals." In the media, he defended and strengthened the museum's ideology: to open up for people that may not have any prior knowledge of art. That something else always follows as well. That the museum is a mass medium with a strong power of attraction. That one should not set oneself up as a judge of people's art experiences.

The South Wing was not even 20 years old when it began to rain
into the building. It had been built too quickly and too cheaply back
then, and Tøjner had to clear up after his over-enterprising predecessor. In the foreground César's 'Victory at Villetaneuse' (1965).

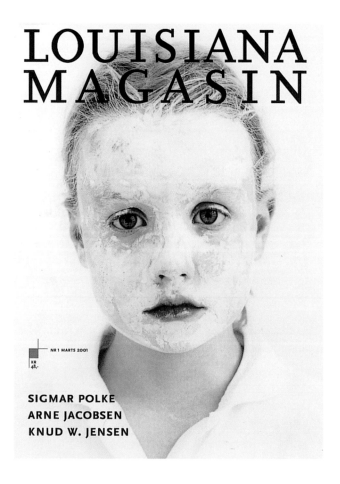

LOUISIANA MAGASIN

NR 1 MARTS 2001
KR 48,-

**SIGMAR POLKE
ARNE JACOBSEN
KNUD W. JENSEN**

"At any rate I myself will never venture to pronounce on people's experience on seeing Magritte without having asked them myself. There is a general suspicion that if anything sells in large quantities or has high visitor figures, then it is probably because it panders to the public or is superficial, and those who have arranged it have merely speculated in making money. But, of course, you don't know that."

For Tøjner the good museum visitor has signed an implicit contract before he goes in through the door. He promises to come with an open mind and the wish to be challenged in his habits and views. This is called sensibility, an ability to wish not to absorb and process everything one sees all at once. To look at things as one would meet a new person. One would (should!) not go directly up to that person and say "Jesus, what a big nose" or "What an idiot". Art distinguishes itself from consumption in that it is not just there to be swallowed and disappear. There continues to be something on the plate.

"Some people think it doesn't count if they don't finish with the works. They don't think they are the right kind of viewer if they can't say something about

The first front cover of the new publication *Louisiana Magasin*, which replaced the primitive little members' sheet in 2001.

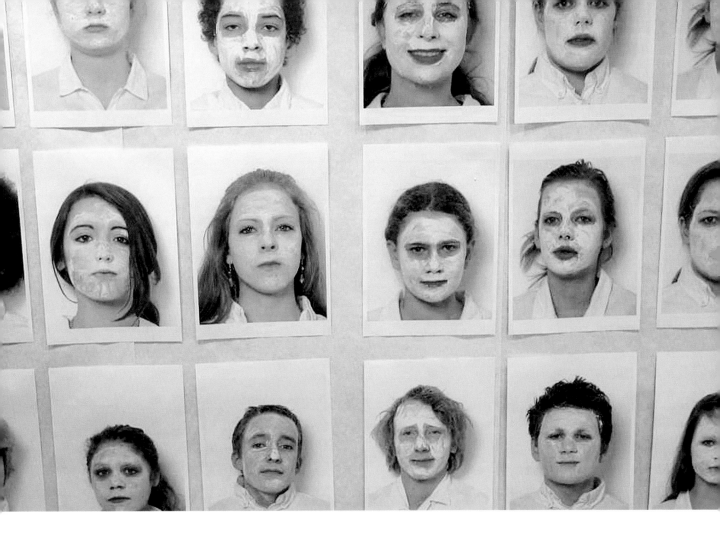

the works or react "correctly". The desire to understand is quite legitimate; nor can one help making a suggestion as to what the picture means, but you don't exhaust art – it is richer than you are and in some way or other always gets the last word if it is good art."

In comparison with the way in which classical art history presents art Louisiana still takes liberties. The important thing is to make the works live, to establish contact between the pictures and the public. So the exhibitions focus on the visual as opposed to the historical and theoretical. Sometimes Louisiana departs from the chronological order preferred by most other museums in order to arrange a thematic or purely visual effect. Baselitz in 2006, in which his old and new paintings hung among one another, was like that. One could walk around without knowing anything and just *see*. On the other hand, there was no art historical assistance available to trace the artist's development. The museum refrained from explanations and interpretations, because it is not possible directly to translate visual art. If it had been, the artist would have written a text.

White-powdered children from the Children's House imitate Mari Slaattelid's photograph from the series 'Protective', 2000.

Delighted by the exhibition Baselitz presented the museum with a reversed painting of his wife Elke – 'Finger Painting – Study of Nude Woman' (1972) – before anyone had even begun to pester him.

◄ Made in China (2007). Performance with soy and ketchup on the beach.

Tøjner feels convinced that the absence of art historians in the first three decades has been all-important for Louisiana, because they often – also in their own self-view – lack a physical enthusiasm for art. At university, they are brought up with slides and reproductions, and many of them feel most comfortable in collections and archives. Instead of on theoretical knowledge, Louisiana was founded con amore and on Knud W. Jensen's flair for what was going on and what affected people before they were aware of it. The museum rested on the ability to cross genres, involve photography and architecture and shuffle the cards at the major exhibitions. And then on the ability to see exhibitions as a new and independent medium that required all the stops to be pulled out in its staging and scenography.

Once when the staff of the National Museum re-encountered some of the things they had lent in Louisiana's rooms, they were astonished at how *amazingly good* they suddenly looked. But it cost respect in some places; the resistance among specialists and intellectuals was primarily due to the fact that the museum had become a mass medium, almost a place where people were entertained, but

also to the view that Louisiana was not serious about art history. The exhibitions were not based on research but on aesthetics, and that's how it still is.

Louisiana's deliberate hesitation

Basically, Poul Erik Tøjner knew nothing about running a museum, nor did he have any international connections, and he went out into the world equipped only with a letter of recommendation from Knud W. Jensen, Louisiana's name and his talent for becoming the natural focus of attention in most contexts. That was enough to borrow on, it turned out. Despite Lars Nittve's fear of the opposite Louisiana's reputation had been preserved.

Tøjner pestered the artists. Tried to convince a reluctant David Hockney that an exhibition in Humlebæk would stress neither the artist nor his assistant in the slightest. "That would really be something new," the assistant said dryly. "But I *am* very new!" answered Tøjner quite truthfully. Later, he also pestered Jørn Utzon. Didn't take a no thank you to be a no thank you but more or less a thank you. Both ended up by agreeing.

Where Nittve said: "It takes time before one can turn the ship around" and thereby clearly indicated his course – to attract a different public via the new and provocative – his successor stuck to the familiar Louisiana. Tøjner did not show the new as demonstratively as Nittve, nor the popular as demonstratively as ARoS with its racing cars or *Statens Museum for Kunst* with Parisian dresses and Tage Andersen flowers. Tøjner is not facile. On the contrary, he finds it difficult to arrange something crazy, as critics of Louisiana's earnestness could wish. He wants to arrange large, intelligent exhibitions. With "The Flower as Image" (2004) he was nervous that it would be said that he had chosen a seductively pretty, light and popular theme. At any rate, he vigorously defended his concept in the catalogue. Louisiana's own exhibitions began to travel on to other well-reputed museums of modern art, which is the closest one can come to an accolade in that world. Roy Lichtenstein (2003) was sent on to the Hayward Gallery in London, to Reina Sofia in Madrid and ended in the artist's home country at the San Francisco Museum of Modern Art, and that sort of thing doesn't happen if the exhibition is "a load of crap", as one curator put it briefly.

The new team under Poul Erik Tøjner works with greater transparency and openness than the elderly silverbacks that would combat one another during exhibition meetings in the old days. Whereas in Knud W. Jensen's day the museum bought works by fully or semi-mature artists, Louisiana today buys things by the younger generation, even though there are some people on the Danish art scene who never think that the acquisitions are young or soon enough. Despite Louisiana's declared goal – to be a museum for international

Louise Bourgeois' enormous female spider at Nytorv in Copenhagen in connection with the exhibition at Louisiana. In 1982 she was the first female artist to have a major retrospective exhibition at MoMA in New York. In 2003 she was shown at Louisiana for the second time.

art without any form of special treatment for Danish art – some critics miss Nittve's focus on Danish art. Everything has changed during the past decade, they say. Danish art has become professionalised and is no longer marginalised. It is here things are happening! While collectors are queuing up to buy the works of academy students before they become too expensive, the museums are hesitant about acquiring contemporary art.

"With few exceptions they are tending to miss the bus and therefore fail to buy what are gradually becoming expensive names," *Weekendavisen's* two art critics Lisbeth Bonde and Mette Sandbye write in 2006. "It is still mostly paintings that find their way to the walls of the museums, and far more art by men than by women is still being bought despite the fact that the sum of talent among young artists is distributed fifty-fifty between the sexes. Furthermore, they are all too often hesitant in face of the 'more difficult' genres, which make use of new materials and forms of expression."

But Louisiana wants to have the right to hesitate before the colossal supply of young artists. It is the museum's task to take thought and have a historical awareness that can for example see that much of today's art has been imported directly from the 1960s. The museum should wait and see what happens to the individual artist over the years and beyond the first exhibitions. In an answer to critics Tøjner says that the museums should by no means see themselves as part of the intensified food chain that one would automatically be forced into if it were merely a matter of seizing opportunities There is no reason to buy more simply

An established and canonised Roy Lichtenstein in 2003. He caused a total scandal the first time he was shown at Louisiana in the 1964 exhibition "American Pop Art" with his pictures painted as magnified strip cartoons. "The great pop fraud," as a shocked *B.T.* called the genre, later became the museum's speciality.

because the market is booming. The museums should be the critical authority that considers things one extra time, also at a distance from the intoxication of the contemporary scene with its collector's mania and social ambition, rampant market economy and youth-fixated philosophical fashion. Tøjner has experienced the hysterical hype at the opening of the Basel Art Fair in Switzerland at 11 a.m. on the classical Tuesday at the beginning of June and seen respectable billionaires running down the corridors to secure some object before anyone else. The ugly side of contemporary art.

"Our task is not to document everything that happens, but to take a qualitative cross-section that gives meaning. And that things are going well for the artists doesn't necessarily mean that they are going well for art."

With a provocative image he sees contemporary art as "a business that is screaming for state recognition". It insists that the youngest artists' expression is of the very greatest importance, and that it is now-now-now it is happening and all the time and hurry! They tell people that so much is happening in contemporary art, so they begin to believe it. That's a trick that is used by all businesses that want to attain power without admitting it. "Imagine what you could do for Danish art," is often whispered in the ears of Louisiana's curators. In fact, the museum has acquired more Danish art over the past five years than it had collected since 1958 – if we don't count *the quantities* of Kirkeby and Jorn.

When Tøjner himself was a critic on *Weekendavisen*, he wrote an editorial about the distribution of roles among *Statens Museum for Kunst*, Arken and

Louisiana. The first two had just emerged from the mists after the big extension project and museum director Anna Castberg's false examination qualifications respectively. The Copenhagen region suddenly had three art institutions, which ought to have different profiles, but which on the contrary were beginning to be dangerously alike. The problem was that they all resembled Louisiana with railway excursion schemes, cafés, bookstores, views of the landscape and children's houses. Sometimes also the same artists. Tøjner suggested a clean cut, so Arken dropped any idea of obtaining its own collection, but became an exhibition hall for experimental contemporary art. *Statens Museum* should constantly arrange exhibitions based on its own collections. And Louisiana?

"One could then keep Louisiana as the cultural forum it is with all its historical weight and experience, as an institution that has the interaction between art and culture as its core, and as a museum that with its point of departure in the twentieth century has the coming classics as the guiding principle for its exhibition policy, of course still with its gaze directed towards the future."

Tøjner has followed his own advice to Louisiana and shows "the coming classics". The chosen. This means that you take your time and do not bring young artists into the museum direct from the academy. Louisiana would rather choose them at 35 than at 25 and lets them first exhibit and sell further down in the hierarchy. The young Danish painter Tal R had to go by way of Horsens Museum of Art before coming to Louisiana. The opposite would look strange; nor would it be in the artist's interest, according to Humlebæk. Louisiana is the highest a

Louisiana is the highest a Danish artist can reach in Denmark, says Humlebæk self-confidently.

Tøjner, Gerhard Richter and the picture 'Three Sisters', painted after a chance cutting from a weekly magazine in 1965, when Richter had no idea who the girls were. Their identities were revealed by the Danish art collector Jytte Dresing, who saw the picture at Sotheby's in New York. She recognised three of her compatriots: Princesses Margrethe, Anne-Marie and Benedikte.

Danish painter can attain, says Tøjner in his matter-of-fact way. Louisiana wishes to be the same in Copenhagen as Tate Modern is in London and MoMA in New York. The two supernovas do not have a particular responsibility for local art life. They have a global view and show artists and artistic experience without regard to nationality, gender or age. As Knud W. Jensen said: "There is so much art in the world. Why should the very best have been produced right here in Denmark?"

Mentioned in no particular order, Tøjner's Louisiana has opened major retrospective exhibitions with the German painters Polke, Richter and Baselitz, shown the architects Norman Foster, Renzo Piano, Arne Jacobsen, Jørn Utzon, Jean Nouvel and Poul Kjærholm, the photographers William Eggleston, Brassaï, Cindy Shermann and Richard Avedon, the rapidly up- and-coming young and youngish Thomas Demand, Michael Bevilacqua, Janet Cardiff, Keith Tyson, Julie Mehretu and Tal R, the classical and semi-classical Matisse, Louise Bourgeois, Lucian Freud, Roy Lichtenstein and David Hockney. And in the 50th anniversary year of 2008 it will be the turn of Cézanne & Giacometti, his dream.

The old artists from the first half of the previous century must continue to be represented, since all the time there are new visitors who may not know that the artists of today are working on the backs of the insights attained by their predecessors. Art is not just a private language – it has a historical dimension.

The difference between Knud W. Jensen and Poul Erik Tøjner is that Tøjner not only associates with the country's intellectuals, but is himself an intellectual.

Matisse exhibition in 2005. Louisiana was visited by more than four times as many people (95.000) as the small exhibition with the same artist, called a parasite exhibition by *Politiken's* Karsten Ivfersen, at *Statens Museum for Kunst*.

"Why should the very best have bee

He is an ironist, an aesthete and elitist, but he tries to divest himself of the first characteristic, which is second nature for him, and to replace it with ordinary human attentiveness. The irony could be accepted at a family-type workplace like *Weekendavisen*, but not at the much larger and more feminine Louisiana, where he discovered that importance was attached to openness and being able to talk properly together about how one was feeling. A feature that probably became inherent to the place from the beginning because it was person-centred and built up with Knud W. Jensen's well-being as the pivotal point.

Tøjner can conceive ideas himself, realise them himself and write about them in the catalogue himself. There is a lot of *himself* in him. As opposed to the founder he is not so dependent on what other people think, and he doesn't talk things through quite as long and as many times. He is impatient, makes up his own mind – and quickly – is in control all the way through and doesn't enthusiastically ask to be contradicted. He doesn't care to be No. 2 anywhere. Finds it hard to tolerate fools. A close friend describes him as the typical elder brother, which he actually is. A boy of whom high demands were made at home, and who almost routinely had to rebel, kick over the traces, break windows, play truant and cause his mother concern only suddenly to pull himself together and dutifully continue his life with great confidence in himself and with an awe-inspiring work capacity. To irritable people it seems as though everything has been easy for him, that he is the incarnation of an Aladdin type, a golden boy, but he has worked like a horse from the moment he pulled himself together. It's just the outcome that seems so effortless. In the museum world, there still exists a certain animosity against him and the museum because he is not an art historian, and Louisiana has that commercial taint about it.

Another difference between Jensen and Tøjner is that the latter has to get out of the house in order to be able to breathe. He is on the boards of the University of Copenhagen, the David Collection and Gyldendal and is an adviser to the coming art museum Tjuvholmen in Oslo, as well as being a member of a number of advisory committees. He neither can nor will make do with Louisiana alone, as Knud W. Jensen could.

Tøjner was a director long before he became director. Where other chiefs in the art world live in modest terraced houses and wait to move into representative villas until they have been appointed only to feel uncomfortable and wander restlessly around in their new surroundings, he did it the other way round. Tøjner had ambitious plans from the very start. He bought the enormous director's villa at an early stage and renovated it himself with original leather hangings in the smoking room. Bought big German cars. And just as early he smoked cigars and drank claret every day. In that way, everything was in place for Georg Baselitz and the others, who years later would be standing in the reception rooms and talking with collectors and borrowers and museum people or queuing up for the buffet in the kitchen.

It's gone excellently, everyone says. Also the group that doesn't think Louisiana sufficiently avantgarde, sufficiently experimental, sufficiently crazy – even when the museum does in fact show *contemporary contemporary*. Louisiana doesn't have street credibility among the merciless young radicals. For them Humlebæk is establishment, but all the same everyone goes up there to see the youngest things – Sip my Ocean, Online, Janet Cardiff – but not Matisse and the historical stuff. No one doubts the museum's expertise, but a man like Mikkel Bogh, the rector of the Royal Academy of Fine Art, is a representative voice when he says that at Louisiana one can't see all the young artists who are working across more than one medium. The museum is cautious and focuses on the authoritative, the established and the safe. Typically: major painters. Last time Mikkel Bogh saw the museum tackle young contemporary art was in Lars Nittve's 'Nowhere' in 1996. He would like to see more 'Tabernakel' to stimulate the art that will end up at Louisiana some time anyway:

"A sense for the visual in art is greater in Louisiana than in many young artists at the Academy. They are interested in the discursive, where meaning lies not in the work itself but in the social idea, dreams and fantasies that are to be found around it, the non-visible part of the work. If we add Documenta in Kassel to the Biennale in Venice, perhaps 75 % of the art is of such a discursive nature."

The criticism has always been there, will always be there and changing directors mark their positions in the art scene by moving closer to the group or moving away from it. It hurts economically to move closer because problem-oriented contemporary art at one and the same time attracts the "right" people and scares off the many. Tøjner often uses the phrase "a qualified popular institution" about Louisiana and has accepted the historical requirement that the museum has to make money. The museum pays two-thirds of its running costs, while the remainder is paid by the State, which is roughly the opposite of the situation for the other museums – they earn the smaller part themselves and are given the larger part. Some receive everything.

A typical characteristic of Louisiana is that it is visited by many people, and it has been able to take on tasks that no one else could manage – from a large-scale Egyptian exhibition to four Picassos – but the visitor figures must not become a goal in themselves. "We want a lot of people to come to something good, not to anything whatsoever," says the director, who now and then expresses deep frustration about visitor figures because they remove the focus from the art and prevent the curators from showing what they know is good but will not attract

Planning in the museum director's office. A discreet orgy of good taste.

Michael Sheridan, American architect and connoisseur of Scandinavian modernism, unfolded/displayed Poul Kjærholm's life and work at Louisiana. The American journal *Art Forum* called the exhibition one of the world's 15 most interesting in 2006.

as large a public. Tøjner's policy is like Knud W. Jensen's to show "a little of everything" and to let warm exhibitions alternate with cold ones, but in 2006 the visiting figures fell below the level that led to Lars Nittve's dismissal. The difference is that Tøjner was able to get on with Knud W. Jensen and still remain within Louisiana's tradition. He is not in the process of changing course.

Nevertheless, something classical has disappeared somewhere between Knud W. Jensen and Tøjner. What has happened to the peace people, the Arabs, the Russians and the feminists? In the old days, Louisiana was a meeting place, which always delivered *more* than art: a meeting with Germaine Greer on the female menopause; a lecture by the LSD researcher Stanislav Grof on holotropic breathwork; or folk dancers from Wales, the children's theatre Bimmer, Marilyn Mazur's Future Song or Troels Kløvedal with slides. The world's conflicting parties came to Louisiana. Where in the 1980s it was exiled Russian writers who met critics and writers from their home country, it became the turn in the 1990s of Arabs and Israelis to discuss in the Boathouse down by the beach. Only the children in the Children's House and the music in the concert hall are left. Louisiana's chamber music is world class, and according to the British newspaper the *Independent*, the concert programme could more than fill the Royal Festival Hall. After Isaac Stern the violinist Gidon Kremer has become artist in residence, but the politicians, writers, the hippies and the wild debaters have disappeared.

"Knud believed in the necessity of establish dialogue between opposing parties," says Pundik, whose activist newspaper matched the museum perfectly. More than anything else both men wanted their institutions to be *alive*. They wanted to influence and change society. Louisiana's interpretation of what constitutes art was very, very broad. In Nittve and Tøjner's years the concept has become narrower and the political dimension has been dropped. But from 2008 the debates will return under the name of "Louisiana Live" – where the public will again meet writers, researchers and debaters. And Louisiana will become complete again.

Louisiana Manifesto

The tonsured French super architect Jean Nouvel sat in the sun with Vilhelm Wohlert and interviewed him. "Thank you because you have created this place, which is so natural and comes out of the ground like a spring," he said to the elderly gentleman with the cane. Wohlert looked embarrassed. The Frenchman is one of a handful of the world's most prominent architects; he has designed Institut du Monde Arabe in Paris and a number of other modern cult places from museums to opera houses. The Dane has designed Louisiana, which Jean Nouvel praises with such affection and empathy that it is almost too much. The buildings in Humlebæk fit perfectly into his view of architecture: that each site

After a concert at Louisiana in 2006 the Japanese pianist Mitsuko Uchida said of the museum's grand piano: "It's one of the worst I have played on for a long time." She therefore had to help music chief Lars Fengér to find the best of eight grand pianos at Steinway & Sons in Hamburg. "Grand piano no. 7 has an unusual amount of personality," she said, so now it stands in the concert hall.

Bookmark for the Schumann series with Eric le Sage, the French pianist, who is scheduled to play Schumann's collected piano works at Louisiana in 2006-2010.

requires a new architecture, that architecture is therefore to relate to a place, not just to throw up a spectacular model in international style. In Louisiana's case: to be sensitive to the park and the old villa, the slopes clad with beech trees all the way down to the Sound, the Danish tradition for brick and wood, the white garden walls of North Zealand, the air, the light and the history. And then draw it out a little further with flat roofs, which were not part of the traditions, Japanese simplicity and elegant Californian modernity. Nouvel's signature is not to have a signature, but to take time to get to know the site, which is Knud W. Jensen and his ideas about the spirit of the place all over again. He did not care for the dominating effect on the landscape of these autonomous masterpieces, which are almost unsuited for showing art in.

To have a trademark or a special style that one imposes on all that one gets near from Dubai via Beijing to London is self-assertive and harmful in Nouvel's eyes. The functionalists were quite wrong when they claimed that the same style could fulfil everybody's needs. They flatten out the differences that one can't live without. "Architecture that kills feeling is not Louisianian", said Nouvel and insisted on letting the museum itself be the heart in the exhibition of his own work since it would be in the middle of a perfect example of architectonic insight anyway. But it surprised the museum nonetheless that he wanted to go so far as to call his exhibition "Louisiana Manifest". In the pillared room, he wrote his manifesto on architecture directly on the walls.

It begins:

> "In 2005, more than ever, architecture is annihilating places, banalizing them, violating them.
>
> Sometimes it replaces the landscape, creates it in its own image, which is nothing but another way of effacing it.
>
> And then there is Louisiana, an emotional shock.
>
> The living proof of a forgotten truth: architecture has the power to transcend.
>
> It can reveal geographies, histories, colours, vegetations, horizons, qualities of light.
>
> Impertinent and natural, it is in the world. It lives. It is unique. It is *Louisianan*."

Lena Willemark in a voluminous dress with pockets for the audience. At their concert.

Curator Anders Kold with model of a room at the China exhibition in 2007. All exhibitions are first set up in miniature.

In reality, he is not particularly occupied by Louisiana's style, but by Vilhelm Wohlert and Jørgen Bo's understanding of the site, the calm it gives that their buildings are not in noisy conflict with the surroundings. Nouvel speaks of a "transcending power", and he is not alone in that. As incredible art museums spring up all over the globe, one can feel a longing for Louisiana's natural simplicity and meditative calm, especially abroad, where some people have had enough of an extreme sport architecture that is ever striving to go further out, higher up and deeper down than its predecessors. Present-day museum architects are engaged in a global competition in attention-demanding buildings designed to have so powerful an impact that they can literally attract crowds of people from a neighbouring town, country or continent. A stronger contrast to that way of thinking than the flat building along the edge of a park in Humlebæk is not to be found. The big guns have been there to look at its special quality – the fusion of architecture, art and landscape.

"If one wants to build art museums, it is necessary to have seen Louisiana," says the Japanese architect Tadeo Ando. And the founder of the mysterious and wildly different Museum Insel Hombroich, which is laid out in twelve pavilions in an extensive Rhine landscape, cites two private modern museums as his models: Kröller-Müller in Holland and Louisiana in Humlebæk, because both bring their rural situation right into the architecture, especially at Louisiana, where the pavilions are linked by glass corridors. Louisiana is first and foremost an inspiration for rural museums with space around them and a landscape to take into account, not for big city museums that are squeezed onto small building sites. *The Architectural Review* calls Louisiana one of the 20th century's finest museums, precisely because it was not conceived as a treasure house, department store, theatre, theme park or any other hypermodern phenomenon, but simply as a real place.

"Perhaps we have been mistaken in recent years in spending so much time on thinking about museums as the cathedrals of our day and worrying about their external appearance and expression, Bo and Wohlert's early work hardly appears to have a style, but in a wonderful fashion it creates space and allows the art and the landscape to speak for themselves. Strangely, it is rarely discussed and has barely exerted any influence. It is time to reassess what it teaches us: intensity, quietness, balance, calm, all desperately necessary in an increasingly crazed world."

The founder's endless attention to detail could seem comic or tiring for some. He could not pass through the house without pointing out something that had to be fixed, removed, improved or just picked up, and in time everyone around him became just like him. The next generation inherited his supreme feeling for the

An enthusiastic Jean Nouvel
interviews Vilhelm Wohlert
(with his back to the camera).

place. It was never a matter of indifference how things looked. The carpenters altered an apparently banal wooden staircase from the glass corridor to the Lake Garden ten times in the course of two months before he was satisfied. The same with the banisters. On the other hand, it is beautifully finished, and this modernistic perfection gets people to relax. The *New York Times'* correspondent thinks that Louisiana has a therapeutic effect and is entirely different from most other museums. In the more than 30 years in which John Russell has been coming to the museum, he has never seen a visitor who looked flustered or troubled, tired or bad-tempered. "This is on the contrary a museum where people spontaneously hold hands," he writes. A female visitor calls it friendliness.

"There is a friendliness at Louisiana even when there are so damn many people and Swedish ladies in fur coats. The atmosphere never becomes really stressed, the attendants are calm elderly men who stand around quietly smiling. Slippers types with home knit sweaters. They remind me of my father."

Louisiana had to be conquered and become Tøjner's own place, but how? He emptied the rooms in the South Wing of Warhol, Kirkeby, Kiefer, Lichtenstein & Co. and cycled through the empty white rooms in order to feel his freedom to do as he wished

"The first time I sensed that I had anything at all to do here besides being director and working together with a lot of people, having a balanced relationship with Knud and so on was when I began to hang the collection up. It was in fact quite concretely the case that I couldn't link myself with Louisiana in any other way than that I was a newly appointed emissary or governor in this little state. I had not had any relation to the museum physically, substantially, before I began to hang the collection up. It is a very concrete way of conquering the rooms, for it is quite true that the rooms here at Louisiana are quite concrete, but at the same time imaginary because one has seen so many exhibitions in them that one can't actually see them. One just walks around thinking – how delightfully Louisiana-like it is here."

He also had the liberty to accept Louisiana as it stood even though a young architect immediately begged him to break up the red floor tiles and in that way

◄ "Why is the star architect building a bathing jetty?" *Berlingske Tidende* asked Jean Nouvel. "From this spot one can see how beautiful it is here. Louisiana is really an incredibly inspiring place for architects. Everything is just right here. The scale of things and the interaction with nature, the understanding of the landscape's character," he answered.

The exhibition 'Sip My Ocean'
with videos from Louisiana's
own collection was named
after Pippilotti Ris's underwa-
ter work, which can be seen
here. Bought in Lars Nittve's
era in 1996 together with a
number of other major works.

Louisiana worked for five years to be allowed to acquire the David Hockney picture. It is a painting costing in the region of 50 million kroner, donated by the A. P. Møller Foundation, which ventured for the first time into the field of modern art.

remove some of the homely suburban atmosphere that permeated the museum. Young artists think that the place is so *nice* that nothing really barrier-breaking can take place in it. But that is something Tøjner doesn't want to change. He finds it a strangely puritanical viewpoint. Louisiana is as Louisiana is – a kind of museum for itself and the architecture of the past. Louisiana can easily stand firm while art is on the move within it.

This duality fascinates him. That the museum is a place where one can do and show things that are inconceivable outside. One can scare the life out of people without fatal consequences and put them to the test in a situationm that resembles a state of emergency. True it is fiction, true it is staged. The museum performs aesthetic experiments that have to do with people's view of existence just as at the theatre. That is why we have such institutions – to try things out on

From 2008 the museum will be open on 200 evenings a year. As the only museum in the country.

people. Perhaps they will be able to see something they have already seen, but didn't know that they saw.

If art is fundamentally about crises – in love, in sexuality, in the self, in our relations with our mothers, our fathers, in love, in boredom – the museum is one big smouldering crisis centre, where someone comes and looks at the patients, walks around among them and says: "That looks good, that does." Modern art has to do with what is lacking, uncertainty, scepticism, but we stand looking at it in a secure and good space. We deliberately expose ourselves to it. As the writer Per Højholt has said, we are museum-forming mammals.

That is in fact a very strange and very human phenomenon.

Notes and references

The 1950s

10 "The journalist from the ladies' magazine *Tidens Kvinder*": The article was called "At 'Louisiana' in Humlebæk. Visit to Landowner Busky-Neergaard", *Tidens Kvinder*, no. 26, 1942. Text: Lancette.

10 "Named by the first owner after his wives": Alexander Brun built Louisiana in 1855. His first "Louise marriage" lasted only 25 days. Alice Louise was the daughter of the politician and Master of the Royal Hunt Peter Tutein from the estate Marienborg on the island of Møn. As a gift to her future husband, Alexander Brun, the 18-year-old girl had a miniature portrait of herself executed by Johannes Müller. The painter made the girl pregnant, and Alexander only agreed to marry her on condition of a quick divorce. The child was given up for adoption.

10 "North Zealand makes me want to throw up!": Carsten Jensen in "Sjælen sidder i øjet" [The Soul Resides in the Eye], Gyldendal 1985.

14 "In *Bo Bedre* Louisiana's architects defend": *Bo Bedre*, no. 1, March 1961.

14 "The first catalogue": Edited by art critic Pierre Lübecker, designed by Austin Grandjean.

16 "The heavily reliable": Hans Edvard Nørregård-Nielsen in "Ny Carlsbergfondet 1902-2002" [The Ny Carlsberg Foundation 1902-2002], Gyldendal, 2005.

16 "In this museum": *Kristeligt Dagblad* 14.8.1958

16 "It may seem peculiar": *Berlingske Tidende* 14.3.1958

16 "A visit to Louisiana was nice": Conversation with journalist and editor Dan Tschernia.

19 "So when he catches sight of the painter Jeppe Vontillius": *Information* 15.8.1958.

19 "Even the Communist paper *Land og Folk* surrenders": Otto Gelsted in *Land og Folk* 14.8.1958.

19 "Louisiana must be *used*": *Berlingske Tidende* 15.8.1958.

22 "A Danish historian compares this tiger's leap": Henrik S. Nissen in Gyldendal og Politiken's Danmarkshistorie [History of Denmark] 1950-70, vol. 14, 1991/2004.

22 "You can say what you like": Thorkild Bjørnvig in Knud – her er dit liv! [Knud – This is Your Life!], 1996.

22 "Knud was right": Conversation with Knud W. Jensen's wife Vivi Jensen.

24 "I remember it as if": Conversation with writer and critic Niels Barfoed.

24 "Quite a few people who shook their heads": Architect Vilhelm Wohlert in "Knud – her er dit liv!" [Knud – This is Your Life!], 1996

24 "They underestimated him": Conversation with journalist Bo Bjørnvig, son of Thorkild Bjørnvig.

25 "It may seem immaterial": Klaus Rifbjerg in "Knud – her er dit liv!" [Knud – This is Your Life!], 1996.

25 "It doesn't matter how much I read": Conversation with journalist Karen Fougner.

27 "The opposition is comic": Conversation with writer and critic Torben Brostrøm.

27 "Christ, that was Knud W. Jensen!": Torben Brostrøm in "Knud – This is Your Life!", 1996.

28 "At the steps and the entrance portal one was received": Knud W. Jensen in "Mit Louisiana-liv" [My Louisiana Life], 1983/93.

28 "They agree that Louisiana was not really first-rate": Conversation with art historian and curator Hanne Finsen.

30 "A valuable art work can be trodden flat": Museum inspector Erik Fischer from *Statens Museum for Kunst* in *Louisiana Revy*, March 1963.

32 "Louisiana was a breach with everything": Conversation with director and haberdasher Jørgen Nørgaard from Nørgaard on Strøget.

36 "At Louisiana importance was attached from the start": Hans Edvard Nørregård-Nielsen in "Knud – her er dit liv!" [Knud – This is Your Life!], 1996.

36 "When Moderna Museet in Stockholm visited Louisiana": The problem of the beautiful view is mentioned in *Louisiana Revy*, no. 1, September 1960.

36 "An important person like Thorlacius-Ussing": Hans Edvard Nørregård-Nielsen in "Ny Carlsbergfondet 1902-2002" [The Ny Carlsberg Foundation 1902-2002], 2005.

36 "Jensen must find some tricks": *Louisiana Revy*, no. 1, September 1960.

38 "There the art is 'given a calm setting'": Critic Peter Iden in *Frankfurter Rundschau* 16.10.1982.

38 "Both places have lots of glass": *Politiken* 10.6.1959.

39 "I think that art is better served": *Politiken* 15.8.1959.

39 "The debate on 'Louisiana' came to concern trivialities": *Dagens Nyheder* 13.9.1959.

40 "Knud W. Jensen 'a piece of filthy luck' for Denmark": Hans Edvard Nørregård-Nielsen in "Ny Carlsbergfondet 1902-2002" [The Ny Carlsberg Foundation 1902-2002], 2005.

40 "Art at the Workplace": Founded on 23.11.1954 by Knud W. Jensen from the cheese firm A/S P. Jensen and the then director of the Royal Copenhagen Porcelain Factory. Christian Christensen. The Confederation of Danish Employers and the Trade Unions Council put money on the table together with a number of enterprises. The idea was to buy Danish art and send exhibitions round to the workplaces. Knud W. Jensen was the first chairman of the association. The sculptor Peter Bonnén is the present chairman.

43 "From going around in a strange freedom": Thorkild Bjørnvig in "Knud – her er dit liv!" [Knud – This is Your Life!], 1996.

43 "Lottery winners always say": Conversation with former Danish Broadcasting Corporation Head of Programmes Werner Svendsen.

43 "The slow and organic power": Clara Selborn "Notater om Karen Blixen" [Notes on Karen Blixen], 1974.

43 "The radio is such a miserable institution": Frans Lasson and Tom Engelbrecht: "Karen Blixen i Danmark. Breve 1931-62" [Karen Blixen in Denmark. Letters 1931-62], vol. 2, 1996.

44 "Such a spiritual pachyderm": Clara Selborn: "Notater om Karen Blixen" [Notes on Karen Blixen], 1974.

44 "You'd better be off": Conversation with Niels Barfoed.

44 "We freely spent Knud's money": Ole Wivel in "Lys og mørke. Mit venskab med Knud W. Jensen" [Light and Dark]. My Friendship with Knud W. Jensen], 1994.

44 "Suddenly you were in safety": Tage Skou-Hansen in "Knud – her er dit liv!" [Knud – This is Your Life!], 1996.

44 "Not to use the word *tits*": Jørgen Gustava Brandt in Anders Thyrring Andersen (ed.): "PS. Om Martin A. Hansens korrespondance med kredsen omkring Heretica" [PS. On Martin A. Hansen's Correspondence with the Circle around *Heretica*], 2005.

44 "Thank you for the letter with the invitation": The letter is among Knud W. Jensen's papers at Louisiana.

44 "All this is just due to the fact": *Information* 31.7.1958.

45 "These were difficult years": Letter to Uffe Harder 10.12.1979.

45 "We should find out": Ole Wivel in "Romance for valdhorn" [Romance for French Horn], 1972.

47 "The journal above all": Niels Barfoed in "Farvel så længe!" [Till We Meet Again], 2007.

48 "The 'Heretics' feared that modernism": Hanne Engberg "Kætterne. Kredsen omkring *Heretica* 1948-54" [The Heretics. The Circle around *Heretica* 1948-54], 1995. The author is Knud W. Jensen's niece.

49 "The first year he put": Ibid.

49 "He was capable of getting up at two o'clock": Conversation with Bo Bjørnvig.

49 "When the young poet": Hanne Engberg: "Kætterne. Kredsen omkring Heretica 1948-54" [The Heretics. The Circle around *Heretica* 1948-54], 1995.

49 "While other millionaires keep race horses": *Land og Folk* 18.8.1952.

49 "For me it was the *poet*": Niels Birger Wamberg: "Mens kunsten er ung: en samtale mellem Knud W. Jensen og Niels Birger Wamberg" [While Art is Young: a Conversation between Knud W. Jensen and Niels Birger Wamberg], 1992.

50 "It is an irony of fate": Conversation with Werner Svendsen.

50 "In a long letter to Knud W. Jensen from Martin A. Hansen": Anders Thyrring Andersen (ed.): "PS. Om Martin A. Hansens korrespondance med kredsen omkring Heretica" [PS. On Martin A. Hansen's Correspondence with the Circle around *Heretica*], 2005.

The Secret
50 "In 1928 a charming and gifted": The story of the Ring is primarily taken from Hansaage Bøggild's "Ringen omkring Ole" [The Ring around Ole], 2004.

51 "It is a world by itself": *Louisiana Revy*, no. 2, 1966.

51 "Also Ole Lippmann came to Vedbæk Tennis Club": Niels Barfoed: "En kriger. Portræt af Ole Lippmann" [A Warrior. Portrait of Ole Lippmann], 2005.

52 "Against all that will make no sacrifice": The poem first became known to the general public in Marianne Juhl's article "Forfatter-fortid: Ole Wivel og den vidunderlige krig" [Writer's Past: Ole Wivel and the Wonderful War], 07.03.2001 in *Jyllands-Posten*.

53 "Your defeat is irrevocable": ibid.

53 "Once marched through the streets of Gudhjem": Tage Voss: "Fejemøg fra Parnasset" [Sweepings from Parnassus], 1999.

54 "The serious journal *Nordica*": The article was called "Fuldkommenhedslængslen" [The Longing for Perfection]. *Nordica* 17/2000.

54 "Thanks for the Høst book ": letter dated 27.6.98. Knud W. Jensen's papers at Louisiana.

55 "It would have been a good story": Conversation with Torben Brostrøm.

55 "In a form that never permitted": Bo Lidegaard: "Kampen om Danmark 1933-45" [The Fight for Denmark], 2005.

55 "Everyone loves Knud": Bo Bjørnvig in *Weekendavisen* 2.07.2004.

56 "It's a dark point in my past": Hans Hertel in *Politiken* 27.06.2004.

56 "That was the end of my relationship to Ole Wivel": Marianne Juhl in *Jyllands-Posten* 19.06.2004.

56 "The adjective 'dark' is so difficult": Conversation with Hanne Engberg.

57 "Knud became afraid": Conversation with Knud W. Jensen's secretary for 30 years Skydsgaard.

57 "Knud was much more fluid": Conversation with Niels Barfoed.

57 "I think he was a very banal young man": Conversation with Werner Svendsen.

58 "We never spoke about the War": Conversation with former chief editor Herbert Pundik.

Rite of transition
58 "Knud W. Jensen and Karen Blixen": Conversation with Bo Bjørnvig.

58 "After a year and a half's marriage she fell": Jørgen Stormgaard: "Blixen og Bjørnvig. Pagten der blev brudt" [Blixen and Bjørnvig. The Pact that was Broken], 2005. Here for the first time we find the name of the married woman with whom Bjørnvig fell so passionately in love that it paralysed his ability to work for years and drove his wife to the verge of despair. The infatuation is mentioned elsewhere in the literature, for instance in "Karen Blixen i Danmark" [Karen Blixen in Denmark] (1996) and "Kætterbreve" [Heretical Letters] (2004), but always without the woman's name.

59 "But Benedicte never got over Bjørnvig ": Frans Lasson's postscript in Jørgen Stormgaard: "Blixen og Bjørnvig. Pagten der blev brudt" [Blixen and Bjørnvig. The Pact that was Broken], 2005.

59 "Knud's was a big Airedale Terrier": Thorkild Bjørnvig in "Knud – her er dit liv!" [Knud – This is Your Life!], 1996.

59 "At Rungstedlund she passed the time": Anders Thyrring Andersen (ed.): "PS. Om Martin A. Hansens korrespondance med kredsen omkring Heretica" [PS. On Martin A. Hansen's Correspondence with the Circle around *Heretica*], 2005.

59 "Martin A. Hansen wrote in his diary": Martin A. Hansen – Dagbøger 1947-55 [Martin A. Hansen Diaries – 1947-55].

59 "'Excellent!' answered the young publisher": Conversation with Otto B. Lindhardt.

60 "My understanding was that in the first place Knud": Martin A. Hansen Dagbøger 1947-55 [Martin A. Hansen Diaries 1947-55].

60 "A gambler, reckless as few": Ole Wivel: "Lys og Mørke. Mit venskab med Knud W. Jensen" [Light and Dark. My Friendship with Knud W. Jensen], 1994.

61 "As the lawyer Allan Philip later admitted": Allan Philip in "Knud – her er dit liv!" [Knud – This is Your Life!], 1996.

61 "Your real wedding with fate'": Letter from Thorkild Bjørnvig. Knud W. Jensen's papers at Louisiana.

62 "Of course it might sound a little ambitious": "Mit Louisiana-liv" [My Louisiana Life], 1985/93.

Here it is!
64 "It can't be right ": Ibid.

64 "At this point the minister, Bodil Koch": Ibid.

64 "We have a young man here": Conversation with now deceased architect Vilhelm Wohlert.

66 "In December 1954 his doctor diagnosed": Knud W. Jensen's papers at Louisiana.

66 "He stood there in the wind": Vilhelm Wohlert in "Knud – her er dit liv!" [Knud – This is Your Life!], 1996.

67 "Is there a modern art?": "Mit Louisiana-liv" [My Louisiana Life], 1985/93.

67 "The company's man wrote in an internal memorandum from April 1957": dated 9.4.1957.

71 "The proposal aims to convert": Dated 2.5.1957 and addressed to Director Th. Thorsteinsson, Østifternes Kreditforening.

77 "In terms of museum psychology this was a wise move": Conversation with Vilhelm Wohlert.

78 "It was akin to our Scandinavian approach": Ibid.

79 "They built small Louisiana clones for North Zealanders": Particularly Ole Palsby's house in Vedbæk in 1960 and the project Piniehøj on Strandvejen in Rungsted in 1962.

79 "Everyone believes I'm a compulsive builder": Poul Erik Tøjner's obituary on Knud W. Jensen in *Weekendavisen* 15.12.2000.

The 1960s

84 "A typical Louisiana type": This figure is my invention and entirely fictional. Later he is transformed into a woman.

84 "The Frank Jæger record on the gramophone": Louisiana Grammonfonplader was founded in 1959 and issued five records with classical music, modern Danish music and Danish writers reading their own works. From 1961 the company was called Louisiana/Gyldendal Grammonfonplader and continued to issue records that were typical of the period's progressive cultural trends "Gris på gaflen" [Pork on the Fork] (The Student Council's watershed New Year comedy from 1962], "PH på plade" [PH on Record], Erik Knudsen's "Ned med kulturen" [Down with Culture], etc.

84 "On the coffee table next to the negro sculpture lie a couple of issues of *Louisiana Revy*": The first issue appeared in September 1960 and had an interior from Moderna Museet in Stockholm on the front cover because the Swedish museum had visited Louisiana. Before *Louisiana Revy* three Louisiana Årbøger [Louisiana Yearbooks] appeared: 1958, 1959 and 1960.

84 "His house looks as it should": Knud W. Jensen writes about pretentious "middle class style" in his article "Kunsten og samfundet" [Art and Society] in *Louisiana Revy*, October 1962.

84 "Professor Løgstrup's essay on art and ethics": *Louisiana Revy*, no. 3, 1961.

84 "One man in twelve in Denmark has a beard": Poul Hammerich's Danmarkskrønike [Chronicle of Denmark], "Kagen skæres 1961-68" [The Cake is Cut 1961-68].

86 "If democracy wants to have culture": *Louisiana Revy*, October 1962.

86 "That their need for genuine commitment": *Louisiana Revy*, March 1962.

90 "What is the reason why": Villy Sørensen in the introduction to Kierkegaard's "Begrebet Angst" [The Concept of Anxiety] published 1960.

90 "Critical researchers from a later period call modernism "a holistic theory": Anne Borup (ed.) "Modernismen til debat. Nye historier om dansk litteratur" [Modernism Debated. Recent Stories about Danish Literature], vol. 1, 2005.

90 "Despite our apparent materialism": From Knud W. Jensen's foreword to the questionnaire "Pejling af modernismen" [Taking the Bearings of Modernism] in *Louisiana Revy*, January 1962.

90 "It is the very idea of art that people shouldn't have": Article in *Politisk Revy*, 1963.

91 "One can become lowbrow and hostile to culture": *Louisiana Revy*, January 1967.

91 "A tribute to Europe's best modern museum": *Louisiana Revy*, December 1961.

91 "Will no longer impose on us his egocentric vision": *Louisiana Revy*, December 1967.

U-turn

92 "With rolled up sleeves": At Documenta II 273 artists from the whole world exhibited. 51 of them are represented at Louisiana today, for instance Karel Appel, Francis Bacon, Lucio Fontana, Sam Francis, Alberto Giacometti, Philip Guston, Asger Jorn and Richard Mortensen (the only Danes at Documenta II], Henry Moore, Pablo Picasso, Jackson Pollock, Robert Rauschenberg, Germaine Richier, Mark Rothko.

94 "It is true that we do not possess the artistic mastery of French": *Berlingske Tidende* 15.8.1958.

94 "It was suddenly up in a quite different": Niels Birger Wamberg: "Mens kunsten er ung. En samtale mellem Knud W. Jensen og Niels Birger Wamberg" [While Art is Young: a Conversation between Knud W. Jensen and Niels Birger Wamberg], 1992.

94 "Self-constituted censorship and inquisitorial attitude": Knud W. Jensen: Indtryk fra Documenta: Louisiana Årbog 1959 [Impressions from Documenta: Louisiana Yearbook 1959]. Documenta II was an international exhibition of art after 1945. Open 11.7-11.10 1959. Still exists.

99 "Denmark is certainly an underdeveloped country": Letter from Knud W. Jensen dated 29.3.1960. There is a copy among his papers at Louisiana.

99 "Around 1960 it became known": "KWJ LXX 1986", published on the occasion of Knud W. Jensen's 70th birthday the same year.

100 "Sandberg wrote a kind of love poem": *Louisiana Revy*, November 1961.

The time of scandals

101 "It was like seeing grown-up people": Bernhard Lewkovitch in *BT* 2.10.1961.

101 "The avantgarde's old gardener": *Information* 2.10.1961.

101 "Later in his life Nam June Paik": Louisiana acquired the work "TV Monitor" (1974).

101 "The week before his concert": Tinguely lit his firework sculpture on Friday, 22.9. 1961 at 6 pm on the lawn in front of Louisiana.

106 "Danish prime minister": *Politiken* 23.9.1961.

106 "I was very surprised": *Information* 4.11.1959.

106 "For this reason *Information*'s critic": Ejner Johansson in *Information* 30.10.1959.

108 "The newspaper was happy to print": *Politiken* 26.9.1961.

113 "The majority with their more sporadic concern": *Louisiana Revy*, January 1962.

113 "Only a few people have an artistic": Ibid.

114 "One might say that there": Niels Birger Wamberg: "Mens kunsten er ung. En samtale mellem Knud W. Jensen og Niels Birger Wamberg" [While Art is Young: a conversation between Knud W. Jensen and Niels Birger Wamberg], 1992.

114 "Modern art is a liberation": Conversation with Torben Brostrøm.

115 "So Kirkeby chose": Lars Morell: "Samtaler med Per Kirkeby" [Conversations with Per Kirkeby], 1997.

Rindal comes
115 "In the light of the fact that": All the protests and readers' letters have been taken from Anne Marie Kastrup and Ivar Lærkesen: "Rindalismen. Dokumentations – og studiebind" [Rindalism. Documentation and Study Volume], 1979.

116 "The postman continued to": Hans Sølvhøj: "Rødt på hvidt. Hans Sølvhøj erindrer" [Red on White. Hans Sølvhøj Remembers], 1989.

117 "The workers' movement's mistake": Ibid.

117 "One evening in Ribe": Hans Edvard Nørregård-Nielsen recounts the story in "Riber ret" [Ribe Law], 2001.

120 "They can of course withdraw": Ejvind Larsen: "Da politikerne kom til kunsten og kunstnerne til politikerne eller historien om et kronisk citat" [When the Politicians Came to Art and the Artists to the Politicians or the Story of a Chronic Quotation], 1970.

120 "There was something he needed to say"": Knud W. Jensen: "Mit Louisiana-liv" [My Louisiana Life], 1985/97.

126 "Knud W. Jensen has in a way": Henning Fonsmark in Berlingske Aftenavis 16.10.1962.

127 "Modernism in its special Danish distillation": Nils Gunder Hansen in: Niels Lillelund et. al.: "Velfærd tur-retur – efter socialdemokratismens sammenbrud" [Welfare There and Back – After the Collapse of the Social Democratic Idea], 2005.

127 "It is as if life is slipping away": "Mit Louisiana-liv" [My Louisiana Life], 1985 and 1993.

127 "The Social Democrat Per Hækkerup suggested": "Rødt på hvidt. Sølvhøj erindrer" [Red on White. Hans Sølvhøj Remembers], 1989.

The Americans come
127 "In the mid-1950s the American State Department": Mark Stevens and Annalyn Swan: De Kooning. An American Master. Knopf, 2004.

128 "The sculptor Erik Thommesen did not like": Information 9.1.1960.

128 "Knud W. Jensen suffered almost physically": Ole Wivel: "Lys og mørke. Mit venskab med Knud W. Jensen" [Light and Dark. My Friendship with Knud W. Jensen], 1994.

128 "It's a hard nut to crack": Berlingske Aftenavis 18.4.1964.

128 "We'll probably get it in the neck": Louisiana Revy, April 1964.

131 "Mass culture is the only form of culture": Louisiana Revy, January 1964.

Goodbye Danish art
134 "Documenta made him more restless": Ole Wivel: "Lys og mørke. Mit venskab med Knud W. Jensen" [Light and Dark. My Friendship with Knud W. Jensen], 1994.

134 "In 1966 Knud W. Jensen self-confidently turned 50": The article in Politiken 4.12.1966 was headlined "Knud – the planner" and began: "Further introduction cannot be required. All our readers know Knud W. Jensen and his achievements, indeed many of them know him so well that they will not consider it presumptuous to be on first-name terms with him already in the headline."

134 "We know that, if we want to, we": Wivel's letter is dated 29.4. 1966. Knud W. Jensen's was written the following day.

135 "It took a little time to get used to the provo Knud W. Jensen,": There is a copy of Jørgen Sthyr's speech among Knud W. Jensen's papers at Louisiana.

138 "The problem with Louisiana": Article in Politiken 25.1.1969.

138 "They probably think they are doing it for the sake of the public": Museum inspector Bente Skovgaard in an article in Politiken 16.1.1969.

138 "Calm, respect, indeed humility": Ibid.

139 "A hectic work tempo": Ibid.

139 "An angry Kirsten Strømstad": Financial director at Louisiana Kirsten Strømstad in article in Politiken 4.2.1969.

143 "It makes Knud W. Jensen weak at the knees": Ole Wivel describes Erik Clausen's meeting with Knud W. Jensen in "Romance for valdhorn" [Romance for French Horn], 1972.

143 "Jørgen Nash cuts the head off ": Jørgen Nash: "En havfruemorder krydser sit spor" [A Mermaid Murderer Crosses his Tracks], 1997.

The 1970s
152 "A man like Knud W. Jensen has": Jane Pedersen criticised Louisiana in Information 23.6.1972 for showing 'up-the-ladder art'.

152 *Vindrosen* (yet another Knud W. Jensen product)": The literary magazine *Vindrosen* was published by Gyldendal and appeared for the first time in 1958. Replaced *Heretica*.

152 "The female workers on strike": Conflict at the Royal Copenhagen Factory 1972-73, during which the striking porcelain decorators sold decorated cardboard plates to collect money to pay the fine imposed by the Board of Industrial Relations.

153 "In *Louisiana Revy* Susan Sontag is in love": *Louisiana Revy*, April 1971.

153 "Louisiana Man is slightly shocked": *Louisiana Revy*: Amerikansk kunst 1950-70 [American Art 1950-70], 1971.

A very dead horse
154 "A sharp winter sun shone": *Ekstra Bladet* was present in the field and reported the happening on 31.1.1970.

154 "Afterwards Bjørn Nørgaard opined that people": Torben Weirup: "Man har sine klare øjeblikke. En fortælling om Bjørn Nørgaard" [One has One's Moments of Clarity. A Story about Bjørn Nørgaard], 2000.

156 "There was a lot of rhetorical posing": Per Kirkeby in "Knud – her er dit liv!" [Knud – This is Your Life!], 1996.

156 "A pretty fantastic solution for the radical avantgardists": Ibid.

156 "I slept in a sleeping bag": Lars Morell: "Samtaler med Per Kirkeby" [Conversations with Per Kirkeby], 1997.

156 "Seen in retrospect we": Torben Weirup: "Man har sine klare øjeblikke. En fortælling om Bjørn Nørgaard" [One has One's Moments of Clarity. A Story about Bjørn Nørgaard], 2000.

158 "But twenty years later he said to Bjørn Nørgaard": Bjørn Nørgaard in "Knud – her er dit liv!" [Knud – This is Your Life!], 1996.

159 "When one looks at the circle": Ibid.

159 "Would you, for instance, invite": Lennart Gottlieb: "Forsvar for kunstrummet" [Defence for Art Space], 2006.

161 "It was Beuys who became": On 27 October 1977 Knud W. Jensen was awarded a prize of 10,000 DM by the Association of German Galleries in Cologne. He passed the money on to Joseph Beuys' Freie Universität. In the same year the museum purchased the work "Honey Pump", which Beuys had exhibited at Documenta.

161 "We realise that": Knud W. Jensen in *Louisiana Revy*, no. 3, January 1970.

161 "Jesus Christ, the trouble": Conversation with former Danish Broadcasting Corporation Head of Programmes Werner Svendsen.

161 "His explanation was that": Torben Weirup: "Man har sine klare øjeblikke. En fortælling om Bjørn Nørgaard" [One has One's Moments of Clarity. A Story about Bjørn Nørgaard], 2000.

162 "Using a peculiar Germanic terminology": Knud W. Jensen: "Mit Louisiana-liv" [My Louisiana Life], 1985/93.

163 "A disappointment since despite everything Louisiana": Jane Pedersen: *Information* 23.6.1972.

163 "If an artist wanted to change society": Knud W. Jensen in *Information* 22.8.1970.

Palace revolution
164 "Louisiana was devouring its capital": The two foundations are the Louisiana Foundation, which is responsible for operating the museum, and the Museum Foundation of 7.12.1966, established on Knud W. Jensen's 50th birthday with the object of buying art works for Louisiana. To this foundation he transferred everything he earned above 50,000 kroner a year. This was, in his own words, a "voluntary blood-letting – of income and capital", but on the other hand he saved "a good deal of tax". The boards of the two foundations were identical with Louisiana's board.

164 "According to Wivel, it was particularly a matter": Ole Wivel: "Romance for valdhorn" [Romance for French Horn], 1972.

168 "What could actually go wrong for us?": Knud W. Jensen: "Mit Louisiana-liv" [My Louisiana Life], 1985/93.

168 "It's over. I saved my life!": Conversation with Knud W. Jensen's secretary Hanne Skydsgaard.

169 "In the context of Louisiana": Allan Philip in "Knud – her er dit liv!" [Knud – This is Your Life!], 1996.

170 "In his supermarket chain Vime": Conversation with architect William Hedegaard.

The daily round
170 "Authoritatively and quite undemocratically": former museum inspector Flemming Koefoed in *Information* 31.5.1972.

171 "That's a good figure, that one": Conversation with director and haberdasher Jørgen Nørgaard.

172 "There were very few of us": Conversation with former museum inspector and painter Hugo Arne Buch.

174 "Knud had tons of people": Conversation with writer and critic Niels Barfoed.

174 "God had created Knud in such a way": Conversation with director Peter Augustinus.

176 "Thank you for your kind letter": The letter from Bergman is dated 27 June 1973 and the reply from Knud W. Jensen 16 July 1973.

176 "One does it to make life exciting": *Politiken* 2.9.1973.

176 "New York is as always enormously": Report to the board no. 14, 27 April 1976.

178 "We were thinking American at Louisiana": Conversation with former museum director Steingrim Laursen, died 2007.

178 "Why not spend half or a whole day": *Louisiana Klubben*, no. 1, October 1976.

Free us from art historians
182 "We mediate experiences, not knowledge": *Frankfurter Algemeine Zeitung*, 1992.

183 "His understanding was intuitive": Conversation with Hugo Arne Buch.

184 "Perhaps it is connected with the fact": Bo Nilsson in "Knud – her er dit liv!" [Knud – This is Your Life!], 1996.

184 "Louisiana is a break with": "Louisiana 40 år" [Louisiana 40 Years of Age], 1998.

185 "When art historian Øystein Hjort": Hjort joined the board after having defended Louisiana in a full-page article against charges of having a reactionary view on art under the heading "Art, the museum and the polemic free for all", *Information* 29.6.1972.

185 "This policy, which of course largely rests": Report to the board no. 15, 26 May 1976.

185 "We're in the field of esoteric art": Ibid.

191 "During 'Alternative Architecture' *Louisiana Revy*": *Louisiana Revy* 1977.

195 "A typical example of the decade": Ibid.

195 "Daddy, come and look. I've drawn a hungry child!": *Louisiana Klubben* 10, 1978.

197 "This attitude also permeates the book": Gyldendal's Christmas Book 1976.

197 "The two men had composed": Conversation with Øystein Hjort.

Louisiana fills in holes
200 "We had such sculptures at the Calder exhibition": Report to the board no. 3, 29 May 1975.

200 "All these acquisitions have suddenly become topical": Ibid.

202 "From fairy tales we know": The *New Yorker*, August 1982.

204 "He registered a palpable lack": *Kunst og Museum*, autumn 1977.

211 "May I call you in a week's time": Conversation with Peter Augustinus.

The 1980s
214 "Art worships the darkest chamber of the heart": Martin Hall in *Weekendavisen* 19.8.2005.

215 "The values and norms of capitalism": *Louisiana Revy*, March 1976.

215 "Now the studios are again full of paint cans": *Louisiana Revy*, no. 2, 1982.

216 "History turns yet another notch": *Louisiana Revy*, no. 3, 1985.

216 "Even though we have not definitively": Ibid.

217 "There was something quite wrong about": Søren Ulrik Thomsen: "Farvel til det blå rum" [Goodbye to the Blue Room]: *Kritik*, 1990. Poesi 85 was held in the concert hall on 8.9.1985.

217 "There is not a café, church, institution, library or shopping bag": Frederik Stjernfelt and Poul Erik Tøjner: "Billedstorm – om dansk kunst og kultur på det seneste" [Picture Storm – on Danish Art and Culture Recently], 1989.

217 "In Denmark the number of art museums rises from": *Dansk Kulturstatistik 1970-85*.

217 "The silent, manic collector": Lennart Gottlieb: "Forsvar for kunstrummet" [Defence for Art Space], 2006.

217 "Today the most you risk is a separate": Frederik Stjernfelt and Poul Erik Tøjner: "Billedstorm – om dansk kunst og kultur på det seneste [Picture Storm – on Danish Art and Culture Recently], 1989.

218 "Marx is dead – but there is life": *Politiken* 24.11.1985.

Louisiana twice as big
218 "Everyone's favourite is their first building": Conversation with one of Louisiana's two architects, Vilhelm Wohlert, died 2007.

221 "I can't see": *Louisiana Klubben*, no. 9, 1978.

221 "From the front edge of the veranda": Lawrence Weschler: "Louisiana in Denmark", 1982.

222 "Developments in art have determined": Conversation with Vilhelm Wohlert.

222 "The original thing about Louisiana's architecture": "Mit Louisiana-liv" [My Louisiana Life], 1985/93.

229 "Big museums scare people": *Herald Tribune* 8.7.1983.

Honour and glory
229 "We have no art historians here": *Globe and Mail*, November 1984.

229 "In many of the world's museums": *Reader's Digest*, January 1985.

229 "The *Herald Tribune* describes the museum": 8.7.1983.

234 "I loved Louisiana": *Berlingske Tidende*, November 1988.

234 "The Finnish newspaper *Hufvudstadsbladet* places": 11.12.1985.

234 "Louisiana, which with a broad international horizon": *Berlingske Tidende* 28.4.1986.

237 "Certain members of the aging avantgarde": For instance Jørgen Nash in "En havfruemorder krydser sit spor" [A Mermaid Murderer Crosses his Tracks], 1997.

237 "Louisiana is perhaps the only": *Ystads Allehanda* 12.12.1984.

237 "The Swedes shouldn't be allowed in": Louisiana I love you: *Politiken* 13.7.1985.

237 "The strangest thing is that people": *Göteborg Posten* 8.12.1984.

237 "Where ordinary museums are severe houses": *Dagens Nyheter* 19.01.1986.

238 "I quite simply feel like continuing for the time": Letter in Louisiana's archive.

238 "I cannot imagine a life": 21.2.1989, letter in Louisiana's archive.

Nude-nude
240 "Then give them a picture!": Conversation with former chief editor of *Politiken* Herbert Pundik.

242 "Who still collects ivory works": *Louisiana Klubben*, no. 38, March 1986.

242 "Here it is truly a matter of an international": *Kunstavisen*, no. 7, 1986.

245 "One must *see* and *see* and *see*": Knud W. Jensen: "Mit Louisiana-liv" [My Louisiana Life], 1985/93.

247 "If it wasn't against one's nature": *Louisiana Klubben*, no. 51, 1989.

247 "He threw a rope up into the air and began to climb": Hans Edvard Nørregård-Nielsen's formulation.

Peace
247 "A lot of our sponsors don't like the peace": *Herald Tribune* 8.7.1983.

251 "History's severe verdict on Reagan": Bo Bjørnvig in *Weekendavisen* 6.6.1987.

251 "One invites 'all the usuals'": *Frederiksborg Amtsavis* 29.5.1987.

251 "It is not a question of where nuclear weapons are launched from": *Berlingske Tidende* 14.12.1987.

254 "It sounds all the more improbable": "Knud – her er dit liv!" [Knud – This is Your Life!], 1996.

256 "Six months later Märta-Lisa Magnusson writes": *Politiken* 18.11.1988.

The public
256 "Salvador Dali landed in New York": *Louisiana Revy*, December 1989.

256 "Of the German painter Arnulf Rainer": *Louisiana Revy*, January 1982.

256 "We know that Antonin Artaud": *Louisiana Revy*, June 1982.

256 "And we know that that Gauguin": *Louisiana Revy*, October 1982.

257 "The world's first blockbuster": Bruno Ingemann and Ane Hejlskov Larsen: "Ny dansk museologi" [New Danish Museology], 2005.

257 "It is as if via sensitive signalling": *Louisiana Klubben*, no. 27, June 1983.

257 "What is the message in the huge picture": Reader's letter from Aksel Dreslow in *Politiken* 20.5.1989.

258 "They too were art": Erik Steffensen: "Desperado" [Desperado], 2006.

258 "As a student of art history in the 1970s": *Aktuelt* 13.8.1998.

259 "From 1981 to 1985 Louisiana": *Dansk Kulturstatistik 1970-85*.

259 "When *Berlingske Tidende* asked seven well-known": 13.1.1989.

259 "The newspaper asked again fifteen years later": 15.9.2006.

264 "Kolding's mini-Louisiana": *Jyllands-Posten* 6.7.1987.

264 "First the reviewer drives up the coast road": For instance Professor of Multimedia Lars Qvortrup in *Information* 12.11.2005.

266 "The new intellectual gimmick": *Information* 5.04.1994.

266 "The museum's visitors have done their homework": 9.2.1987.

268 "Lars Fenger, Louisiana's music chief": *Louisiana Magasin*, no, 20. 2006.

269 "The public? Well, they belong": Henrik Winther in *Weekendavisen* 4.3.2005.

The 1990s
272 "The current art world is one big chaos": *Louisiana Klubben*, no. 62, May 1992

272 "Today we are more open": *Louisiana Klubben*, no. 68, September 1993.

272 "And even though Louisiana goes over board": The four videos are "Bruits" and "Bataille" by Absalon, "Peter Land on 5 May 1994" by Peter Land, "Sip my Ocean" by Pipilotti Rist and "Killing Time" by Sam Taylor-Wood.

272 "At an exhibition of young Danish art": "Something is Rotten in the State of Denmark" at Museum Fridericianum, Kassel 1998. Curator: Lars Bang Larsen.

273 "The artists deliberately make social constructions": *Politiken* 18.11.1999.

273 "I connect it with the smell of newly dug earth": *Louisiana Revy*, no.3, June 1990.

Monet and the money
276 "Today there is no doubt": *Louisiana Revy*, no. 1, October 1993.

276 "No bloody way – we'll have nine!": Conversation with gallery owner Bo Bjerggaard.

278 "If you knew the sort of junk": It was to Poul Erik Tøjner in *Weekendavisen* 12.11.1993.

278 "The picture of the museum": Ibid.

278 "Some people hated this new art museum": Mai Misfeldt in *Information* 14.3.1994.

278 "No one is called to answer for the populism": *Information* 21.2.1994.

278 "All this talk reminds me of ": *Politiken* 5.12.1993.

Children
279 "We give the children a piece of paper": *Louisiana Revy*, no. 1, August 1978.

281 "Two generous foundations": The Villum Kann Rasmussen Foundation and the Velux Foundation of 1981.

286 "They become afraid of the materials": The leader of the Children's House Naja Pedersen in a talk to the conference on 12.5.2004.

Everyone wants to be Louisiana
286 "Today, almost 40 years after the first tentative": *Politiken* 7.12.1996.

290 "I am quite convinced that": museum inspector Kasper Monrad in *Politiken* 11.10.1992.

290 "After all it's an old tradition": *Berlingske Tidende* 29.01.2000.

291 "And it must be frustrating to be": Karsten Ifversen in *Politiken* 14.8.2005.

294 "Since Louisiana opened in 1958": *Politiken* 12.11.1994.

The daily round
296 "We owe the board of the Augustinus Foundation": Report to the board on 13.09.1990.

300 "Difficulties often occur": Polke's "Apparizione" is described and interpreted in *Louisiana Revy*, no. 2, 2001.

304 "To pretend that one can write simply": *Louisiana Magasin*, no.8, 2003.

Generation change I
308 "It should be no secret": *Ekstra Bladet* 8.3.1995.

312 "One cannot say no to Knud": Conversation with museum director Lars Nittve.

312 "The interesting thing about the place": *Weekendavisen* 10.3.1995.

315 "I believe that it is clear to most people": The catalogue for 'Nowhere , 1996.

316 "Louisiana has long since qualified itself": *Weekendavisen* 18.4.1997.

316 "It feels good!": "Dansk Kunst 97".

317 "Under Lars Nittve's leadership": *Ekstra Bladet* 14.8.1998.

Years of confusion
321 "Two museum inspectors immediately resigned": They were Anneli Fuchs and Lars Gramby.

322 "From here we express our congratulations": Lisbeth Bonde in 22.4.1998.

Generation change II
325 "Is your father at home?": *Politiken* 10.09.2000.

326 "I hate disinterested criticism": *Information* 29.7.2000.

326 "It is there the discussion of our lives": *Berlingske Tidende* 18.11.1999.

326 "His preference for classical art": *Information* 18.11.1999.

326 "Poul Erik Tøjner has not concealed a his love": *Berlingske Tidende* 17.11.1999.

326 "'Contemporary art?' answered Tøjner": *Berlingske Tidende* 18.11.1999.

The 2000s

330 "She belongs to the *Cosmopolitan* segment": Mediabroker: Louisiana Profilanalyse, 2006.

332 "Irony is as natural a part of the new painting": *Politiken* 26.12.2006.

Desperado

334 "He went to the Ministry of Culture": Conversation with Poul Erik Tøjner.

337 "Louisiana and I can only be satisfied": Letter dated 8.8.2000.

Knud Wadum Jensen 1916-2000

339 "He told Tøjner that": *Louisiana Magasin* replaced the little black-and-white club magazine from 1976. The first issue appeared in March 2001 and was club magazine number 100. It is published four times a year. *Louisiana Revy*, which is the museum's catalogue for the big exhibitions, appears twice a year.

339 "Dear Mother, Would you be so kind": Handwritten note from Knud W. Jensen among his papers at Louisiana.

340 "The momentary possibility for": Frederik Stjernfelt and Poul Erik Tøjner: "Billedstorm – om dansk kunst og kultur på det seneste" [Picture Storm – on Danish Art and Culture Recently], 1989.

340 "He and the other art historians feared". Dagens Nyheder august 1958.

340 "You have the spontaneously happy within you": letter from Thorkild Bjørnvig dated 18.8.1952 among Knud W. Jensen's papers at Louisiana.

Daily life

345 "I'm fundamentally opposed to": *Weekendavisen* 18.11.1999.

345 "We are not running": Conversation with Poul Erik Tøjner.

348 "I myself will never venture": *Berlingske Tidende* 19.02.2000.

348 "Some people think it doesn't": Conversation with Poul Erik Tøjner.

355 "The exhibitions were not based on research but on aesthetics, and that's how it still is Exceptions are, for example, Hanne Finsen's "Matisse – A Second Life" in 2005 and Michael Sheridan's Poul Kjærholm exhibition in 2006. Both are based on the two curators' own research.

Louisiana's deliberate hesitation

355 "With 'The Flower as Image' (2004) he was nervous": The exhibition was arranged in collaboration with Fondation Beyeler in Basel, where it was shown afterwards. At Louisiana it was such a success that it was prolonged for a week.

355 "Louisiana's own exhibitions began to travel": This was also the case for "Matisse – A Second Life", which was seen by more than 300,000 people at Musée du Luxembourg in Paris. The Leon Kossoff exhibition went on to Kunstmuseum Luzern in Switzerland. The exhibition Louisiana Contemporary Keith Tyson Large Field Array was shown at the De Pont museum in Holland in spring 2007.

356 "With few exceptions they are tending to miss the bus": *Weekendavisen* 1.9.2006.

357 "Our task is not to document everything": *Weekendavisen* 7.9.2006.

358 "One could then keep Louisiana as": *Weekendavisen* 6.11.1998.

362 "It's gone excellently, everyone says": Tøjner received Bikuben's Museum Award for 2006 accompanied by, among other things, the following words from culture editor Henrik Wivel of *Weekendavisen*: "You have Knud W. Jensen's dynamism in your own pulse, but in addition you have created a highly qualified team around you – a task force for mutual inspiration and qualification. The latter must be said to be a key word for your first six years at Louisiana. You have qualified the place in depth. Not by having the place expand in volume, but in quality."

362 "A sense for the visual in art": Conversation with Mikkel Bogh, rector of the School of Painting at the Royal Academy of Art.

365 "In 2006 the visiting figures fell below the level": Louisiana had 353,000 visitors in 2006 and was for the first time relegated to a fifth place (after *Statens Museum for Kunst*, the National Museum, ARoS and The Old Town in Århus). In Lars Nittve's worst year, 1997, 410,000 people visited the museum. Possible explanations are that entry to *Statens Museum for Kunst* became free, that Louisiana was encumbered by building activities for three years or/and that the exhibitions were narrower in 2006 than in the other years.

Louisiana Manifesto

367 "More than ever, architecture is annihilating": Jean Nouvel's Louisiana Manifesto, 2005.

368 "If one wants to build art museums": *Louisiana Magasin*, no. 12, 2004.

368 "And the founder of the mysterious": Victoria Newhouse: "Towards a New Museum", 1998.

368 "Perhaps we have been mistaken in recent years": *The Architectural Review*, August 1995.

372 "This is on the contrary a museum where people spontaneously": *New York Times* 16.10.1994.

372 "The first time I sensed": *Weekendavisen* 12.10.2003.

Exhibitions

1958
Louisiana's Greek Collection

1959
Niels Larsen Stevns. Memorial Exhibition
International Design at the Beginning of 1959
"Petroglyphs". Reproductions by R. Broby Johansen
"Dance in Art" – Giersing, Willumsen, Degas
"Czechoslovakian Art". Painting and Sculpture after 1945
Japanese Exhibition
"The Robert Jacobsen Dolls"
"Works from Documenta". Paintings by Dubuffet, Max Ernst,
    Miró, Pollock, de Stael, Tápies, Wols and others

1960
Kasimir Malevitch
Swedish Puppet Theatre. Michael Meschke
Vitality in Art – Vitalita Nell'Arte (arranged by
    Dr. Paolo Marinotti, W. Sandberg and J.J. Sweene)
Moderna Museet visits Louisiana.
Lasar Segall

1960-61
Kenneth Armitage & Lynn Chadwick.
Sonja Henie – Niels Onstad's Collection
Italian Culture Today
Drinking Glasses through 300 Years
Movement in Art
Stedelijk Museum Visits Louisiana

1961-62
Henry Moore
Paolozzi – Pasmore
Icelandic Art – Old and New
5000 Years of Egyptian Art
Luciano Minguzzi

1962-63
Jean Arp
Gold from Peru
August Strindberg – Paintings
100 Years of Norwegian Art
Mexican Masterworks, Part I
Mexican Masterworks, Part II

1963-64
Jackson Pollock
Vincent van Gogh
Sengai
Max Ernst
The Bo Boustedt Collection
Four Sculptors (J. Haugen Sørensen, Ørskov,
    Quinto Ghermandi & Tajiri)

From Bonnard to Today
Foreign Art in Danish Possession
American Pop Art
Grandma Moses

1964-65
Middelheim Visits Louisiana
English Painting Today
Munch-Picasso-Klee from Rolf Stenersen
Graphic Art from the Munch Museum, Oslo
Visionary Architecture from MoMA, N.Y.+
    Danish Architecture Abroad
"What is Man" – World Photo Exhibition
Asger Jorn
The Marzotto Prize 1964
Hidden Treasure – Art from Five Continents
Art in Concrete
Arnaldo & Gio Pomodoro

1965-66
Alberto Giacometti
The Graindorge Collection
The Hulton Collection
James Rosenquist: "F 111"
Selected Works by Olivia Holm-Møller
Bearings 66
The Gothenburg Museum of Art Visits Louisiana

1966-67
COBRA
Memorial Exhibition for Oluf Høst
Robert Jacobsen
The Nordic Youth Biennial for Visual Art
The Marzotto Prize 1966
The Peggy Guggenheim Collection from Venice
Salvador Dali's Illustrations of Hans Christian Andersen's
    Fairytales
Portrait of Carl Th. Dreyer
"Six Surrealists". Dali, Delvaux, Miró, Max Ernst, Magritte,
    Tanguy
Young Danish Art Jubilee Exhibition

1967-68
Pierre Bonnard
Lucio Fontana
Henry Heerup 60
Emil Nolde
Yves Klein
Saul Steinberg
Toulouse-Lautrec
Louisiana Visits Gothenburg Museum of Art
Spanish Art Today

1968-69
Picasso
Works from Documenta
Van Gogh Drawings
Pierre Alechinsky
Carl-Henning Pedersen
Georges Braque & Henri Laurens

1969-70
Alexander Calder
Finland at Louisiana
Arman
Italian Art
Architecture without Architects/Greenlandic Art
Tabernakel
Marc Chagall

1970-71
Richard Mortensen
George Grosz
Naum Gabo
Word and Picture – A Poster Exhibition

1971-72
American Art 1950-70
Klee – Kandinsky

1972
Projection
Robert Indiana
Hasior-Beres
Man Ray
Young Danish Art
Own Collection

1972-73
Svend Wiig Hansen
Asta Nielsen
Naive Art

1973
Extreme Realism
Alfred Jensen
Jean Tinguely
Asger Jorn
Public Design in Holland
Pol Bury "A Forest of Columns"
Salvador Dali

1973-74
Eisenstein
Visible-Invisible, Lennart Nielsson

1974
Christian Boltanski
Tapies
Christo – Valley Curtain
Fellini
Dubuffet

Dewasne
Anonymous Design
Tantra

1974-75
Japan at Louisiana
Miró
Jan Groth
Dario Villalba
Morris Louis
Jacques Monory
Moderna Museet
Duane Hanson
Luginbühl Graphic Art
Willy Ørskov
Jørgen Haugen Sørensen

1975-76
Jean Ipousteguy
Edvard Munch
Navajo Blankets
CAYC
Elementary Forms in Dutch Art
David Hockney's Graphic Works
Nouvelle Peinture Francaise
Louis Cane
Let's mix all feelings together
Henry Moore Sculpture & Drawing
Giacometti
Akhnaton and Nefertiti
Soho Downtown Manhattan
Alechinsky Graphic Art

1977
Ten Artists from Israel
Bob Morris Environment
Claes Oldenburg Drawings
Artists for Amnesty
Bearing on German Art
Art from Bali
Chinese Peasant Paintings
Marginal Architecture + Victor
Alternative Architecture

1978
Pompei 79 A.D.
Sam Francis
The McCrory Collection
Christo Running Fence
Babylon – Art from Mesopotamia
Soto and Hantai
Children Are a People
Sekine & Lee U Fan
Andy Warhol

1979
The CREX Collection – Art of the 70s
Surrealism from MOMA, N.Y.
Günther Grass Etchings

Kienholz
The American Avantgarde Cinema
Mark Boyle
Alechinsky/Appel/Hamilton/Roth
Outsiders

1980
Design Exhibition
American Photography 1920-40
André, Dibbets, Long and Ryman
Homes of the Imagination
Stedelijk Visits Louisiana
Nature-Art Art-Nature
Danish Design Cavalcade
Chinese Treasures
Robert Rauschenberg

1981
Canadian Art
Moroccan Folk Art
Mirrors and Windows
Bram van Velde
Picasso
Standpoints 70
Post-modernism "The House as an Image"
Gold from Eldorado +
Postmodernism "The House as an Image"

1982
Arnulf Rainer
Poul Kjærholm 1950-80
Neil Jenney, Schnabel, Moskowitz, Susan Rothenberg,
    Mimmo Paladino
"Aftermath" 1945-54 – Towards another View of Man
Robert Irwin
Paul Gauguin

1983
Marc Chagall
Chia, Clemente, Cucchi
Henri Cartier-Bresson
Willem de Kooning
Arnulf Rainer: Hiroshima
German Painting around 1980
Carl-Henning Pedersen: The First Years

1984
René Magritte
Jan Borofsky, Tony Cragg, Cindy Sherman
Irish Treasures
The Frozen Image – Scandinavian Photos
Robert Smithson
New York Graffiti
Expressionism from the Buchheim Collection

1985
Henri Matisse
Jan Schoonhoven
Time – The Fourth Dimension

Enzo Cucchi. Three New Pictures
Homo Decorans – The Decorated Human
Lucas Samaras – Polaroid Photographs 1969 – 1983
Russian Avantgarde 1910 – 1930
Georg Oddner, Photographs
Colour in French Art after Matisse

1986
Sculpture – 9 Artists from Great Britain
Jan Groth. Drawings 1975 – 1985
Portrait of a collector: Stephane Janssen
The Global Dialogue – Primitive and Modern Art
Constructivism in Louisiana's Collection after the Gift from the
    Riklis McCrory Collection
Richard Serra. Drawings
Jean Tinguely
Yoshiaki Tono: Akvademic Photographs
Sam Francis from the Idemitsu Museum
Barnett Newman. Graphic Art
Emil Nolde – The Nolde Museum Visits Louisiana

1987
Art from the Islamic World
Sitings: Sculpture and Place
The London School
Mexico's Art – Before the Spanish Came
Tierra y Libertad! Land and Liberty! – Mexican Photography
    1900-1935

1988
Irving Penn – Photography
Michael Buthe – Environments
Edvard Munch – Painter and Photographer
Robert Capa – Photographs 1932-54
Mario Merz
"Blow Up" – Pictures of the Time
Roberto Matta
Germaine Richier
Art & Comics
Picasso 1960 – 1973
Enzo Cucchi "La Disegna" – Drawings 1975-88

1989
Antony Gormley
New Art – 12 Artists from Switzerland
Master Photographers 1959-88
Africa, Africa!
Yousuf Karsh
Borealis 4
Turkish Treasures
Human Rights – An International Poster Exhibition
Erik Levine – Sculpture
Salvador Dali

1990
Marc Chagall "La Dation" – the Heritage after Chagall
Poetry and Reality – Soviet Photography after the Revolution
Per Kirkeby
Innovation via Design

Walker Ewans: American Photographs
Joel Shapiro – Sculptures
Andy Warhol
Stephan von Huene. Sound – Sculpture – Installation
Marina Abramovic/Ulay. "The Lovers – The Great Wall Walk"

1991
Vienna 1900 – Art & Design
Imogen Cunningham – Frontiers – Photographs 1906-76
Jenny Holzer – Venice Installation
Eric Fischl
The World Seen by MAGNUM – 50 Years of Photography
Oceania – Art from Melanesia

1992
Edward Hopper
Robert Mapplethorpe
Spain at Louisiana – Photography and Design 1970-92
Jeff Wall
William Eggleston. Past and Present
Pierre Bonnard
Jasper Johns – Graphic Art and Drawings from Leo Castellis'
    Collection

1993
On the Brink of Chaos – New Pictures of the World
Georg Baselitz – Works from 1990-93
Jana Sterbak
Mistaken Identities
Morris Louis
Wim Wenders: Film and Photo

1994
Claude Monet. Works from 1880 to 1926
ARATJARA – Art by the Original Australians
Kiki Smith
BILD – Photography in German Contemporary Art
From van Gogh to Gerhard Richter.
    Major Works from Museum Folkwang, Essen
Duane Michals

1994-1995
Toulouse-Lautrec and Paris

1995
Lewis Baltz
Asger Jorn
The Calas Legacy
Japan Today
Sam Francis -The Shadow of Colors

1995-1996
Tony Smith
Alexander Calder
BOREALIS 7 – Desire

1996
Design and identity – Aspects of European Design
Andrea Zittel – A-Z Travel Trailer Unit

Per Kirkeby "The Art of Architecture"
NowHere

1996-1997
Picasso and the Mediterranean

1997
Menn and Gods
New Discoveries from Ancient China
Cai Guo Qiang
Flying Dragon in the Heavens
Sunshine & Noir. Art in L.A. 1960 – 1997
Flamingo
Robert Frank Photographs 1948-1996

1997-1998
The Louisiana Exhibition 1997
    New Art from Denmark and Scania
Alberto Savinio. Paintings 1927-1952
The Continued Evolution of a Collection
    The New Carlsberg Foundation's Gifts to Louisiana
    1988-1997

1998
Francis Bacon
Sam Taylor-Wood
Louisiana at 40. The Collection Today

1998-1999
Joan Miró
The Architect's Studio: Frank O. Gehry

1999
Cities on the Move 4
The Asian City of the 90s
Henri Cartier-Bresson: Europeans
Louisiana's Collection 1999 – New Constellations
Magritte

1999-2000
The Architect's Studio: Henning Larsen
The Cheerful Givers – The Museums' Select Masterpieces

2000
Juan Muñoz. The Nature of Visual Illusion
Andy Warhol and His World

2000-2001
STARDUST, Annie Leibovitz 1970-1999
Vision and Reality – Conceptions of the 20th Century

2001
Magnum – The Turning World
(Separate solo exhibition: Joachim Ladefoged "Albanians")
Sigmar Polke – Alchemist
Anselm Kiefer – Paintings 1998-2000
After the Beginning and Before the End
Instruction Drawings

2001-2002
The Architect's Studio: Norman Foster

David Hockney – Painting 1960-2000
Ola Billgren In Memoriam – 1940-2001

2002
Georgia O'Keeffe
Per Kirkeby – 122x122
Paintings on Masonite. 1963-1978
RISE – Doug Aitken

2002-2003
Arne Jacobsen – Absolutely Modern
The Russian Avantgarde Book 1910-1934

2003
Wolfgang Tillmans – View from Above
Louise Bourgeois – Life as Art
Arnold Newman. Master Portraits
"Against the Wind". A Collection of Weathercocks at Louisiana
Renzo Piano Building Workshop
The Architect's Studio

2003-2004
Roy Lichtenstein – All About Art

2003
Thomas Demand

2003-2004
Kingdom of the Sun. Pre-Columbian Art from the Wessel
    Bagge Collection

2004
"I Hate You"
Painting, photo, video, installation from 1960 to Today
William Eggleston
Los Alamos
Jørn Utzon – The Architect's Universe
Works and Days
    Acquisitions for the Louisiana Collection – 2000-2004

2004-2005
The Flower as Image
Leon Kossoff. Selected Paintings 1956-2000

2005
Gerhard Richter. Image after Image
Jean Nouvel – Louisiana Manifesto
LOUISIANA CONTEMPORARY – Michael Bevilacqua
Matisse – A Second Life

2005-2006
LOUISIANA CONTEMPORARY – ON LINE
Brassaï – The Photographer of the Night

2006
Georg Baselitz – Painter
Sip My Ocean
Video from Louisiana's Collection:
    Bill Viola · Candice Breitz · Pipilotti Rist · Peter Land · Gary
    Hill · Absalon · Doug Aitken · Johan Grimonprez · Sam Tay-
    lor-Wood · Nam June Paik · Salla Tykkä · Paul McCarthy ·
    Runa Islam · Aernout Mik
LOUISIANA CONTEMPORARY –
    Janet Cardiff & George Bures Miller
Poul Kjærholm
    The Furniture Architect

2006-2007
STARLIGHT
    100 Years of Film Stills
LOUISIANA CONTEMPORARY – Keith Tyson – Large Field Array

2007
Cindy Sherman – 30 years of staged photography
MADE IN CHINA – CHINA ART NOW!
LOUISIANA CONTEMPORARY – Julie Mehretu – Black City
Philip Guston – Works on Paper – 1946-1980
Frontiers of Architecture I – Cecil Balmond – Unfolding New
    Dimensions

2007-08
Richard Avedon – Photographs 1946-2004
LOUISIANA CONTEMPORARY – Tal R: The Sum
Lucian Freud
Miniatures from the David Collection

2008
LOUISIANA CONTEMPORARY: Candice Breitz
    Cézanne & Giacometti
    Prestige or Paradise
    Per Kirkeby Retrospective
    Manga
    Collection I
    Collection II
    Collection III
    Collection IV

Literature

Andersen, Anders Thyrring (ed.): PS. Om Martin A. Hansens korrespondance med kredsen omkring Heretica [PS. On Martin A. Hansen's Correspondence with the Circle around *Heretica*]. Gyldendal 2005.

Barfoed, Niels: En kriger. Portræt af Ole Lippmann [A Warrior. Portrait of Ole Lippmann]. Gyldendal 2005. Farvel så længe! [Till We Meet Again]. Gyldendal 2007.

Bille, Trine et al.: Danskernes kultur- og fritidsaktiviteter 2004 – med udviklingslinjer tilbage til 1964 [Cultural and Leisure Activities in Denmark in 2004 – and Tracing the Development Back to 1964]. Akf Forlaget 2005.

Bjørnvig, Thorkild et al.: Knud – her er dit liv! [Knud – This is Your Life!], Published on the occasion of Knud W. Jensen's 80th birthday on 7 December 1996.

Borup, Anne, Morten Lassen, Jon Helt Haarder: Modernismen til debat [Modernism Debated]. Gyldendal. Syddansk Universitetsforlag 2005.

Bøggild, Hansaage: Ringen omkring Ole [The Ring around Ole]. Gudhjem 2004.

Coolidge; John: Patrons and Architects: Designing Art Museums in the Twentieth Century. Fort Worth 1989.

Engberg, Hanne: Kætterne. Kredsen omkring Heretica 1948-54 [The Heretics. The Circle around *Heretica* 1848-54]. Gyldendal 1995.

Engelbrecht, Tom and Frans Lasson: Karen Blixen i Danmark. Breve [Karen Blixen in Denmark. Letters] 1931-62. Gyldendal 1996.

Gottlieb, Lennart: Forsvar for kunstrummet [Defence for Art Space]. Gads Forlag 2006.

Hammerich, Paul: En Danmarkskrønike 1945-72 [A Chronicle of Denmark 1945-72]. Gyldendal 1976.

Hansen, Martin A.: Dagbøger 1947-55 [Diaries 1947-1955]. Gyldendal 1999.

Hornung, Peter Michael: M.A. degree lecture on the development of Danish art museums 1960-1980, unpublished, 1981.

Hornung, Peter Michael (editor): Ny dansk kunsthistorie. Kunsten i mediernes tid [Recent Danish History. Art in the Era of the Media]. Vol. 10. Fogtdal 1996.

Hunosøe, Jørgen: Fuldkommenhedslængslen [The Longing for Perfection]. In *Nordica* – Tidsskrift for nordisk teksthistorie og æstetik [Journal for Nordic Text History and Aesthetics], no. 17, 2000.

Ingemann, Bruno and Ane Hejlskov Larsen: Ny dansk museologi [New Danish Museology]. Aarhus Universitetsforlag 2005.

Jensen, Knud: Mit Louisiana-liv [My Louisiana Life], Gyldendal 1985 and 1993 (revised edition).
Stedets ånd [The Spirit of the Place]. Gyldendal 1994.
Slaraffenland eller Utopia [Land of Milk and Honey or Utopia]. Gyldendal 1966.

Kastrup, Anne Marie and Ivar Lærkesen: Rindalismen. Dokumentations – og studiebind [Rindalism. Documentation and Study Volume]. Hans Reitzel 1979.

Kongstad, Martin and Henrik Vesterberg: Dengang i 80érne [That Time in the 80s]. Gyldendal 2003.

Lidegaard, Bo: Kampen om Danmark 1933-45 [The Fight for Denmark 1933-45]. Gyldendal 2005.

Lillelund, Niels and Flemming Rose (eds.): Velfærd tur-retur – efter socialdemokratismens sammenbrud [Welfare There and Back – After the Collapse of the Social Democratic Idea]. Gyldendal 2005.

Louisiana Årbog [Louisiana Yearbook] 1958, 1959, 1960.
Louisiana Revy 1961-2008.
Louisiana Klubben 1976-2000.
Louisiana Magasin 2000-2008.
Louisiana Profilanalyse. Mediabroker, 2006.

Morell, Lars: Per Kirkeby. Bygningskunst [Art of Building]. Aristo 1996.
Samtaler med Per Kirkeby [Conversations with Per Kirkeby]. Borgen 1997.

Nash, Jørgen: En havfruemorder krydser sit spor [A Mermaid Murderer Crosses his Tracks]. Aschehoug 1997.

Newhouse, Victoria: Towards a New Museum. The Monacelli Press 1998.

Nørregård-Nielsen, Hans Edvard: Ny Carlsbergfondet 1902-2002 [The Ny Carsberg Foundation]. Gyldendal 2005.
Riber ret [Ribe Law]. Gyldendal 2001.

Pardey, John: Louisianas arkitekt Vilhelm Wohlert [Louisiana's Architect Vilhelm Wohlert]. Edition Bløndal 2007.

Scherfig, Hans: Den fortabte abe [The Lost Ape]. Gyldendal 1964.

Selborn, Clara: Notater om Karen Blixen [Notes on Karen Blixen]. Gyldendal 1974.

Steffensen, Erik: Desperado [Desperado]. Gyldendal 2006.

Stevens, Mark and Annalyn Swann: De Kooning. An American Master. Knopf 2004.

Stjernfelt, Frederik and Poul Erik Tøjner: Billedstorm – om dansk kunst og kultur på det seneste [Picture Storm – on Danish Art and Culture Recently]. Amadeus 1989.

Stjernfelt; Frederik og Søren Ulrik Thomsen: Kritik af den negative opbyggelighed [Critique of Negative Edification]. Vindrose, 2005

Stormgaard, Jørgen: Blixen and Bjørnvig. Pagten der blev brudt [Blixen and Bjørnvig. The Pact that was Broken]. Haase 2005.

Sølvhøj, Hans: Rødt på hvidt. Hans Sølvhøj erindrer [Red on Whire. Hans Sølvhøj Remembers]. Gyldendal 1989.

Thomsen, Søren Ulrik: Farvel til det blå rum [Goodbye to the Blue Room]. *Kritik* 1990.

Voss, Tage: Fejemøg fra Parnasset [Sweepings from Parnassus]. Cervus 1999.

Wamberg, Niels Birger: Mens kunsten er ung: en samtale mellem Knud W. Jensen og Niels Birger Wamberg [While Art is Young: a Conversation between Knud W. Jensen and Niels Birger Wamberg]. Gyldendal 1992.

Weirup, Torben: Man har sine klare øjeblikke. En fortælling om Bjørn Nørgaard. Møntergården 2000.
Dansk kunst 97 [Danish Art 97]. Søren Fogtdal 1997.

Weschler, Lawrence: Louisiana in Denmark, *The New Yorker* 30 August 1982.

Wivel, Ole: Erindringsmotiver (indeholder Romance for valdhorn (1972), Tranedans (1975) og Kontrapunkt (1989) [Remembered Motifs (contains Romance for French Horn (1972), Crane Dance (1975) and Counterpoint (1989)]
Lys og mørke. Mit venskab med Knud W. Jensen [Light and Dark. My Friendship with Knud W. Jensen]. Poul Kristensen 1994.
En ondskabsfuld klodsmajor: bemærkninger til Jørgen Hunosøe [A Malicious Bull in a China Shop: Remarks to Jørgen Hunosøe]. Poul Kristensen 2001.

Index

Photo credits

Ekstra Bladet 155 **Palle Fogtdal Publishers** (Illustreret Tidende 1997) 61 **Gyldendal's Picture Library** (Otto F.) 24, (Bo Bojesen) 114, (Herluf Jensenius) 126 **Louisiana Archive** (The Royal Library) 14ff, (Mobilia) 16ff, (The Royal Library) 18, (Photographer: Wolfgang Etzold) 20ff, 23, (Mobilia) 29, 30, (Photographer: Mogens von Haven) 34ff, (Photographer: Virginia Garner) 36ff, 41, (Knud W. Jensen) 42, 46ff, 62ff, (Photographer: Ole Olsen) 65, 66, 68ff, 70ff, (Photographer: Jens Frederiksen) 72ff, 74ff, (Photographer: Lennart Larsen) 76, 78, 80ff, 85, 86ff, 88ff, (Photographer: Vivi Jensen) 93, (Photographer: Jørn Freddie) 96ff, (Photographer: Børge Venge) 98, 99, (Photographer: Jørn Freddie) 104ff, (Photographer: Jørn Freddie) 110ff, (Photographer: Jørn Freddie) 112, (Photographer: Børge Venge) 120ff, (Photographer: Børge Venge) 122ff, 124ff, (Louisiana Revy nr. 1 1963) 129, (Photographer: Vittus Nielsen) 132, 133, (Photographer: Carl Rasmussen) 136v, 144ff, (Photographer: Louis Schnackenburg) 146, (Photographer: Louis Schnackenburg) 147, (Photographer: Jesper Høm) 148ff, (Louisiana Revy nr. 3 1970) 158, (Louisiana Revy nr. 3 1970) 159, 160, (Photographer: Teit Jørgensen) 162, (Photographer: Jens Frederiksen) 164ff, (Photographer: Ole Werlin) 166ff, 171, (Photographer: Morten Bo/Delta) 173, 180ø, (Photographer: Steen Møller Rasmussen) 180n, (Photographer: Anders Bentzon) 181ø, 181n, 194, (Photographer: Susanne Mertz) 196ø, (Photographer: Susanne Mertz) 196n, (Photographer: Susanne Mertz) 198ff, 201, 202ff, 204ff, 206ff, 208ff, 210, (Photographer: Morten Langkilde) 220, (Photographer: Poul Buchard) 223, 224ff, 226ff, 228ff, 330ff, 332ff, 234ff, 236ff, (Photographer: Marianne Grøndahl) 240ff, 244ff, (Photographer: Marianne Grøndahl) 246ff, 248ff, (Photographer: Marianne Grøndahl) 250, (Photographer: Anders Bentzon) 252ff, (Photographer: Erik Petersen) 254, (Photographer: Finn Frandsen) 255, 258, (Photographer: Anders Bentzon) 262ff, (Photographer: Anders Bentzon) 265, (Photographer: Marianne Grøndahl) 267, 268ff, (Louisiana Klubben) 277, (Mobilia) 280ff, (Photographer: Strüwning) 282, (Photographer: Søren Thomsen) 284, 285, (Photographer: Marianne Grøndahl) 287, (Photographer: Marianne Grøndahl) 288, (Photographer: Marianne Grøndahl) 289, (Photographer: Gregers Nielsen) 292ø, (Photographer: Gregers Nielsen) 292n, 293ø, 297, (Photographer: Tommy Verting) 298ff, (Photographer: Jens Frederiksen) 300ff, (Photographer: Tove Kurtzweil) 307, (Photographer: Marianne Grøndahl) 309, (Photographer: Poul Buchard) 310ff, 312ff, (Photographer: Jens Frederiksen) 314, (Louisiana 40 år) 317, (Photographer: Kim Hansen), 322ff, 327, 341, (Photographer: Marianne Grøndahl) 342, 346ff, (Louisiana Magasin 2001) 348, 349, (Photographer: Kim Hansen) 350, (Photographer: Steen Møller Rasmussen) 351, 354, 356ff, (Photographer: Kim Hansen) 358, 363ø, 364ø, 364n, (Photographer: Kim Hansen) 366ø, (Photographer: Steen Møller Rasmussen) 368ff, 374, 376ff **Hans Ole Madsen** 177, 238ff, 242ff, 334ff, 352ff, 373 **Polfoto** (Photographer: Lars Hansen) 102ff, (Photographer: Erik Petersen) 107, (Photographer: Lilian Petersen) 118ff, (Photographer: John McConnico) 136ff, (Photographer: Ebbe Andersen) 140ff, (PPF) 156ff, (Photographer: Peer Pedersen) 175, (Photographer: Finn Frandsen) 186ff, (Photographer: Anne-Marie G.) 188ff, (Photographer: Kim Agersten) 190, (Photographer: Erik Gleie) 192ff, 218ff, (Photographer: Ole Buntzen) 259, (Photographer: Nicolai Perjesi) 260ff, (Photographer: Finn Frandsen) 275, (Photographer: Morten Langkilde) 283, (Photographer: Mette Ragner) 320, (Photographer: Jakob Carlsen) 336, (Photographer: Steen Wrem) 366n, (Photographer: Kim Agersten) 375 **Politiken** 109, (Photographer: Erik Petersen) 182ff **Scanpix** 31, 45, (Photographer: Kurt Nielsen) 48, (Photographer: Steen Friis) 117, (Photographer: Emil Christensen) 130ff, (Photographer: Allan Petersen) 142, (Photographer: Linda Henriksen) 293n, (Photographer: Marianne Grøndahl) 295, (Photographer: Mogens Ladegaard) 302ff, (Photographer: Jan Jørgensen) 305, (Photographer: Kaspar Wenstrup) 324ff, (Photographer: Jakob Dall) 332ff, (Photographer: Bo Tornvig) 338, (Photographer: Carl Redhead) 244, (Photographer: Keld Navntoft) 359, (Photographer: Bjarne Oersted/AFP) 360ff, (Photographer: Reimar Juul) 363n, (Photographer: Ditte Valente) 370ff **Statens Museum for Kunst** 33 **Svikmøllen 1952** (Des Asmussen) 25 **Tidens Kvinder** (Photographer: Rie Nissen) 11, (Photographer: Rie Nissen) 12ff, (John Jørgensen) 26ff **Weekendavisen** (22-28. oktober 2004) 53

Thanks to my invaluable oral sources:

Director Peter Augustinus, former member of Louisiana's board.
Literary critic, journalist and author Niels Barfoed.
Art historian and rector of the Schools of Visual Arts at the Royal Academy Mikkel Bogh.
Gallery owner and former head of activities at Louisiana Bo Bjerggaard.
Journalist Bo Bjørnvig.
Literary critic, author and professor at the Danish School of Education Torben Brostrøm.
Painter and former museum inspector at Louisiana Hugo Arne Buch.
Museum inspector at Louisiana Helle Crenzien.
Museum inspector at Louisiana Kirsten Degel.
Author Hanne Engberg, niece of Knud W. Jensen.
Art historian, former museum director Hanne Finsen.
Journalist Karen Fougner, formerly at the Danish Broadcasting Corporation
Publisher, former director of Gyldendal and chairman of Louisiana's board Kurt Fromberg.
Art historian and former museum inspector at Louisiana Anneli Fuchs.
Architect William Hedegaard, briefly employed as a receptionist in Knud W. Jensen's company Vime.
Professor of art history Øystein Hjort, former member of Louisiana's board.
Vivi Jensen, married to Knud W. Jensen.
Architect, museum inspector Kjeld Kjeldsen.
Art historian, museum inspector at Louisiana Anders Kold.
Jurist, former museum inspector and director at Louisiana Steingrim Laursen, deceased 2007.
Publisher and former director at Gyldendal Otto B. Lindhardt.
Former head of personnel at Louisiana Annette Lindholm.
Head of the Louisiana Club Katrine Mølstrøm.
Former museum director at Louisiana Lars Nittve, now Moderna Museet in Stockholm.
Director Jørgen Nørgaard.
Art historian, author and chairman of the Carlsberg Foundation Hans Edvard Nørregård-Nielsen.
Head of the Children's House at Louisiana Naja Pedersen.
Journalist and former chief editor at Politiken Herbert Pundik.
Art historian and former museum inspector at Louisiana Tove Vejlstrup.
Culture editor at Weekendavisen, author and art critic Henrik Wivel.
Louisiana's architect Vilhelm Wohlert, deceased 2007.
Head of Finances at Louisiana Agatha Rasmussen.
Publisher and literary director at Gyldendal Johannes Riis.
Secretary to the management at Louisiana Lisbeth Ruben.
Art historian and former museum inspector at Louisiana Jens Henrik Sandberg.
Hanne Skydsgaard, Knud W. Jensen's secretary for 30 years.
Former head of programming at the Danish Broadcasting Corporation Werner Svendsen.
Artist Erik Steffensen, professor at the Schools of Visual Arts at the Royal Academy.
Journalist and editor Dan Tschernia.
Museum director Poul Erik Tøjner.

And thanks to the Augustinus Foundation for generous support for my work on this book. The support made it possible for me to devote all my working time to a task that was a source of pleasure every single day.